Geography and Spatiality in Hosea 1–3

Geography and Spatiality in Hosea 1–3

A Model for Using Critical Spatial Theory as a Hermeneutical Tool

Richard Halloran

◆PICKWICK *Publications* • Eugene, Oregon

GEOGRAPHY AND SPATIALITY IN HOSEA 1–3
A Model for Using Critical Spatial Theory as a Hermeneutical Tool

Copyright © 2025 Richard Halloran. All rights reserved. Except for brief quotations in critical publications or reviews, no part of this book may be reproduced in any manner without prior written permission from the publisher. Write: Permissions, Wipf and Stock Publishers, 199 W. 8th Ave., Suite 3, Eugene, OR 97401.

Pickwick Publications
An Imprint of Wipf and Stock Publishers
199 W. 8th Ave., Suite 3
Eugene, OR 97401

www.wipfandstock.com

PAPERBACK ISBN: 979-8-3852-4572-7
HARDCOVER ISBN: 979-8-3852-4573-4
EBOOK ISBN: 979-8-3852-4574-1

Cataloguing-in-Publication data:

Names: Halloran, Richard, author.
Title: Geography and spatiality in Hosea 1–3 : a model for using critical spatial theory as a hermeneutical tool / Richard Halloran.
Description: Eugene, OR: Pickwick Publications, 2025. | Includes bibliographical references and index.
Identifiers: ISBN 979-8-3852-4572-7 (paperback). | ISBN 979-8-3852-4573-4 (hardcover). | ISBN 979-8-3852-4574-1 (ebook).
Subjects: LCSH: Bible.—Hosea—Criticism, interpretation, etc. | Space perception.
Classification: BS1565.2 H35 2025 (print). | BS1565.2 (ebook).

VERSION NUMBER 12/04/25

The Prophetic Mission chart was taken from *Plowshares & Pruning Hooks* by D. Brent Sandy. Copyright © 2002 by D. Brent Sandy. Used by permission of InterVarsity Press, P.O. Box 1400, Downers Grove, IL 60515, USA. www.ivpress.com.

Maps in book were taken from *Satellite Bible Atlas* by William Schlegel. Copyright © by W. Schlegel, *Satellite Bible Atlas*. Used by permission of William Schlegel.

Scripture quotations marked (RSV) are taken from Revised Standard Version of the Bible—Second Catholic Edition (Ignatius Edition) Copyright © 2006 National Council of the Churches of Christ in the United States of America. Used by permission. All rights reserved worldwide.

Scripture quotations marked (NIV) are taken from The Holy Bible, New International Version®, NIV®. Copyright © 1973, 1978, 1984, 2011 by Biblica, Inc. Used with permission of Zondervan. All rights reserved worldwide. www.zondervan.com.

Scripture quotations marked (NASB) are taken from the (NASB®) New American Standard Bible®, Copyright © 1960, 1971, 1977, 1995, 2020 by The Lockman Foundation. Used by permission. All rights reserved. lockman.org.

Scripture quotations marked (NKJV) are taken from the New King James Version®. Copyright © 1982 by Thomas Nelson. Used by permission. All rights reserved.

Scripture quoted by permission. Quotations designated (NET) are from the NET Bible® copyright ©1996, 2019 by Biblical Studies Press, L.L.C. http://netbible.com. All rights reserved.

Scripture quotations marked (ESV) are taken from the ESV® Bible (The Holy Bible, English Standard Version®), © 2001 by Crossway, a publishing ministry of Good News Publishers. ESV Text Edition: 2025.

This book is dedicated to my loving wife, Mikki, who has been a steadfast encourager and companion throughout this journey. It is also dedicated to my children, mother, and mother-in-law: CJ, Bella, and Teddy; my mom; and Bubbe, who each made sacrifices so that I could pursue and complete this work. I thank you all from the depths of my heart.

Contents

List of Illustrations | x
Preface | xi
Acknowledgments | xiii
List of Abbreviations | xv

1 Introduction | 1
2 The Hermeneutical Method | 11
3 The Rhetorical Situation | 33
4 The Rhetorical Use of Jezreel | 50
5 The Rhetorical Usage of Spatial Images | 103
6 Conclusion | 120

Appendix: Structure of Hosea 1:2–9 | 125
Bibliography | 127
Scripture Index | 151

Illustrations

Figure 1. The Prophetic Mission | 14
Figure 2. Map of Jezreel Valley | 52
Figure 3. Topography of Travel through the Jezreel Valley | 58
Figure 4. Hazael's Campaign | 60
Figure 5. Optional Sites for the Valley of Achor | 112

Preface

Adding Another Tool to One's Hermeneutical Toolbox

DURING MY STUDIES AT Dallas Theological Seminary, I was increasingly drawn to the literary, rhetorical, and communicative dimensions of the Scriptures. Alongside these interests, I developed a deep appreciation for how the geography of the land of Israel shapes and informs the meaning of the biblical text. These twin interests, literary analysis and geographical awareness, ultimately converged in my research.

As I explored the intersection of these fields, I encountered a relatively recent development in hermeneutics: the application of critical spatial theory to biblical studies. This framework, though still emerging, provides fresh insight into the way ancient audiences may have conceived of and experienced space and place. I recognized that my dissertation could contribute uniquely to this conversation, particularly since spatial dimensions are often overlooked in biblical interpretation.

This book, originally my doctoral dissertation, reflects that commitment. Specifically, it focuses on the book of Hosea, particularly chapters 1–3, and examines how an understanding of space and geography within the text aids interpretation. My purpose in this study is fourfold:

1. To explore how critical spatial theories can equip readers to better grasp the shared cognitive and cultural world of Hosea and his implied audience;
2. To demonstrate the multidimensional nature of Hosea's geographic and spatial references within that cultural context;

PREFACE

3. To analyze how these references function rhetorically to persuade Hosea's audience; and

4. To offer a methodology by which critical spatial theory can serve as a hermeneutical tool.

What follows is an interdisciplinary investigation that weaves together rhetorical criticism, critical spatial theory, and the distinct interpretive challenges of prophetic literature. After a survey of relevant scholarship and a detailed discussion of method, the study turns to a close reading of Hosea 1–3. The findings suggest that Hosea skillfully employs spatial and geographic language to engage his eighth-century audience, and that modern interpreters stand to gain a more nuanced and persuasive understanding of the text when these dimensions are taken seriously.

My hope is that this work will not only advance scholarly discussion but also enrich the reader's own interpretive journey through Hosea and the prophetic literature more broadly.

Acknowledgments

This work was originally my dissertation at Dallas Theological Seminary. It represents not only years of research and writing, but also the culmination of relationships, mentorships, and support that have shaped both the scholar and person I have become.

I am deeply indebted to my advisors, Robert Chisholm Jr. and Gordon Johnston, who were far more than advisors, they were mentors, teachers, and friends. My relationship with both of these men stretches back to my ThM studies. In fact, it was during my very first semester, in a class with Dr. Chisholm, that I was persuaded to shift my academic focus from the New Testament to the Old Testament. Dr. Johnston was my first Hebrew professor. I was fortunate to continue learning from both of these remarkable scholars through every opportunity I could seize. Their wisdom, insight, and example inspired me to return to DTS to complete my PhD studies.

I also owe a debt of gratitude to my outside reader, Dr. Victor H. Matthews. His pioneering work in applying critical spatial theory to biblical studies had a direct influence on the development of my dissertation topic. I am thankful that he agreed to serve on my committee, and his expertise, probing questions, and thoughtful feedback helped me sharpen my thinking and refine this work.

My academic journey has been further shaped by the many professors at Dallas Theological Seminary who invested themselves in teaching students to think critically while upholding a high view of God and the Scriptures. For that, I am truly grateful.

I would also like to thank Mark and Becky Lanier, David Fleming, Holly Johnson, Jennie Enright, and the entire staff at the Lanier Theological Library. Their gracious hospitality and their kindness in granting me

ACKNOWLEDGMENTS

off-hours access to the library made it possible for me to complete this research in such an enriching environment. Last but not least, thank you Carmen Watson for your encouragement and willingness to be an extra set of eyes for reviewing and making edits.

Abbreviations

B. Bat.	Bava Batra
CEB	Common English Bible
COS	*The Context of Scripture: Monumental Inscriptions from the Biblical World*
Eng	English Bible as opposed to the Hebrew Bible
LXX	Septuagint
MT	Masoretic Text
NASB	New American Standard Bible
NET	New English Translation
NIV	New International Version
NJPS	*Tanakh: The Holy Scriptures: The New JPS Translation according to the Traditional Hebrew Text*
NKJV	New King James Version
NRSV	New Revised Standard Version
RSV	Revised Standard Version
WYC	Wycliffe Bible

1

Introduction

The Rationale for the Study

BIBLICAL SCHOLARSHIP HAS WRITTEN much regarding aspects of Hosea's literary style, including his vast use of metaphor and his rhetoric. Yet, an interdisciplinary analysis of the use of geography and space in Hosea's rhetorical approach has yet to be undertaken, especially in light of recent studies in spatial theory. Critical spatial theorists have shown how space and geography have often been ignored amidst the rise of social and historical studies. Flanagan recognized this challenge, stating, "omitting, ignoring, or suppressing spatiality leads to imbalanced, distorted, and continually flawed understandings and practices in the real world."[1] While the historical and social aspects of life have been the focus of much scholarship, it is essential to recognize that both of these aspects occur in space. A balanced approach must look at history, sociality, and spatiality together as a trialectic methodology.[2] The use of such a balanced methodology provides the interpreter a more balanced hermeneutical process to assist in appreciating the ancient world of the author and audience. When this balanced approach is applied, fresh insight can be gained into the rhetorical approach of biblical authors, and, in this case, Hosea.

Though sometimes ignored, geography and spatiality are significant components of interpretation. Furthermore, when geography is discussed, it

---

1. Flanagan, "Ancient Perceptions of Space," 26.
2. Soja refers to this as the "Trialectics of Being" in Soja, *Thirdspace*, 70–73.

is most often considered solely from a historical perspective, taking into consideration questions regarding a place's historical location or physical attributes. However, a geographical or spatial reference entails more than a place on a map. Places encompass the space where people live and experience life.[3] As such, space "comprises both physical location and a set of cognitive associations that have come to be attached to that specific location."[4]

The proposal of this book is that Hosea 1–3 provides an example of how biblical authors often use both the physical and cognitive dimensions of spatial references to effectively communicate with their audiences, with the goal of persuading them towards a greater level of covenant faithfulness. Therefore, the modern interpreter should take a comprehensive approach to spatiality. Any communication "presupposes a speaker who resorts to certain linguistic and structural tools in order to produce certain effects on the addressee."[5] Spatiality frequently becomes one such tool in the communicator's repertoire to shape a message and emotionally engage an audience. Such references are frequently intended to evoke the audience's memories, feelings, and experiences.

This functional use of space is clearly seen in the rhetoric of some modern speeches. Consider Martin Luther King Jr.'s *I Have a Dream* civil rights speech. Geography became a tool that Dr. King used to evoke the emotions of his audience. For example, he referenced Georgia, Alabama, and Mississippi, three states where violent abuses were occurring. King mentioned Mississippi four times, epitomizing the struggle of the civil rights movement. This historical referent was shared between the speaker and the audience. As such, when King said, "Go back to Mississippi . . . knowing that somehow this situation can and will be changed," he assumed the audience was aware of the injustices occurring in Mississippi.[6]

---

3. Many geographers distinguish between "location," "space," and "place." The term "location" can be relative in relation to something or someplace else or can be absolute (based on specific coordinates). For example, the town of Klein is a location northwest of Houston but is specifically at 30.0477°N, 95.5324°W. "Space" is used to refer to abstract areas, while the term "place" can be used to denote more significance and personal meaning. "Place" is specified to refer to a space to which people have attached meaning. However, for the sake of this book, such a distinction is not taken. "Place" is sometimes used as a synonym for "space" and the significance and meanings associated with a space are discussed using other terminology.

4. Matthews, *More than Meets the Ear*, 131.

5. Sternberg, *The Poetics of Biblical Narrative*, 9.

6. King's command, "Go back to Mississippi, go back to Alabama, go back to South Carolina, go back to Georgia, go back to Louisiana, go back to the slums and ghettos of

There was no need to elaborate any further. The mere mention of the place conjured pictures of vicious racism and injustice. King was able to stir the emotions of his audience and, at the same time, communicate his argument for change.[7]

King's rhetorical use of geography served as a model for President Barack Obama's 2013 Inaugural Address. In it, like King, he mentioned three locations: Seneca Falls, Selma, and Stonewall.[8] Unlike King's references, Obama's allusions were rooted in past history and were not common knowledge for everyone in his audience. The Seneca Falls reference alluded to the 1848 protest over women's rights in Seneca Falls, NY. The mention of Selma pointed to the 1965 brutal attacks and subsequent march for civil rights in Selma, AL. Less well known to many was his reference to Stonewall. Riots occurred in Manhattan in 1969 in response to a police raid on a homosexual bar at the Stonewall Inn. President Obama used three spatial referents to attempt to link his work for homosexual rights to the prior efforts of the nation to provide equal rights for women and African Americans. One clearly can see his rhetorical use of spatiality to attempt to persuade his audience.

Both of these speeches illustrate more than just the rhetorical use of geographical space. They highlight the reality that places are multivalent in character. Space is not simply a physical or topographical location. It encompasses cognitive associations that include historical events and sociality.

---

our northern cities, knowing that somehow this situation can and will be changed" is reminiscent of Amos's call to "Go to Bethel and rebel" (Amos 4:4). Yet, King used these geographical references in hopes that things would change. Amos, on the other hand, used Bethel ironically, condemning the people's hypocritical worship.

7. Similarly, Jeremiah mentions the destruction of Shiloh, an incident in Israel's earlier history that would be familiar with his audience, to stir their emotions by conjuring up images of judgment in his threat against the temple in Jerusalem (Jer 7:12, 14). The people trusted that the ark's presence in Shiloh was some sort of magical promise of protection. Yet, Shiloh was destroyed by the Philistines. Now, over 400 years later, the people were guilty of the same false sense of security. Jeremiah rhetorically warns the people that just because the Lord picked Jerusalem as a place where his presence would be worshipped, safety and protection were still contingent on the people's obedience.

8. The following provides the further context of the references: "We, the people, declare today that the most evident of truths—that all of us are created equal—is the star that guides us still; just as it guided our forebears through Seneca Falls, and Selma, and Stonewall; just as it guided all those men and women, sung and unsung, who left footprints along this great Mall, to hear a preacher say that we cannot walk alone; to hear a King proclaim that our individual freedom is inextricably bound to the freedom of every soul on Earth." Obama, "Inaugural Address" (2013).

A communicator assumes that he/she and his/her audience share a cultural and referential context. Sperber and Wilson elaborate: "A context in this sense is not limited to information about the physical environment or the immediately preceding utterances: expectations about the future, scientific hypothesis or religious beliefs, anecdotal memories, general cultural assumptions, beliefs about the mental state of the speaker, may all play a role in interpretation."[9] Thus, an author may use information accessed from a shared cognitive environment to communicate ideas and arguments.

While an original audience shares these associations, rules, and conventions of the culture with the author, readers from other cultures often do not share the same cultural referents, coming from an etic perspective.[10] Even during the President's Inaugural Address, large portions of his audience did not share knowledge of his spatial references, having been removed from the events by time and space.[11] A lack of shared cultural background hinders the communicative impact upon the audience. Geographical and spatial referents pose a barrier that can prohibit a reader from comprehending the message and intent of an author/speaker.

As in King's and Obama's speeches, biblical texts use spatial allusions and references in a multi-dimensional manner, characteristically implying connotations derived from the society in which the place existed. The modern interpreter comes to biblical texts, reading references to spaces and locations, and is often unfamiliar with the shared cultural cognitive environment. Those who study and travel to Israel or other biblical lands can become more familiar with elements of the topography and physical aspects of the land. Archaeologists have illuminated other physical elements as well (e.g., walls, houses, streets, administrative buildings, temples, military training sites, etc.). However, these physical elements only contribute to part of the cultural world of a space. How does one approach the mention of a geographic location or a reference to a spatial concept in a manner that does justice to the original cultural world of the author and audience?

Fortunately, over the past forty years, geographic scholarship has advanced studies of space to emphasize a more comprehensive approach, including the social context that accompanies space. These developments in

---

9. Sperber and Wilson, *Relevance: Communication and Cognition*, 15–16.

10. McNutt, *Reconstructing the Society of Ancient Israel*, 247.

11. One could argue that this was purposeful, knowing that the reference would resonate with those who were passionate for the cause of the LGBTQ community while being overlooked by those who opposed such a cause.

geographic studies are often referred to as critical spatial theory. Critical spatial studies have extended well beyond the discipline of geography into all aspects of the social sciences. As the prominent spatial theorist Edward Soja notes, "Never before has a critical spatial perspective been so widespread in its recognition and application—from archaeology and poetry to religious studies, literary criticism, legal studies, and accounting."[12] For the biblical interpreter, this critical spatial perspective provides another tool for interpreters to better understand the society in which the biblical text originated, the rhetorical situation that prompted the text, and the rhetorical message of the biblical author.

Geographical allusions and references are multi-dimensional, characteristically implying connotations derived from the society in which the place existed. Furthermore, the author also shared a cultural and referential framework with his audience in relation to spatial practices and assumptions. These referential aspects are assumed in the rhetoric of the author. As this book suggests, this is particularly true in the book of Hosea.

The book of Hosea's references to geography and space reveal its multivalent character. The historical nature of a geographical site is only one dimension of a geographical space, albeit an extremely important one. Building on Soja's foundational theories, this book addresses the need for a more comprehensive approach. Hosea shared a cultural context with his audience that attributed significant imagined and real meanings to locations. While a mere geographical reference appears minor on the surface, the shared meaning of such a reference can have inferred significance. A comprehensive approach to unpacking Hosea's rhetorical usage of geography and space helps to answer the question, "Does a geographical space (e.g., Jezreel), or a spatial reference, function rhetorically within Hosea's texts?" If so, how does the reference contribute to Hosea's persuasive intent? This study addresses the need to consider spatiality as a significant aspect of the trialectics of life (not simply historicality and sociality). In so doing, it provides the reader with a greater ability to hypothesize the context of

---

12. Soja, "The City and Spatial Justice," 1. It is worth noting that critical spatial theory developed partly in response to the conditions and circumstances of the theorists' times. For example, Lefebvre's writings reflect his brand of Marxism and reflect his responses to class discrimination and government involvement in French universities. One may disagree with the conclusions and applications of spatial thinking to modern situations; nevertheless, these developments in spatiality provide helpful considerations for reading ancient texts.

Hosea's message, gain new insights into the meaning of the text of Hosea, and gain a greater appreciation for Hosea's rhetoric.

The Thesis

Hosea 1–3 reflects Hosea's rhetorical usage of space and geography to effectively communicate with the eighth-century, original implied audience, that they must return to covenantal faithfulness to experience the blessings of God, or else they would experience His wrath. The modern interpreter's hermeneutic will be enhanced by applying the following methodology that engages the principles of critical spatial theory.

The Method of the Study

This study approaches the use of geography and space in the rhetoric of Hosea 1–3 from an interdisciplinary approach. The methodology is intended to provide a tool to correct the error of "reading back into" the text what is not in the ancient culture, while also illuminating aspects of the ancient culture that are often ignored or read incompletely. While taking such an interdisciplinary approach runs the risk of becoming overly complex, Chisholm's insights regarding hermeneutical methods should be considered. "Though interpretation has its technical aspects . . . it should not be reduced to a mathematical formula . . . The process of considering these issues need not be understood as linear, nor should it be viewed as mechanical. Many of the guidelines are interrelated. In actual practice they end up being concurrent."[13] This book attempts to approach the intersection of these disciplines in a manner that enlivens the picture of the rhetorical setting and provides clarity to how geography and space contribute to the rhetoric of Hosea 1–3. To accomplish this, the following proposed method is adopted.[14]

13. Chisholm, *Interpreting the Historical Books*, 185.

14. This methodology has been influenced by two sources that provide literary methods as hermeneutical guides to interpretation. James Resseguie provides an applicational methodology for reading narrative criticism in the New Testament and Robert Chisholm provides an applicational methodology for interpreting the historical books of the Old Testament. Both of these methods contribute to this proposed method for interpreting prophetic literature with an awareness of critical spatial theory. This book does not provide a completely comprehensive approach to interpreting the prophets but seeks to add an emphasis on how geographical and spatial references add another tool to the process.

INTRODUCTION

Overview of the Proposed Method

To provide a holistic approach that is contextually understood within its literary genre, adequately accounts for the rhetorical intentions of the author of a prophetic passage, and includes a holistic awareness of spatial references, an interpreter should apply the following methodology.

1. Approach the passage within its context. This includes its historical and religious context, and the broader context of the book as a whole. When possible, identify the rhetorical situation that prompted the prophetic message.
2. Evaluate the text with a sensitivity to the genre of prophetic literature, the nature of prophetic rhetoric, and the principles of critical spatial theory (this will require engaging in the archaeology of locations and the nature of the social structures of the time of writing).
3. When working with a unit, summarize how the passage should have rhetorically impacted the different social groups within the implied audience.

Following these three steps provides the general framework of the methodology. The details of the steps include asking several questions consistently of the text's geography and space. These questions do not provide a mechanical process to follow, and as mentioned above, are often interrelated. While not providing a formula to follow step by step, they provide the interpreter with a range of questions that assist the process of understanding spatial references more holistically.

Questions Regarding Prophetic Hermeneutics

Prophetic books should be approached with sensitivity to hermeneutical principles that are specific to the prophetic genre (see chapter 2). The following are questions that are considered regarding the relationship of the thesis with prophetic hermeneutics:[15]

Certainly, more could be added for a complete approach (e.g., analyzing forms of judgment speeches, exhortations, calls to repentance, analyzing parallelisms, etc.). Resseguie, *Narrative Criticism of the New Testament*, 241–54; Chisholm, *Interpreting the Historical Books*, 184–86.

15. To ease categorization of these questions, key words are written in *italics* font.

1. How does the prophet's use of geography and space reflect *emotional and functional* language? Does the function of the reference differ from the normal use?
2. What implications does the *contingent* nature of prophecy have upon the prophet's rhetorical use of geography and space?
3. What is the *context* that allows for an *utterance* to be made?[16] Does the prophet expect his audience to provide further information to understand his point? If so, what information? How do the prophet's geographic or spatial references serve as a stimulus for the audience to draw *inferential meaning*?[17]
4. How does the *contextual* nature of the prophet's use of geography and space affect the immediate impact upon the audience, even if the message's fulfillment is in the distant future?
5. Do the details of a prophetic foretelling demand *literal fulfillment* regarding its geographic nature (e.g., the Valley of Achor in Hos 2:15)?
6. How does *archaeology* contribute to the understanding of the *shared cognitive environment* of the prophet and his audience and the contextualized nature of the message?
7. In light of considering these questions, what is the intended *illocutionary* and *perlocutionary* meaning of the geographical and spatial references?

Questions Regarding Rhetoric

In light of the reality that prophets spoke from a functional perspective (see next chapter), their messages were highly rhetorical, designed to persuade their audiences. The following are questions that are considered regarding the relationship of the thesis with rhetoric:

---

16. Sperber and Wilson define context as "the set of premises used in interpreting an utterance." They further state, "A context in this sense is not limited to information about the immediate physical environment or the immediately preceding utterances: expectations about the future, scientific hypothesis or religious beliefs, anecdotal memories, general cultural assumptions, beliefs about the mental state of the speaker, may all play a role in interpretation." Sperber and Wilson, *Relevance: Communication and Cognition*, 15–16.

17. Klingler notes, "It is the author's responsibility to provide material of maximum relevance so that a desired cognitive goal can be achieved." Klingler, "Validity in Identification and Interpretation," 151.

1. How do geography and space contribute to the message of the prophet in regard to its *creation*, its *arrangement*, and its *style*? Does the use of *parallelism* in connection with geography and space have rhetorical impact?
2. How does the use of *wordplay* impact the prophet's rhetorical use of geography and space? Is there a rhetorical use of key words, phrases, themes, or patterns that relate to the use of space and geography?
3. In what ways do the *metaphors* and *allusions* used contribute to the rhetoric? Does verbal or situational *irony* come into play in the prophet's rhetoric? If so, what impact does it have on the audience (e.g., help convince the audience of the prophet's views; encourage a supportive audience; persuade opponents)?
4. Does the use of geographic or spatial references cause the audience to pause and consider the message? Does such usage "*ground*" his message with the audience?
5. Does the rhetorical use of geography and space *challenge the views* of the elite or the societal norms?

Questions Regarding Critical Spatial Theory

The following are questions that are considered regarding the relationship of the thesis with critical spatial theory:

1. Based on the information at our disposal, how did the *physical* and *material* aspects of a geographical site impact the prophet's message?
2. Based on the information at our disposal, what were the *everyday practices* and interactions with the physical space, and did these actions have an impact on the prophet's message?
3. Were there *modifications* made to a place (e.g., the fortress at Tel Jezreel)? How was a site occupied, manipulated, or modified? If so, how might those modifications have *impacted the conception* of that place in people's minds? How might this be rhetorically influential? If a location's significance is transformed, how does its *memory contribute to its developed meaning*?[18]

---

18. Matthews highlights a community's remembrance of a space's past, stating, "the memory of its former state lingers on and to an extent continues to at least partially define that space." Matthews, "Remembered Space in Biblical Narrative," 67.

4. Does the prophet himself *transform* spaces in a manner that plays on the audience's shared cognition? Given the religious apostasy in eighth century Israel, is there a *polemical* value to space being transformed?

5. Did the place have *symbolic value* and identity? If so, how did the audience remember locations (e.g., Jezreel)? Does the prophet engage the *memory* of his audience for rhetorical purposes (e.g., serve as a stimulus for *inferential meaning*)? How does such an engagement affect the audience?

6. Are there spatial references that represent *contested space*?[19]

7. Are there spatial references that represent violations of *cultural norms* (in/out of place)?

8. How did various *social groups* (e.g., kings, the elite, the prophet, commoners) use and view the spatiality (e.g., the land)? How do these views relate to the rhetoric of the prophetic message?

Limitations

Given the interdisciplinary nature of this study, it must limit its scope to the use of the broad principles from each discipline to their specific application of the rhetorical usage of geography and spatiality. The text will be approached synchronically, with limited references to the potential of the text's diachronic nature.

---

19. Flanagan's illustration of Rosa Parks is helpful. While the front of the bus was literally in the front of the bus, it also represented a place of preference. As he states, "spatiality is constructed through social practice." Flanagan, "Ancient Perceptions of Space," 26–27.

2

The Hermeneutical Method

THIS STUDY CONSIDERS THE use of geography and space in the rhetoric of Hosea 1–3 from an interdisciplinary approach. It recognizes that communication, by its nature, requires that a speaker uses linguistic and structural tools to produce an intended impact on the recipient.[1] Hosea shared a cognitive environment with his audience, one that included the multivalent nature of geography and a cultural understanding of places and space. An approach that is sensitive to the functional nature of the prophetic genre, rhetorical criticism, and critical spatiality provides the reader with a greater ability to understand the text within its original rhetorical setting.

Prophetic Hermeneutics

Prophets were the means of God's communication to the people. The nature of their message was most often polemical, being charged with confronting the people in their state of disobedience.[2] For this reason, the

---

1. See the previously quoted statement regarding this by Sternberg. Sternberg, *The Poetics of Biblical Narrative*, 9.

2. This reality is best displayed in 2 Kgs 17:13 (NET), where it is said, "The Lord solemnly warned Israel and Judah through all his prophets and all the seers, 'Turn back from your evil ways; obey my commandments and rules that are recorded in the law. I ordered your ancestors to keep this law and sent my servants the prophets to remind you of its demands.'" Clendenen considers this passage as a paradigmatic one, highlighting the function of prophets as covenant mediators or enforcers. Clendenen, "Textlinguistics and Prophecy," 386.

prophets were often hated and ridiculed.³ Their messages often challenged the cultural norms and the religious and political institutions of the day. The confrontational nature of their messages required that they appeal to the people through varied rhetorical means.

Prophets rarely used mere propositional descriptive statements since they would not be remembered to the same degree as a rich word picture or a creatively crafted argument. Austin's work on speech act theory is helpful here. He distinguishes between constatives and performatives. Constatives are propositional descriptive statements. Performatives focus on performing an act and are classified into his three categories of locution, illocution, and perlocution. Locution is the initial act of saying or writing words within a certain context. The force or intent behind what is actually said is termed illocution. The illocutionary force refers to what the speaker means by his words. The locution and illocution together influence the recipient. This desired impact is referred to as the speech's perlocution. In summary, words stated or written (locution) have an intentional function (illocution) and are designed to lead the recipient to an action (perlocution).⁴ For the prophets, mere propositional descriptive statements were not persuasive enough. Thus, prophetic language was filled with poetry, where images abound and thoughts were commonly expressed in parallelism. Poetry, figures of speech, satire, irony, and even symbolic actions and naming⁵ became tools used to persuade the audience to change their actions.

Many of the poetic devices found in the poetical books are also used in the prophets; however, the nature of prophetic poetry is distinct from poetry used elsewhere. "Prophetic poetry . . . is devised as a form of direct address to a historically real audience."⁶ The conditions and circumstances in a historical era required a response from God's spokesmen. This rhetorical situation was best suited to be addressed using poetry. Prophetic poetry

---

3. 1 Kgs 18:4; 2 Chr 36:15–16; Jer 26:1–19; 37:14; Hos 9:7; Amos 7:10–17; Matt 5:12; 23:37; Acts 7:57; Heb 11:37.

4. Austin, *How to Do Things with Words*, 101–07.

5. For example, the names of Hosea and Isaiah's children had significant rhetorical meaning, and prophets were often led to perform symbolic actions for rhetorical meaning (e.g., Isa 20). Willis discusses how Isaiah contains two clusters (Isa 7:1—9:6 and 60–62) where the naming of people, places, and God emphasize and impress major theological themes on the minds of his hearers and readers. Willis, "Symbolic Names and Theological Themes," 72–92.

6. Alter, *The Art of Biblical Poetry*, 148.

had a powerfully persuasive "vocative character."[7] It provided a way for the prophet to attempt to shock the people out of their disobedience.

The poetic language of the prophets is memorable, leaving a vivid impression upon the audience. Sandy notes the power of prophetic literature and clearly shows how the prophets' use of imagery displays "God at the extreme limit of His attributes, humanity at the limits of disobedience, calamity that seems unlimited, and prosperity of peace and joy beyond limit."[8] Rhetorically, the use of such imagery enabled the speaker to achieve his intended persuasive goals, or at least to powerfully present before his audience the need to make a decision to change or to encourage the audience to remain faithful to the covenant. By describing these areas in their most powerful terms, the prophet stirred the audience's emotions. Feelings of fear, guilt, hopelessness, and desperation could overtake the listeners. The prophets desired that their audiences acknowledge their own guilt and turn from it. Without such change, they faced extraordinary impending judgment. Rather than using a mere propositional descriptive statement, the poetry communicated emphatically by providing a picture.[9]

While direct accusations using poetry highlighted the emotional appeals, these appeals were not simply created to stir the emotions. There was a logical basis for the argument. The prophets' statements of judgment had an illocutionary force that intended to remind the audience of their covenant with Yahweh. The people of Israel and Judah entered a treaty with Yahweh as their suzerain. The curses and the blessings mentioned in the covenant as found in Deuteronomy 6–7 and 28–30 provided the basis for God's responses. Consequently, when the prophets announced their judgment speeches to the people, they were based on a logical argument,

---

7. Alter, *The Art of Biblical Poetry*, 139. Alter states that this is the key distinction between prophetic poetry and poetry elsewhere in the Scriptures. Alter also makes the point that poetry best fits the divine speech that the prophets conveyed to the audience since it is our most intricate and rich form of communication.

8. Sandy, *Plowshares and Pruning Hooks*, 19–23.

9. To illustrate this point, consider the differences between an organization or ministry's mission statement and its vision statement. A mission statement declares an institution's goal and reason for its existence. In contrast, a vision statement paints a picture of what the mission statement looks like fulfilled. Instead of a simple statement often posted on a wall, it provides a picture that should stir the emotions of those who are a part of the organization or ministry. By seeing what could be, constituents become engaged, excited, and committed. Similarly, the prophets painted vivid pictures of who God is, of the people's utter sinfulness, and of His intentions of calamity and blessing. These pictures were much more emotionally engaging than a simple statement of intention or goal.

reasoned from Israel's covenantal relationship with Yahweh. God expected obedience, allegiance, and ethical living to characterize Israel's relationship with Him. When this expectation was violated, the prophets brought messages of God's intentions to respond to His disobedient vassal.

These prophetic messages must be approached with an awareness of key hermeneutical principles that are specific to their corpus. Chisholm highlights three key hermeneutical principles that are integrated with the poetic and rhetorical nature of the prophets. Prophecy is primarily functional, contingent, and contextualized.[10]

The prophets' foundational role was functional and accusatory in nature, directly accusing the listeners of disobedience while exhorting them to change their ways. Similarly, Sandy displays the relationship between the prophets' roles of prosecution, persuasion, and prediction.[11]

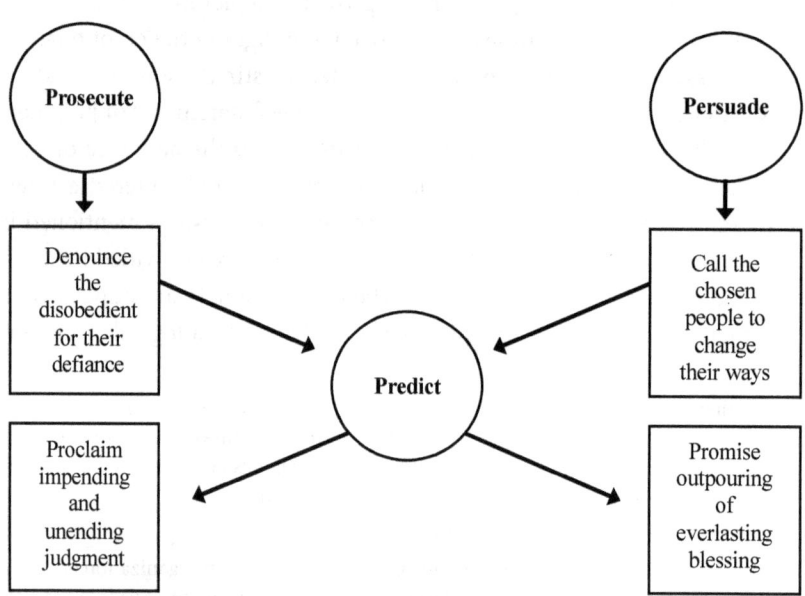

10. Chisholm, "When Prophecy Appears to Fail," 561–77.

11. Sandy, *Plowshares and Pruning Hooks*, 132. Taken from Plowshares & Pruning Hooks. Copyright (c) 2002 by D. Brent Sandy. Used by permission of InterVarsity Press, P.O. Box 1400, Downers Grove, IL 60515, USA. www.ivpress.com.

Sandy's chart reflects the primary role as one of prosecution, denouncing the disobedient for their defiance. The secondary role was that of persuasion, calling the chosen people to change their ways. From these two roles came the role of prediction. An unchanged response would result in impending and unending judgment. A repentant response provided the potential for a promise of everlasting blessing.[12]

In light of the functional role of prophecy, it is helpful to consider the aforementioned speech act theory.[13] Rather than emphasizing what is said in the Scriptures as simply a transmission of information, speech act theory brings to center-stage the functional aspect of the message. Regarding biblical studies, speech act theory is used by the interpreter to look at what is said (locution) and determine its intended meaning (illocutionary force) in order to determine the intended impact upon the audience (perlocution), all within the original contextual setting. Patte acknowledges that this often challenges the exegete, who is forced to take into consideration what is not in the text.[14] By this, Patte refers to the need to share the author's illocution, which is not simply the text written on the page. Sandy rightly states, "The *function* of statements in the Bible can be as important for understanding their meaning as the *content* of the statements . . . Ignorance of illocution leads to exegetical fallacies."[15]

---

12. Clendenen and Chisholm make similar points. Clendenen builds on Longacre's system of discourse types and highlights that the prophet books are hortatory by nature and include: "(1) the situation that needs to be changed; (2) the change being called for; and (3) the arguments or factors used to motivate that change." Clendenen, "Textual Linguistics and Prophecy in the Book of the Twelve," 388. Chisholm references the distinctions between expository-hortatory discourse and predictive discourse. The expository-hortatory discourse is similar to Sandy's terms of "prosecute" and "persuade." The prophets evaluated the disobedient behavior and challenged the hearers to change. The predictive discourse parallels Sandy's prediction. Chisholm also points out that predictive discourse, in light of its typical conditional nature, also is intended to persuade the hearers to change. Chisholm, "When Prophecy Appears to Fail, Check Your Hermeneutic," 562–63.

13. It should be noted that speech act theory is useful but has been a debated topic. One cannot make a simple categorization of all those that use speech act theory in biblical interpretation. Its uses are broad, and scholarly work varies as to the extent of its usage. Brevard Childs, Vern Sheridan Poythress, and Kevin Vanhoozer are among those who have written concerning the distinctions and limitations of speech act theory. Childs, "Speech-Act Theory and Biblical Interpretation," 375–92; Poythress, "Canon and Speech Act," 337–54; Vanhoozer, *Is There a Meaning in This Text?*

14. Patte, "Speech Act Theory and Biblical Exegesis," 90.

15. Sandy, *Plowshares and Pruning Hooks*, 82.

The second hermeneutical principle is closely related to prophecy's functional nature. Prophecy is primarily contingent, also referred to as conditional, rather than deterministic. Since the prophets sought to persuade their audiences, the announcements made were most often conditional. As Richard Pratt notes, "They spoke of *potential* and not *necessary* future events. Thus, their predictions warned of judgment and offered blessings in order to motivate listeners to participate in determining their own future."[16] They announced the Lord's intentions, which were typically subject to change based on the people's response. The prophets stressed a cause-and-effect relationship in both the looming judgment and the potential for restoration. Defiance was the cause of the impending doom, but repentance could be a catalyst for Divine mercy.

Within the covenant treaty curses, Deuteronomy 28:68 makes the contingent nature of prophecy evident. The Lord threatened to "bring you back in ships to Egypt, a journey that I promised that you should never take again." Despite the prior promise of blessing, this curse depicts that the promise of blessing was conditional upon obedience. This hermeneutic principle of contingency is most clearly reflected in Jeremiah 18:1–12. Following an illustration of a potter and clay, the Lord declared that an announced judgment could be averted if that nation repented. Likewise, if a nation chose to do evil, it could miss out on an announced blessing. Thus, the potter, while free to do as he pleases, allows the clay to impact his decision in the clay's formation.[17] The principle of contingency is illustrated numerous other times in the prophetic books.

Isaiah expressed this principle in 1:19–20, where obedience would lead to prosperous crops, but disobedience would result in death.[18] Joel 2:12–18 recorded judgment being averted through repentance.[19] The Ninevites were spared destruction through repentance in Jonah 3–4. After two destructive visions, Amos interceded on behalf of Israel to temporarily withhold judgment (7:1–6). Micah 3:12 recorded a message of judgment against Jerusalem. Although there is no hint at its conditionality in Micah,

---

16. Pratt, "Historical Contingencies and Biblical Predictions," 184.

17. Wessels, "At the Potter's Workshop," 4.

18. Isaiah's use of prophetic poetry is displayed in these verses. Obedience would literally lead to their ability to "eat" (תֹּאכֵלוּ) of the good of the land, but disobedience would cause them to be "eaten" (תְּאֻכְּלוּ) by the sword.

19. For a discussion on the Hebrew verbs in Joel 2:18 as narratival, see Allen, Barker, or Chisholm. Allen, *The Books of Joel, Obadiah, Jonah, and Micah*, 85–90; Barker, *Joel: Despair and Deliverance*, 113–19; Chisholm, *Handbook on the Prophets*, 373.

Jeremiah 26:18–19 recorded that the disaster was averted through Hezekiah's intercession and repentance.

In addition to being recognized as functional and contingent, prophecies must also be read within their contextualized setting to avoid drawing fallacious conclusions from the text. As noted previously, the message arose out of a rhetorical situation rooted in the culture and context of the prophet's time. The normal prophetic message was understandable to the original audience, the author's contemporaries. Thus, even the future predictions were described, "as being realized in their own contemporary geopolitical context."[20]

Relevance theory provides a helpful tool to the interpreter when considering the contextual nature of prophecy. Relevance theory suggests that the author and the audience shared a cultural and rhetorical context.[21] Therefore, when an utterance is given, the author assumes that the audience can infer more than simply the propositions stated. The meaning of any utterance is always found within a rhetorical context. This communicative theory mandates that a text's meaning be understood within its original contextual setting. Communication is highly inferential. Therefore, "it is important to attend to what is implicit in a speaker's meaning as well as what is explicit, since both are essential for understanding meaning."[22] As Brown relates it, "linguistic expression + background context assumptions = meaning (i.e., utterance meaning, which includes both explicit and implicit meaning.)"[23]

When an interpreter lacks contextual knowledge of a period and the rhetorical setting of a piece of historic writing, communication stalls. Successful interpretation requires effort to provide the adequate contextual effects of the original rhetorical setting. In many ways, relevance theory challenges the modern interpreter to overcome the contextual gap that exists and to consider the shared contextual environment in the meaning of a text. Gutt captures the idea well: "even with a good background in biblical studies, for many biblical passages, we are a long way from the communicative impact of the original, a long way from the rich and exciting interpretation it yielded to its readers."[24]

---

20. Chisholm, "When Prophecy Appears to Fail," 573.
21. Sperber and Wilson, *Relevance: Communication and Cognition*, 41–42.
22. Brown, *Scripture as Communication*, 36.
23. Brown, *Scripture as Communication*, 38.
24. Gutt, *Relevance Theory: A Guide*, 33.

While certainly one can address other hermeneutical principles encountered in the prophetic texts, the functional, contingent, and contextualized aspects of prophecy provide a solid foundation for understanding the rhetorical nature of prophecy. While approaching Hosea 1–3, the interpretation of the text will rely on these principles.

Rhetorical Criticism

The term rhetoric has been defined variously. Corbett and Connors define rhetoric as "the art or the discipline that deals with the use of discourse, either spoken or written, to inform or persuade or motivate an audience, whether that audience is made up of one person or a group of persons."[25] Rhetoric finds its roots in the beginning of communication itself; yet, the study of rhetoric as an art or science owes its beginnings to Aristotle.[26] Aristotle defined rhetoric as "the faculty of discovering the possible means of persuasion in reference to any subject whatever."[27] He saw rhetoric as a counterpart to dialectic, a means of intellectual investigation by process of discussion and reasoning, often through the process of logic and detection of logical fallacies. In classical studies, rhetoric was a vitally important broad field of study. Its goal was to master the art of persuasion. Since many decisions rested on one's communication of a view, speech was seen as a weapon.[28] Aristotle recognized three elements of speech: a speaker, a subject, and a person addressed.[29] The speaker seeks to persuade an audience by learning to say things well.

---

25. Corbett and Connors, *Classical Rhetoric for the Modern Student*, 1. Various other modern authors provide helpful definitions as well. Patrick and Scult define rhetoric as "the means by which a text establishes and manages its relationship to its audience in order to achieve a particular effect." Patrick and Scult, *Rhetoric and Biblical Interpretation*, 12.

26. Prior to Aristotle, rhetoric was studied by the Sophists and Plato; however, Aristotle's thoughts on rhetoric redeemed the study of rhetoric as something positive and not to be scorned. It is recognized that Aristotle's writings came after the writings of the Old Testament text. While some rhetorical critics use classical rhetoric's terminology, this study will refrain from such usage, recognizing the primary knowledge of Old Testament literary devices and persuasive technique must rely most heavily on the Old Testament itself and writings from other ancient Near Eastern contemporary cultures.

27. Aristotle, *Rhetoric*, 1.2.1.

28. Ricoeur, *The Rule of Metaphor*, 9. Ricoeur elaborates on the tension between the ethics of rhetoric and philosophy.

29. It should be noted that modern communication studies have rightly recognized

The application of rhetorical studies to the biblical text has flourished in the last fifty years.[30] By the late twentieth century, many Old Testament scholars became disenchanted with the results of historical-critical approaches to the text. The constant detailed analysis and reconstruction left an impression that the books had little literary purpose and structure. Allowing for editorial work within a text, a new literary, theological, and rhetorical approach arose that emphasized the structure and thematic messages of the final form of the text.

In 1968, James Muilenburg challenged Old Testament scholarship to go beyond mere form criticism.[31] Muilenburg appreciated form criticism but saw limitations within it. He urged biblical scholarship to build upon form criticism and begin to study other literary features that were being ignored. While form criticism tends to emphasize individual pericopes, Muilenburg argued for scholarship to study the text in its entirety. He described his process and method as being interested "in understanding the nature of Hebrew literary composition, in exhibiting the structural patterns that are employed for the fashioning of a literary unit, whether in poetry or in prose, and in discerning the many and various devices in which the predications are formulated and ordered into a unified whole."[32] He entitled this method "rhetorical criticism," and his address led to the field of biblical studies entitled accordingly.

Although Muilenburg's charge initially sought to see rhetorical criticism as an additional aspect of form criticism, rhetorical criticism has become a discipline in and of itself. Watson and Hauser's work traces the breadth of rhetorical studies since Muilenburg's challenge.[33] Much of the

---

more elements that are involved in the communication process— elements such as outside "noise" that may hinder the communication process and the reality of nonverbal communication that comes from the audience back to the speaker. Further, classical rhetoric is divided into five elements: *inventio* (invention), *dispositio* (arrangement), *elocutio* (style), *memoria* (memory), and *pronuntiatio* (delivery).

30. Trible has provided a helpful history of rhetorical studies. Trible, *Rhetorical Criticism: Context, Method, and the Book of Jonah*, 5–54.

31. Muilenburg, "Form Criticism and Beyond," 1–18.

32. Muilenburg, "Form Criticism and Beyond," 8. Muilenburg offered some clear guidelines to follow. His first step urged the interpreter to define the literary unit, where it begins and where it ends. The second step was to recognize the structure of a composition and discern the configuration of its component parts, noting the rhetorical devices that are employed, the sequence and movement of the pericope, and the shifts and breaks in the author's thoughts.

33. Watson and Hauser, *Rhetorical Criticism of the Bible*.

early work addressed narrative literature, especially studies in the Torah.[34] Robert Alter, Adele Berlin, Jan Fokkelman, Meir Sternberg, and Robert Chisholm have made significant contributions in the field of both biblical narrative and biblical poetry.[35] The study of metaphor has also benefited greatly from these literary advances.[36] Regarding Hosea specifically, Gerald Morris, Göran Eidvall, Jack R. Lundbom, G. W. Light, and Francis Landy are among more recent scholars who offer studies on the literary nature of the book.[37] Brad E. Kelle's rhetorical study of Hosea 2 considers Hosea's rhetoric in light of a specific historical and political setting.[38]

Rhetorical criticism attempts to study the overall structure of a literary unit and how its rhetorical devices contribute to the expression of its message, thus enabling the reader to trace the writer's/editor's thought. What was lacking in Muilenburg's charge was an emphasis on the persuasive nature of rhetoric.[39] Trible stresses that rhetorical criticism is interested in both the "art of composition" and the "art of persuasion" of the text.[40] A close consideration of the structure and devices enables one to

34. Jan P. Fokkelman produced an early work on the entirety of Genesis in 1975 and has continued to produce rhetorical works. Fokkelman, *Narrative Art in Genesis*, and Fokkelman, *Reading Biblical Narrative*. Clines also wrote in the late 1970s on the Pentateuch. His work presented the Pentateuch as a literary whole, arguing that the historical-critical method, with its tendencies towards *atomism* and *geneticism*, had hindered Pentateuchal studies. Clines, *The Theme of the Pentateuch*, 7–9. *Atomism* referred to the reduction of the text to excessive sources. *Geneticism* referred to the overemphasis of "the origins and development of the extant Biblical text."

35. Alter, *The Art of Biblical Narrative*; Alter, *The Art of Biblical Poetry*; Chisholm, *A Commentary of Judges and Ruth*; Chisholm, *From Exegesis to Exposition*; Sternberg, *The Poetics of Biblical Narrative*; Berlin, *Poetics and Interpretation of Biblical Narrative*.

36. Studies on the rhetorical nature of metaphor are vast. Contributions in metaphorical studies include work from Paul Ricoeur, Wayne Booth, J. S. Mio and A. N. Katz, J. David Sapir and J. Christopher Crocker, George Lakoff and Mark Johnson, G. B. Caird, Harold Fisch, Adele Berlin, J. Cheryl Exum, Göran Eidvall, Gerald Morris, and Peter Macky. Full bibliographic data are given in the bibliography.

37. Eidevall, *Grapes in the Desert*; Morris, *Prophecy, Poetry, and Hosea*; Lundbom, "Poetic Structure and Rhetoric in Hosea"; Landy, "In the Wilderness of Speech."

38. Kelle, *Hosea 2*.

39. While Muilenburg's article did not emphasize the persuasive aspect of rhetorical criticism, his work on Isaiah 40–66 did engage persuasion. Muilenburg, "The Book of Isaiah: Chapters 40–66," 381–773. Similarly, Gitay's work on Isaiah 40–48 uses Aristotelian rhetoric to emphasize how Deutero-Isaiah carefully crafted his arguments to persuade the audience to make a decision. Gitay, *Prophecy and Persuasion: A Study of Isaiah 40–48*.

40. Trible, *Rhetorical Criticism*, 25–52. See also Barton, *Reading the Old Testament*,

consider the author's point in the discourse. Yet, as Sternberg aptly states, "form has no value or meaning apart from communicative (historical, ideological, aesthetic) function."[41] Thus, rhetorical criticism should not be merely interested in a formal examination of literary structure, but should also seek to understand how the text communicates ideas and desires for a performative purpose, seeking a particular effect upon the audience.[42] The prophets spoke and wrote persuasive messages to address specific conditions and circumstances facing the people. The persuasive nature of their messages reinforces the functional aspect of prophetic hermeneutics mentioned earlier.

Rhetorical studies, growing out of form-critical studies, have also highlighted a message's oral nature. The original audiences most often received the communication by oral means. In ancient Israel, few people would read a text. Most would hear it, either when it was initially spoken or when it was read to them after it was written.

Möller highlights the rhetorical nature of reading practices in antiquity. First, reading was a social event and almost always done aloud. Even solitary reading was typically done aloud. Secondly, ancient writers likely wrote for public reading, so they often used oral indicators. Lastly, since oral reading was a fluid process that expected readers' responses, rhetorical signals needed to be easily recognized to be effective.[43] Thus, the oral nature of communication in ancient Israel prompted a need for the careful crafting of a persuasive message.

With an emphasis on rhetoric, rhetorical critics look at the structure, devices, and details within a passage, as well as both the oral and written rhetorical setting to understand the message and persuasive intent of the author. Watson and Hauser have defined rhetorical criticism well in relation to the Old Testament. Rhetorical criticism is "a form of literary criticism which uses our knowledge of the conventions of literary composition practiced in ancient Israel and its environment to discover and analyze the particular literary artistry found in a specific unit of the Old Testament text.

---

199. Some rhetorical critics see their emphasis on the persuasion to be a corrective or in opposition to Muilenburg's approach.

41. Sternberg, *The Poetics of Biblical Narrative*, xii.

42. Patrick engages the performative nature of revelation, stating, "Speech acts are pragmatic, and that requires speakers to calculate strategies for achieving desired results." Patrick, *The Rhetoric of Revelation*, 12.

43. Möller, *A Prophet in Debate*, 50–60.

This analysis then provides a basis for discussing the message of the text and the impact it had on its audience."[44]

Though often overlooked, geography and spatiality are included in the details and devices used by the ancient authors. These elements provided common referents for the ancient authors to build their cases or to stir up the audience's emotions. Patrick says it well: "All persuasion requires that the rhetor build on the knowledge, beliefs, and affections of the audience."[45] Geography and spatiality are additional building blocks that a biblical rhetor often used to be persuasive. As will be seen in chapter 4 and 5, this is certainly the case for Hosea.

Critical Spatial Theory

While there are a variety of approaches to critical spatial theory, this book adopts the model and principles of Edward Soja, believing that he offers principles that can be universalized beyond his purposes and applied to biblical studies, and in this case, to the analysis of the rhetoric of the eighth century prophet Hosea.[46] In this case, his categories are being used to provide the biblical interpreter with another set of tools that help the process of observing the text, asking proper questions, and understanding the message more wholistically. Biblical studies remain text-focused, but Soja's categories are helpful as one approaches spatial references from an etic perspective, attempting to see the text closer to the original emic audience. Furthermore, the use of these principles contributes to an understanding of how spaces are transformed or changed, as sometimes this is the result of social groups in conflict.

Critical spatial theorists have argued that space and geography have often been ignored amidst the rise of social and historical studies. Regarding this disparity, Flanagan states that "omitting, ignoring, or suppressing

---

44. Watson and Hauser, *Rhetorical Criticism of the Bible*, 4.

45. Patrick, *The Rhetoric of Revelation*, 7.

46. For further discussion on the use of Soja's principles and a response to a critique of the use of them, see n71 below. A biblical scholar, who seeks to apply the Bible's principles to life, interprets a text that is contextualized in an ancient setting to de-contextualize the timeless principle from the text so that the principle can then be recontextualized and applied to the current context. Similarly, this book is interpreting Soja's work to see what universal principles are helpful for understanding spatial concepts more fully so that those principles can be reapplied to the study of Hosea's rhetorical use of geography and spatiality.

spatiality leads to imbalanced, distorted, and continually flawed understandings and practices in the real world." While the historical and social aspects of life have rightly been a focus of scholarship, it is essential to recognize that both of these aspects occur in space. A balanced approach must look at history, sociality, and spatiality together in a trialectic methodology.[47] One cannot properly understand history, society, or spatiality in isolation.[48] These three disciplines are intricately related and dependent on one another. Considering the principles and applications of critical spatial theory offers the interpreter the opportunity to attain a more balanced and undistorted understanding of the real world.

Key Principles of Critical Spatial Theory

Soja captures the three key principles upon which critical spatial thinking center:

a. The ontological spatiality of being (we are all spatial as well as social and temporal beings).
b. The social production of spatiality (space is socially produced and can therefore be socially changed).
c. The socio-spatial dialectic (the spatial shapes the social as much as the social shapes the spatial).[49]

These three principles are somewhat intuitive but not commonly considered. They highlight the impact that space has on human beings and can spur the biblical interpreter to reconsider how space is referenced and used by biblical authors.

The Ontological Spatiality of Being

Humans are social and temporal beings, living in a historical time period and within societal groups. These two aspects of being always occur in the third aspect: space. While the fact that life is lived in space appears simplistic, the spatial element of life has most often been studied marginally in comparison to social and historical studies.

47. Soja calls this the "Trialectics of Being."
48. Soja, *Thirdspace*, 72.
49. Soja, "The City and Spatial Justice," 2.

Meaning is centered in human experiences, which occur in space. Thus, there is an intricate relationship between what happens in a space and that space's multidimensional meaning. Tuan emphasizes that it is life experiences that provide a place its aura. He defines experience as "a cover-all term for the various modes through which a person knows and constructs a reality."[50] The experiential shapes the significance of a space.[51]

Experiences can be approached at both the personal and corporate level. Individuals attribute meaning to places based on their own experiences. When biblical authors refer to places, it is often the case that the original audience was experientially aware of the place. They had been there and experienced life in its midst.[52] Furthermore, since individuals may have different experiences from others, the meaning of a space may be polysemous. Corporately, a place becomes identified with daily life and well-known events experienced in its history. For example, Matthews highlights how the cultic experiences at Bethel, with all of its politically appointed systems, became a key point in the polemics of Amos and Hosea.[53] The prophets' simple references to Bethel tapped into the corporate experiences of the people.

Life is lived in space, and space "holds memories that implicate people and events."[54] People attribute meaning to places based on what individuals and groups experienced. Consider how the meaning or aura of the ancient steps outside of the Huldah gates changes for modern

---

50. Tuan, *Space and Place: The Perspective of Experience*, 8.

51. Kosal follows Tuan on differentiating place as a distinctive part of space, a relational space. Kosal, "Society, Spatiality, and the Sacred," 57. Similar to this book, Kosal proposes an interdisciplinary approach to build a new methodology. He proposes to: (1) "derive conceptual and theoretical discussions on the notions of sacred from sociology and the anthropology of religion;" (2) "draw on the analyses of cultural and historical studies and adapt their concepts appropriate to the intricate social, cultural, and political context in which the sacred is embedded;" and (3) take place seriously, pulling together a conceptual and theoretical framework that rethinks the sacred so that it is both socially and spatially constructed.

52. Consider the modern commercials for Las Vegas that base their whole marketing plea on one's past or future experiences there. Biblically, consider Jesus's message of woe in Matthew 23. His message was intricately tied to where he was speaking, providing clear imagery from their experiences of Moses's seat in the synagogues, the Hinnom Valley (Gehenna), and the white-washed tombs on the Mount of Olives.

53. Matthews, "Back to Bethel," 161–65.

54. Low and Lawrence-Zúñiga, "Locating Culture," 13.

Christians when they realize that Jesus may have actually walked on those steps and taught from them.

This dynamic affirms that symbolic value is ascribed to space. Past history, both recent and extended, occurred in space and thus shaped and defined space. As Matthews writes, "Memory lingers. It attaches itself to events, persons, and places creating a mental map that guides, consciously or unconsciously, much of our everyday activities and allows us to make a virtual journey back in time."[55] When activities and events become accepted among groups, they become part of the group's collective memory.[56] They are part of the cognitive environment shared between an author and his/her audience. This becomes part of the culture's "social frame."[57]

The Social Production of Spatiality

The principle of ontological spatiality of being is directly related to the principle of the social production of spatiality. Life is lived by individuals and societies in space. As societies live in space, they shape and create it. Henri Lefebvre, a pioneer in critical spatial studies, recognized that a geographical space is a product of a society.[58] Societies attribute social meanings to spaces, and as previously noted, these meanings are most often based on experiences.[59] Rodman notes, "Places are not inert containers. They are politicized, culturally relative, historically specific, local and multiple constructions."[60] Places can have shared meanings (e.g., collective memory)

---

55. Matthews, "Remembered Space in Biblical Narrative," 61.

56. Assmann discusses how memories become shared and collective: "Once they are verbalized in the form of a narrative or represented by a visual image, the individual's memories become part of an intersubjective symbolic system and are, strictly speaking, no longer a purely exclusive and unalienable property." Assmann, "Transformations between History and Memory," 50. See also Assmann, *Religion and Cultural Memory*; Bommas, ed., *Cultural Memory and Identity*; Rogerson, *A Theology of the Old Testament*; Un-Sok Ro and Vikander eds., *Collective Memory and Collective Identity*; Erll and Nünning, eds., *Companion to Cultural Memory Studies*.

57. Assmann defines social frame as "an implicit or explicit structure of shared concerns, values, experiences, narratives. The family, the neighborhood, the peer group, the generation, the nation, the culture are such larger groups that individuals incorporate into their identity by referring to them as 'we.'" Assmann, "Transformations between History and Memory," 52.

58. Lefebvre, *The Production of Space*, 26.

59. Tuan, *Space and Place*, 3–7.

60. Rodman, "Empowering Place," 205.

or contested meanings (i.e., when social groups are in opposition). The experiences of people affect how a space is thought about and how life is practiced in it.[61] Again, Rodman states, "Places have multiple meanings that are constructed spatially. The physical, emotional, and experiential realities places hold for their inhabitants at particular times need to be understood apart from their creation as the locales of ethnography."[62]

As societies change over time, so too the meanings of spaces change and evolve over time. Space is not a fixed entity but a dynamic one, best understood through the historical progression of time. A space is not static, maintaining its meaning throughout its existence; rather, space is variable, as meanings associated with it develop and change. As society changes, space changes, both physically and due to the meanings associated with it. As Matthews notes, space can be transformed and repurposed. A space, "which had physical qualities and a social reality associated with its use or its perceived use, becomes a newly designed product with new social possibilities associated with the persons who inhabit and use it."[63]

The modern reader comes to the text from an etic perspective, living outside of the ancient culture. As a result, one runs the risk of reading the text anachronistically, reading a later culture or even one's own culture back into the text, or ignoring the social meanings associated with spatiality. It is impossible to live within the ancient culture of the biblical world, making one thus unable to read the text with a "direct and intimate" experiential or emic knowledge.[64] However, since biblical scholarship attempts to read

---

61. Winter reflects how Europeans organically and collectively remembered the loss of life from World War I. He addresses this within the context of different 'sites of memory,' reflecting how physical places are filled with emotional and experiential reality. In Europe, he concludes that the human catastrophes were culturally encoded throughout the community via the visual images of the dead, through prose and writing, and through social action. This reflects Soja's principle of the social production of spatiality. For example, in response to the great loss, war memorials are seen throughout Europe. These memorials communicate various messages, but they clearly point to the harshness of life and death during a time of war. Winter, *Sites of Memory, Sites of Mourning*.

62. Rodman, "Empowering Place," 205. In context, Rodman is expressing concern over anthropologists creating western, industrialized concepts of a people group's places, urging an understanding rooted in the experiences of the indigenous people group. Her point is also well-applied to biblical societies and places.

63. Matthews, "Remembered Space in Biblical Narrative," 67. Elsewhere Matthews uses the term "geographic reiteration" to refer to the process by which place names evolve and are thereby used as a strategy for scribal and political purposes. Matthews, "Back to Bethel," 149–65.

64. Tuan, *Space and Place*, 6.

a historical piece of writing within the setting of the society in which it originated, critical spatial theory can be used as a tool to conceptually understand space from the perspective of the society that produced it.

The Socio-Spatial Dialectic

Social life both contributes to the shaping of a space and is also shaped by that space. This dialectic relationship is exemplified in Winston Churchill's *House of Commons Rebuilding*. On October 28, 1943, more than two years after the House of Commons had been destroyed by bombings, Churchill stated, "We shape our buildings; thereafter they shape us." He made a plea to rebuild the chamber in the same shape because he had too "great pleasure and advantage" from the building. He attributed the two-party system to the shape of the chamber, stating, "It has a collective personality which enjoys the regard of the public and which imposes itself upon the conduct not only of Individual Members but of parties."[65]

People have a role in the structure of a place, but the structure of a place also influences people. Mary Mills engages this same principle in her discussion of psycho-geography. She emphasizes that cities affect people's minds, and in turn, the human imagination affects the cities.[66] This mutual process is evident in the daily activities of life and the relationships between social groups.

Spaces are used to communicate messages regarding social relationships.[67] As noted earlier, they can be a means of rhetoric, providing emotional impact and reflecting authority. Those in power often shape space, resulting in various effects upon different classes in a society. Boundaries, buildings, property, and structures in worship influence social structures. It is often over space that social groups collide in conflict. Rabinow writes, "space could be used as one of several tools to locate and identify the relations of knowledge and power."[68] When space is used as a means of controlling social structures, this is referred to as spatial tactics.

---

65. "Churchill and the Commons Chamber."
66. Mills, *Urban Imagination in Biblical Prophecy*.
67. Kuper, "The Language of Sites in the Politics of Space," 258.
68. Rabinow, "Ordonnance, Discipline, Regulations," 354.

Trialectics of Spatiality

The three principles of critical spatial theory provide a foundation to consider the multi-dimensional character of spatiality. As noted earlier, Edward Soja proposed that the state of "being" is composed of the interrelated nature of history, sociality, and spatiality, which he terms the "trialectics of being." Similarly, he proposes that space also has a trialectic nature. Responding to the work of Henri Lefebvre, he acknowledges three key dimensions of space: Firstspace, Secondspace, and Thirdspace.[69] These three dimensions are not independent of each other. They are not different types of space.[70] Rather, all three are concurrently a reality of a geographic space.[71]

Firstspace involves two components: the physical and material aspects of a space, and the everyday practices and interactions with the physical space. It speaks to the physical description of a space and its environment, including a space's topographical aspects, its physical location, and the constructions (e.g., buildings) located within it. Further, it considers the "everyday spatial practices such as 'job routines', 'travel routes', 'urban life', and 'leisure.'"[72] It is that which can be measured and mapped.

When approaching a biblical spatial reference, an interpreter should take into consideration the reference's Firstspace. How did the intended audience see the physical nature of the space? What are the characteristics that were shared with the author but are no longer shared with the modern

---

69. While it is common to see Soja's and Lefebvre's categories made synonymous, Meredith has argued that Soja has oversimplified Lefebvre's categories, and that Soja's oversimplification has become the norm by which people now read Lefebvre. Soja's Firstspace is related to Lefebvre's "perceived space;" Secondspace is related to Lefebvre's "conceived space;" and Thirdspace is related to Lefebvre's "lived space." Meredith, "Taking Issue with Thirdspace," 82–89.

70. Soja, *Thirdspace*, 70–82.

71. Christopher Meredith has urged biblical scholarship to be more critical of using Soja and Lefebvre's principles in biblical studies. He argues that Soja's Thirdspace is "a more troublesome and nebulous concept than is often advertised." He highlights that Soja's motivations are tied to modern applications in an attempt to promote social emancipation. Yet, he states "The Sojan trialectic acknowledges the inter-relationship of arena, idea and praxis, certainly, but it only presents us with tools for isolating each of these three aspects of space from the fellows." This is the benefit that this book finds in using Soja's categories. They are not being used in an attempt to see how a marginalized group sought to override some political or economic system, but the categories provide the biblical interpreter with another set of tools that help the process of observing the text and understanding it more wholistically. Meredith, "Taking Issue with Thirdspace," 76, 77, 79.

72. Allen, "The Socio-Spatial Making and Marking of 'Us,'" 259.

audience? Has archaeological research provided further insight into our understanding of the Firstspace of the reference?[73] Had there been recent changes to the space (e.g., new or destroyed buildings, sacred sites, walls, roads, etc.)? What everyday activities were involved with this space?

Secondspace refers to how a space is conceived in people's minds. It refers to the mental constructs, the "imagined representations" that are thought about a space.[74] This entails the meanings, purposes, and feelings attributed to the location. It is the subjective element of space that is intangible. It is the space that is produced by language and ideologies, known through thought. Kuper writes that a site "becomes a symbol within the total and complex system of communication in the total social universe."[75] Firstspace is important, but a space's symbolic meaning adds a new dimension to what its reference communicates.

Since conceived space embraces the thought process, one must take into account the previously mentioned memory of a place. Memory is directly related to space.[76] Since human experiences occur in physical spaces, they are naturally identified with space. Of memory, Matthews states, "It attaches itself to events, persons, and places creating a mental map that guides, consciously or unconsciously, much of our everyday activities and also allows us to make a virtual journey back in time."[77] In fact, Matthews even advances Soja's categories, labeling "remembered space" as "Fourthspace."[78] This study will consider memory within Soja's category of Secondspace.[79]

---

73. Soja promotes this wholistic approach within archaeology too. He states, "archaeologists should not weaken their focus on temporality and historical explanation but strengthen it through an adaptation of an equally rich critical spatial perspective, always conceiving history as geohistory, with neither temporality nor spatiality privileged over the other." Blake, "Spatiality Past and Present: An Interview with Edward Soja," 144.

74. Soja, *Thirdspace*, 79.

75. Kuper, "The Language of Sites in the Politics of Space," 258.

76. Richard Flores discusses the relationship of space and memory while covering the memory of the Alamo. He states, "collective memory is semiotically grounded in geographic sites, providing physical and spatial locations upon which social meanings, and concomitantly, social identities are fabricated. As such, collective memories, disguised as the workings of historical discourse, are spatially and physically embedded in geographically fixed sites of public history." Flores, "Memory-Place, Meaning the Alamo," 429.

77. Matthews, "Remembered Space in Biblical Narrative," 61.

78. Matthews, "Remembered Space in Biblical Narrative," 62.

79. Given the breadth of research on memory, Matthews's Fourthspace is an attractive consideration for future studies. Memory seems to be comprised within Soja's concept

Since experiences in a place vary from person to person and group to group, the memory of a place, while sometimes becoming a collective memory, is often diverse. Hartmann captures this diversity: "there is not one ultimate memory, but rather diverse cultures of remembrance at different times, societal structures and societal strata, and these cultures of remembrance are dynamic, creative and discursive."[80] This dynamic of memory theory must be considered when studying the use of geography and space in the rhetoric of a biblical message. On the one hand, a space is perceived in light of its current setting. Yet, the perception and meaning of a space are also shaped by its historical memory, both in its recent and distant past. A space can be "transformed and literally repurposed" while its former memory continues to "define that space."[81]

The interpreter must therefore account for Secondspace as well. How was the space considered within the biblical culture? Was it a space that was contested? Is there a reason why the event occurred at this space and not somewhere else? Was the space considered negatively?[82] Conversely, was the space considered positively? Was the space perceived to have different meanings based on gender and the role of men, women, or children? What memories were attached to the space? Did different social groups hold

---

of Secondspace but could also be considered separately as it would expand beyond the conceived meaning of the original audience. The memory of prior and future audiences would also be considered. Such an approach would be most beneficial when considering a comprehensive study of a place. While it has value for considering the rhetorical significance to Hosea's implied audience as well, this work will attempt to narrow the scope and include memory in Secondspace as to avoid introducing further complexities to the model. In addition to the aforementioned work on cultural memory (see fn 55 and 56 above), Pierre Nora's work on 'sites of memory' in France has been widely applied to various historical studies (e.g., see the aforementioned work of Jay Winter in fn 61 above). Nora describes a 'site of memory' (*lieux de* mémoire) as a place where "memory crystallizes and secretes itself." It is "any significant entity, whether material or nonmaterial in nature, which by dint of human will or work of time has become a symbolic element of the memorial heritage of any community." These "sites of memory" include the material, the symbolic, and the functional. Without the will to remember, a place simply become a historical site. Nora, *The Realms of Memory*; Nora and Jordan, eds., *Rethinking France: Les Lieux de mémoire*.

80. Hartmann, "Mental maps, Cognitive Mapping and Mental Space," 330.

81. Matthews, "Remembered Space in Biblical Narrative," 67.

82. Munn describes types of space that are excluded because they are viewed as negative in nature and thus avoided. Munn, "Excluded Spaces," 95.

those memories differently?[83] Was the space considered public or private? Was the space considered sacred?

For Soja, the two dimensions of Firstspace and Secondspace are incomplete. One must also consider what he terms "Thirdspace." Thirdspace is a "flexible term that attempts to capture what is actually a constantly shifting and changing milieu of ideas, events, appearances, and meanings."[84] Space encompasses both the real (Firstspace) and imagined (Secondspace), but also includes more, an "Other" space. It is the space where "everything comes together . . . subjectivity and objectivity, the abstract and the concrete, the real and the imagined, the knowable and the unimaginable, the repetitive and the differential, structure and agency, mind and body, consciousness and the unconscious, the disciplined and the transdisciplinary, everyday life and unending history."[85] This social space reflects how Firstspace and Secondspace cannot be reduced to simplistic understandings. In "lived space" ideologies are often in conflict over space. It is in Thirdspace where opposing social groups collide with their various views, where often the dominant power group's ideology is in tension with those not in power. It is because of Thirdspace that we see how space is socially changed.

When considering Thirdspace, the interpreter should ask questions of the text that consider the various ways life was lived in a space. What is the dominant social group's perspective on the Firstspace and Secondspace of a location? Did this view align with the principles and instructions of the covenant Israel made with Yahweh?[86] Is the author/speaker confronting a dominant or secondary social group's views (i.e., is there polemical value)? Is a spatial meaning being challenged or transformed? What is the rhetorical significance of such a challenge or modification? Are there norms in spatiality that are being violated (e.g., is a person or group in/out of place)?

As a result of considering these dimensions, a geographical space becomes the ever-expansive cultural concept discussed earlier. It is influenced and socially produced by renegotiations of power, social changes, and realignment of boundaries. It reflects both the physical realities and the mental/cultural constructions. It has a dialectical relationship with

---

83. Matthews, "Remembered Space in Biblical Narrative," 61.

84. Soja, *Thirdspace*, 2.

85. Soja, *Thirdspace*, 57. Allen provides a helpful analysis of the distinctions and interconnectedness of the trialectics of spatiality. Allen, "The Socio-Spatial Making and Marking of 'Us.'"

86. If applying the principles to the New Testament, consider NT teachings as well.

those living in it. For biblical studies, this component of space is vital. Geography has to be read within its historical and cultural setting. While the biblical text offers a source for the cultural context of a location, extra-biblical sources and archaeological evidence also play a significant role. A comprehensive approach opens a cultural window into the significance of a space. Only when one considers space within this cultural window is one able to fully appreciate the rhetorical significance of geographical and spatial references.[87]

---

[87]. Beck uses the term "narrative geography" to highlight how writers of biblical narratives carefully used geography in the storytelling process. In the narrative of Elijah's showdown with the prophets of Baal, Beck highlights how the author used the geographical and spatial concepts of drought, Mt. Carmel, and rainfall to reflect the reversal of what appeared to be a geographic advantage for the prophets. In doing so, the biblical author ironically displayed these prophets' lack of power. Beck, "Geography as Irony," 291–302.

3

The Rhetorical Situation[1]

HAVING INTRODUCED THE PRINCIPLES of prophetic hermeneutics, rhetorical criticism, and critical spatial theory, the process of applying the proposed method to Hosea 1–3 can now begin. The first step in the process is to consider the passage within its context. This includes the historical and religious context, the broader context of the book as a whole, and the rhetorical situation that prompted Hosea's message.

Identifying these elements for the book of Hosea is a complex task. Scholarship shows little unity and is divided on several major textual issues. The book's superscription asserts that the prophetic speeches were those of the prophet Hosea from the eighth century (Hos 1:1).[2] Yet, two challenges arise which complicate determining the historical and rhetorical setting. First, the speeches in Hosea contain few significant specific references to times, places, people, and events, making it difficult to be certain as to the

---

1. Much has been written regarding rhetorical situation, and there is great debate regarding its nature within the academic world of rhetorical studies. A brief summary of the issues and this book's usage of the term is explained later in this chapter.

2. Hosea 1:1 identifies the prophet's ministry as the time period of four kings of Judah and only one of Israel. The kings of Judah mentioned are: Uzziah (792–739; Uzziah served parts of his time as king as a co-regent with his father Amaziah and his son Jotham during his time of illness.), Jotham (750–731), Ahaz (735–716), and Hezekiah (716–687). Jeroboam II (793–753) is the only king of Israel mentioned. This single referent likely functions rhetorically, allowing the writer to make a theological point by arousing curiosity in the recipients by only mentioning one king in Israel (cf. Hos 7:3–7; 8:4; 13:9–11). Additionally, as discussed below, this may also be a way in which Hosea infers meaning to the phrase "House of Jehu" used in Hos 1:4.

33

specific setting of each rhetorical unit. Second, while the messages claim an eighth-century origin, the assembling of the oracles into the book's final form may have a different setting.

When approaching the individual rhetorical units of Hosea, one must proceed with humility and openness. It is impossible to be certain that one situation is definitely the historical setting. Outside of the superscription, Hosea did not mention the specific name of a king, nor did he state the details of events. As Andersen and Freedman note, "Pinpointing historical occasions in the Book of Hosea is a frustrating task . . . and tantalizingly allusive [sic]."[3]

The General Historical Setting of the Eighth Century BC

By the end of the ninth century BC, Israel had experienced a decline in its borders and economic prosperity. Assyria regained prominence and experienced significant expansion during the reigns of Assurnasirpal II (883–859) and Shalmaneser III (858–824). During the expansions, Israel became a vassal of Assyria.[4] Israel also suffered significant loss at the hands of the Arameans. During the reigns of Jehu and his descendants, Israel had experienced a period of defeat to the Arameans and their kings, Hazael (841–801 BC) and his son, Ben-Hadad, thus reducing Israel's territory (2 Kgs 8:12; 10:32–33; 12:17–18; 13:3, 7) and causing significant loss of life (2 Kgs 8:12; Amos 1:3), especially in the Transjordan.[5]

The beginning of the eighth century BC marked a period of prosperity for both Israel and Judah. Relief from the oppression of the Arameans came

---

3. It is likely that Andersen and Freedman meant "elusive" not "allusive." Andersen and Freedman, *Hosea*, 35.

4. In his efforts to expand westward, Shalmaneser fought against Ahab and a coalition of eleven other western kings. The Kurkh Stele of Shalmaneser III dates this battle in the eponym year of Dayyān-Ashur (853 BC). Ahab is mentioned third in the list of kings, contributing 2000 chariots (likely either an exaggeration or a scribal error) and 10,000 soldiers. While Shalmaneser proclaimed victory, other evidence suggests that the battle was a stalemate. Assyria did not proceed further west (i.e., to Hamath) and later faced more western coalitions during years ten, eleven, and fourteen of the reign of Shalmaneser. Shalmaneser's later sovereignty over Israel's king Jehu in 841 BC is reflected in the Black Obelisk (*COS* 2.113F), Calah Bulls inscription (*COS* 2.113C), and the Shalmaneser's Annals on the Marble Slab (*COS* 2.113D), all of which record tribute received from Jehu, the man from the house of Omri. Halloran, *Lexham Bible Dictionary*, s.v. "Qarqar."

5. Hazael's campaign to Gath likely took a route through Jezreel (as discussed below in Chapter 4). Bolen, "The Aramean Oppression of Israel," 152–89.

as Adadnirari III (810–783 BC) and the Assyrians conquered Damascus (7 BC). In his monumental inscriptions, Adad-nirari III claimed, "I marched to the land of Damascus. I confined Mari', the king of Damascus in the city of Damascus, his royal city. The fearful splendor of Aššur, my ("his") lord, overwhelmed him; and he submitted to me. He became my vassal" (*COS* 2.114G).[6] During this westward expansion, Adad-nirari III also received tribute from "Joash (Jehoash), the Samarian" (Tell el Rimah, *COS* 2.114F).[7] Still, Assyria's conquest of Syria provided a reprieve for Israel.

Adad-nirari III died in 783 BC and was succeeded by his son, Shalmaneser IV (782–773 BC). Shalmaneser IV's commander-in-chief (*turtānu*), Shamshi-ilu, led Assyrian troops on behalf of the king.[8] The Maraş Stele records that Shamshi-ilu led a campaign against Damascus and required a heavy tribute from Hadiyāni, the Damascene (*COS* 2.116).[9] The continuation of Assyrian pressure on Syria provided an opportunity for Israel to strengthen its military and prepare for its own expansion.[10]

Furthermore, the conditions for Israel's growth improved even more due to circumstances inside and outside of Assyria. The rapid growth of the Assyrian kingdom had a negative effect on the internal structure of the nation. The success "overwhelmed its administrative capacities and the center was insufficiently unified to function properly under a ruler who was not particularly forceful."[11] As local officials became more powerful, Assyria's central government weakened. Externally, Assyria continued to face the threat from the Urartu in the North. The Urartu gained territory in Syria, causing Assyria to direct its attention away from Israel, Judah, and the rest of the Western nations. For the first half of the eighth century, Assyria

---

6. This inscription is from the Calah Orthostat Slab. His subjection of Damascus is also mentioned in the Saba'a Stele (*COS* 2.114E) and the Tell el Rimah Stele (*COS* 2.114F). For a map of the campaign of Adad-Nirari III to Damascus, see Aharoni, *The Carta Bible Atlas*, 108.

7. It is possible that Adad-nirari III is the "deliverer" who was the answer to Jehoahaz' prayers (2 Kgs 13:4–5). For a list of options held by scholarship, see Cogan and Tadmor, *II Kings*, 143.

8. Shamshi-ilu served as second in command to four different Assyrian kings (see for example Šamši-ilu—Stone Lions Inscriptions *COS* 2.115A). Van De Mieroop, *A History of the Ancient Near East*, 244; Thureau-Dangin, "L'Inscription des Lions de Til-Barsib."

9. See also, Grayson, *Assyrian Rulers of the First Millenium BC*, 239–40.

10. The Aramean's power was further diminished as it suffered a loss in a major battle to Zakir of Hamath.

11. Van De Mieroop, *A History of the Ancient Near East*, 244–45.

struggled with the Urartu, the territory of Syria, and their own internal affairs, thus limiting their influence in the affairs of Israel and Judah.[12]

These struggles provided an opportune occasion for Israel and Judah to press their advantage. Both nations experienced moderate initial success under Jehoash (Joash) in Israel and Amaziah in Judah. Israel regained territory from Syria, and Judah from Edom (2 Kgs 13:18–19, 24–25; 14:7). Jehoash defeated Aram in Aphek, Karnaim, and Lo-debar (2 Kgs 13:17; Amos 6:13). The initial success of Judah led Amaziah to unsuccessfully initiate war with Jehoash (2 Kgs 14:8–14). Both kingdoms would experience tremendous growth during the reigns of Jehoash's and Amaziah's sons, Jeroboam II and Azariah (Uzziah) respectively.

While the overall perspective of Jeroboam II is negative in 2 Kings, the author does highlight his incredible success in expanding Israel's border. He restored the border from "the entrance of Hamath (Central Syria) as far as the Sea of Arabah (the Dead Sea)" (2 Kgs 14:25 author's translation). When considered in conjunction with Uzziah's expansions, their territories equaled the kingdom's territory during the reign of Solomon. The expansion of territory added to the nations' economic prosperity, as well, enabling them to gain control of agriculturally fertile lands and major trade routes (Amos 4:1; Hos 2:10).

As a result of Israel's growth, the nation experienced a change in its social life. Premnath traces how this period's astonishing political power and economic growth impacted the social reality among different classes.[13] The rise in political power resulted in the growth of both an elite class and Israel's military. Trade and commerce flourished and was "initiated, maintained, and monopolized by the crown."[14] Consequently, the majority of the people in the land, namely the peasants, were exploited and gradually deprived of their land (e.g., through taxation and land consolidation) to supply the means of support for the military, the ruling elite, and the judicial bureaucracy (cf. Amos's accusations of injustice and the resulting

---

12. Roux provides a summary of this period. Roux, *Ancient Iraq*, 300–305. The Assyrian eponym lists recorded that the Assyrians faced a series of external wars with the Kingdom of Urartu during Shalmaneser IV's reign (782–773). In addition, during Ashur-dan III's reign (772–755), they faced multiple plagues and internal revolts. This time period coincided with the biblical record of Jonah's visit to Nineveh.

13. Premnath, *Eighth Century Prophets*, 43–98.

14. Premnath, *Eighth Century Prophets*, 77.

luxurious living in the land in 2:6, 8; 3:15; 5:10–13; 6:4–7, 12; cf. also Isa 10:1–2; Hos 10:13–14; 12:8–9; 14:3; Mic 2:1–2, 8–9).[15]

The economic wealth of Israel was displayed in their fortifications, buildings, and use of ivory.[16] Based on the archaeological findings of more than five hundred ivory fragments in Samaria from the eighth century, King refers to Jeroboam II's reign as the "ivory age."[17] The presence of ivory is a significant indicator of Israel's prosperity. As Barnett notes, "Ivory rapidly established itself by reason of its beauty, colour, texture and suitability for carving, and its relative scarcity, as a rare symbol of wealth and status, whether cut, carved or uncut; at times it also served as a medium of tribute or exchange." (cf. 1 Kgs 10:18).[18] Hosea's contemporary prophet Amos referred to Israel's use of ivory in two of his judgment speeches (Amos 3:15; 6:3–4).

The buildings and fortifications from the eighth century also reflect Israel's fortune. They reveal the craftsmanship that manifests itself in a time of prosperity.[19] In addition to the use of ivory, Proto-Aeolic capitals and ashlar masonry are featured in royal administrative buildings.[20] The archaeology of the cities reflects the growth of an urban population. Dever notes,

> Of particular significance here is its hierarchical settlement pattern, with several distinctive capitals and regional administrative centers, characterized by centralized town planning, administrative complexes, monumental architecture, and heavy

---

15. This period has been referred to as an "advanced agrarian society." It was a time when regional specialization occurred. Commodities such as wine and olive oil became very valuable for trade. As a result, pottery also became valuable for the purpose of storing the wine and oil. The Samaria ostraca reflect the trade and potentially even the tax system used during this time. This deprivation of the peasantry is often referred to as latifundialization. See also Coote, *Amos among the Prophets*, 24–32; Chaney, "Micah—Models Matter," 145–60.

16. King, *Amos, Hosea, Micah*, 143.

17. King, *Amos, Hosea, Micah*, 143. There is some debate as to whether the ivory all stems from the eighth century or whether some may originate from the ninth century.

18. Barnett, *Ancient Ivories in the Middle East*, 1.

19. Faust provides a summary of the archaeology of the major Israelite cites from the eighth century. The findings further support the prosperity. For example, at Hazor, one of the houses excavated was a two-story building. Faust categorizes the houses from Hazor into three different social groups: the wealthy, those of mid-level officials, and the poor. Faust, *The Archaeology of Israelite Society*, 45–68.

20. For a discussion of these, see: King, *Amos, Hosea, Micah*, 65–7; Shiloh, *The Proto-Aeolic Capital*; Mazar, *Archaeology of the Land of the Bible*, 409, 412; King, "The Great Eighth Century."

fortifications. These upper-tier sites would include by the 8th century BCE Samaria III–VI and Jerusalem 13–12, of course, but also Dan III; Hazor VIII–V; Megiddo IVA; Beth-shemesh IIb; Lachish IV; and Beersheba IV–III.[21]

Israel's buildings also reflect the need to develop buildings and systems that protect the people from outside threats. With the looming threat of Assyria, Israel was forced to fortify its cities. The Assyrian wall reliefs display fortifications from the eighth century that were conquered by the Assyrian armies. Yadin notes, "the fortifications in Judah and Israel were so strong and the offensive spirit of the defenders so daring that the conquest of the Judean and Israelite cities are given distinct emphasis in the battle portrayals on the Assyrian reliefs."[22] The inclusion of Israel and Judah in these reliefs points to the economic fortune in Judah and Israel. Archaeological findings of water systems also point to these advancements. In efforts to withstand a long-term siege, both Israel and Judah developed elaborate water systems, enabling the city to store water (e.g., in Israel: Hazor and Megiddo; in Judah: Jerusalem, Beth-shemesh, Lachish, and Beersheba).

In addition to fortifying cities, Israel made efforts to strengthen its military. While the Omride dynasty established Tel Jezreel as a military training center, it was no longer used as such in the eighth century (see below in chapter 4). Given the strategic location of the Jezreel valley for trade and travel, a military presence in that area was required. Megiddo had long been used for stabling horses.[23] Mazar states, "The huge stable compounds at Megiddo, intended to hold military chariot horses, are another example of royal efforts of the state to sustain military power."[24] However, the combination of economic prosperity and a growing military provided a false sense of security (cf. Hos 1:5, 7).

After Jeroboam's death, Israel faced great instability in its leadership. Zechariah succeeded his father Jeroboam (2 Kgs 15:8–10) but was

21. Dever, "Archaeology and the Social World of Isaiah," 89.
22. Yadin, *The Art of Warfare in Biblical Lands*, 313–14.
23. For a discussion on the dating of the horse stable at Megiddo (i.e., Solomonic or dating to Ahab), see Finkelstein and Mazar, *The Quest for the Historical Israel*, 101–39.
24. Finkelstein and Mazar, *The Quest for the Historical Israel*, 170. Mazar suggests that these date to Ahab in the ninth century while Finkelstein argues for dating them during Jeroboam II's reign in the eighth century. No matter the dating of the origin of the stables, Megiddo was used for military purposes during the eighth century. Given the lack of the use of the training center at Tel Jezreel in the eighth century, Megiddo's center was likely to feature more prominently.

assassinated after six months by Shallum. Zechariah's death officially ended the dynasty of Jehu (cf. 2 Kgs 10:30). Shallum was only in office briefly, as Menahem assassinated Shallum after only one month (2 Kgs 15:14-17). Menahem reigned for ten years (752-742). Menahem's son Pekahiah followed his reign, but for only two years (742-740) before his assassination by Pekah (740-732).[25] With Assyrian support, Hoshea assassinated Pekah and became Israel's last king (732-722). It is possible that Hosea's reference to only one of these seven Israelite kings in the superscription carried rhetorical significance, suggesting either their insignificance or the wickedness of the political situation.

During Hosea's ministry, both nations regained momentum and sought to expand. Assyria eventually regrouped, however, and became a major threat again, expanding its territory under the strong leadership of Tiglath-pileser III (745-727). Biblical and Assyrian texts mention Menahem paying tribute to him (*COS* 2.1117A).[26] Assyria's power wreaked havoc on the ancient world, setting the stage for chaos in Israel as they were forced to respond.

Menahem and Pekahiah displayed pro-Assyrian policies. In contrast, Pekah opposed Assyrian control. He possibly threatened Menahem's reign from Gilead (see footnote on Pekah above) and later assassinated Pekahiah. His anti-Assyrian stance led to an alliance with Rezin, king of Aram. After Jotham's death in Judah, his young son Ahaz succeeded him (735-716) and refused to join the Israelite-Aramean alliance. Rezin and Pekah attacked Judah, seeking to replace Ahaz with a son of Tabeel. Ahaz responded by seeking intervention from Tiglath-pileser III, sending him tribute from the Lord's temple. In response, Tiglath-pileser III, during his military campaigns against Phoenicia, Philistia, Syria, and Israel (734-732), killed Rezin and captured several cities in Israel (2 Kgs 15:29; Isa 9:1). In addition, with

---

25. Pekah's reign is not without its textual challenges. The biblical text states that he reigned for 20 years (2 Kgs 15:27), which is impossible to reconcile if his years are to be understood at face value. Perhaps his reign entails the years from Zechariah, the last legitimate king. Others suggest that Pekah set up Gilead as an independent capital during Menahem's reign and served as a threat to Menahem. Merrill provides further explanation to the dating of his reign. Merrill, *Kingdom of Priests*, 410-11.

26. The Calah Annals of Tiglath Pileser III recorded tribute received from Menahem. Second Kings 15:19-20 states that Menahem paid Assyria 1000 talents of silver, which he collected from the wealthy.

Assyrian approval, Hoshea assassinated Pekah (2 Kgs 15:30).[27] Israel was forced to pay tribute to Assyria and became a vassal nation.

Upon Tiglath-pileser III's death in 727, his son, Shalmaneser V succeeded him (727–722). Hoshea initially paid tribute to him but then rebelled against Assyria and sought assistance from Osorkon IV, the king of Egypt. In response, Shalmaneser invaded Israel and captured Hoshea (2 Kgs 17:3–4). Samaria was under siege when Shalmaneser died. Sargon II (722–705) succeeded him, finishing the conquest of Samaria between 722 and 720.[28]

The Religious Setting

Hosea challenged the religious norms of his day. Although there were certainly Israelites who were faithful to true Yahweh worship, the nation was known for apostasy. Israel's first king, Jeroboam I (931–910), instituted the worship of golden calves in Dan and Bethel (1 Kgs 12:28–32). Under Ahab (874–853), Baal worship and Canaanite practices flourished, including Ahab's erection of an altar for Baal and creation of an Asherah in Samaria (1 Kgs 16:31–33; 18:19). While Jehu slaughtered a host of Baal worshippers and destroyed the house of Baal (2 Kgs 10:18–28), he did not abandon the worship of the golden calves in Dan and Bethel (2 Kgs 10:29).

It is also clear that Jehu's acts did not eradicate Baalism from Israel. The onomastic evidence from the Samaria ostraca reflects Baal elements.[29]

---

27. These events are recorded in several parts of Scripture (2 Kgs 15:37—16:9; 2 Chr 28:1–21; and Isa 7). In addition, they are mentioned in Pritchard, *Ancient Near Eastern Texts*, 283–84.

28. For a discussion on the unfolding of the last years of Israel, see: Matthews, *A Brief History of Ancient Israel*, 73; Galil, "The Last Years of the Kingdom of Israel," 52–65; Hayes and Kuan, "The Final Years of Samaria," 153–81.

29. When considering inscriptional evidence, Tigay argues the opposite, stating, "—as far as our evidence goes—deities other than YHWH were not widely regarded by Israelites as sources of beneficence, blessing, protection, and justice." Tigay, *You Shall Have No Other Gods*, 37. While his research is thorough, the conclusion that the preponderance of Yahwistic elements in names suggests Israel's faithfulness to Yahweh is questioned. The Samaria ostraca provide a clear picture of one geographic setting, within the time period of the eighth century, where Baal elements were more common. Furthermore, the biblical text demonstrates that even Baal-worshipping Ahab named his sons with Yahwistic elements (Aha*ziah* and *Je*horam). Perhaps one can make the claim that the evidence suggests that there was not a complete abandonment of Yahweh for Baal or other deities, but that is as far as the evidence goes.

THE RHETORICAL SITUATION

Six of the ostraca contain names with Baal elements, referring to five different names.[30] Yahwistic elements only occur in nine of the names. Exclusive Yahweh worship was not existent for the nation as a whole, and there were still allegiances to Baal influences present in the eighth century. Hess writes, "In the north in the eighth century BC the presence of Baal names as well as the extrabiblical personal name ʿglyw, "Yahweh is a calf" (or "calf of Yahweh") testify, along with Kings, Amos, and Hosea, to the continuing presence of various divinities and images."[31]

The syncretistic nature of Israelite worship is also evident in the eighth century. This is perhaps best depicted in the Kuntillet ʿAjrud *pithoi* inscriptions of blessings and curses found from this period that associate Yahweh with an Asherah. Part of the first *pithos* reads, ברכת אתכם ליהוה שמרן ולאשרתה ("I have blessed you to YHWH of Samaria and to his Asherah"). The second *pithos* similarly contains a reference to YHWH of Teman and his Asherah (ליהוה תמן ולאשרתה).[32] While Kuntillet ʿAjrud is in Judah, south of Kadesh Barnea, Naʾaman proposes that as a result of Jeroboam II restoring an ally relationship with Judah, Kuntillet ʿAjrud became a center for Israelite travelers conducting trade on the route to the Gulf of Elath.[33] This is further supported by the inscriptional references to Samaria as opposed to Jerusalem or other locations in Judah.

During this same time period, Bethel continued to be a center for religious and political activity. Its significance stemmed from ancestral traditions.[34] Jeroboam I made Shechem his capital but established his rival

---

30. Ostracon 2 contains לגדיו and לגדיש; Ostracon 3 לגעל; Ostracon 12 בעל לגעל; Ostracon 28 לגעל; Ostracon 31a also has לגעל; and Ostracon 37 בעל לעגל. This analysis is based on the pictures and renderings of the ostraca from 1910 with their proposed readings by Aḥituv. Aḥituv, *Echoes from the Past*, 260–310.

31. Hess, *Israelite Religions: An Archaeological and Biblical Survey*, 250. For a summary of the opposing argument, see Kelle's argument that the Baal cult was not widespread in the eighth century. Kelle, *Hosea 2*, 122–66.

32. Hess discusses the importance of this find for understanding Israelite religion in the eighth century. Hess, *Israelite Religions: An Archaeological and Biblical Survey*, 283–90. Aḥituv provides pictures and illustrations of the *pithoi*. He also provides commentary on them. Aḥituv, *Echoes from the Past*, 315–22. Hess also reviews several other cultic evidence that suggest the worship of multiple deities (297–314).

33. Naʾaman, *Ancient Israel's History and Historiography*, 230–34. Similarly, one could point to the Israelite Temple in Arad that evidences two standing stones in the temple, presumably one for Yahweh and one for Asherah.

34. For example, Abraham built an altar at Bethel (Gen 12:8); Jacob met with God there (Gen 28:11–22; 31:13; 35:7); Samuel visited Bethel annually (1 Sam 7:16; 10:3). For a comprehensive look at how this geographic location's significance is developed and

cult centers in Dan and Bethel. As previously noted, Matthews highlights how the cultic experiences at Bethel, with all of its politically appointed systems, became a key point in the polemics of Amos and Hosea (Amos 3:14; 4:4; 5:5; 7:13; Hos 4:15; 5:8; 10:5).[35] Amos sarcastically highlights the wickedness of Bethel. He states, "Go to Bethel (בֵּית־אֵל "house of God") and transgress" (Amos 4:4). While they oppressed the poor (4:1), they still loved to go present tithes and make offerings (4:4–5). He then warns that Bethel would become "nothing/iniquity" (לְאָוֶן). Similarly, Hosea did not even refer to Bethel by its name but instead called it Beth-aven (אָוֶן), ironically calling the "house of God" the "house of iniquity."

Hosea confronted Israel's cultic apostasy throughout his book. He alluded to Baal worship (2:15, 19; 7:14), cultic prostitution (4:10–14), hilltop shrines (4:13–14), the false worship at Bethel (4:15; 5:8; 10:5), and calf images (8:4–6; 10:5–8; 13:1–2). The theme of idolatry is throughout, especially within the motif of an adulterous people.[36]

The Rhetorical Situation

As stated in the "Overview of the Proposed Method," when possible, it is helpful to identify the rhetorical situation that prompted the prophetic message. Prior to discussing the rhetorical situation of Hosea, it is helpful to consider the broader academic discussions regarding rhetorical situation.

The Debate Over Rhetorical Situation

Lloyd Bitzer's "The Rhetorical Situation" became a significant work that has sparked much discussion and debate.[37] Bitzer's premise was that rhetoric is situational and pragmatic, coming into existence as a response to a circumstance and "functions ultimately to produce action or change in the world."[38] He proposed that every rhetorical situation has three components:

---

reiterated throughout the scriptures, see Matthews, "Back to Bethel."

35. Matthews, "Back to Bethel," 161–65.

36. Amos, Hosea's contemporary, addresses the *marzeah* festivals in Amos 6:3–7 and likely 2:7. See King, *Amos, Hosea, Micah*, 137–62.

37. Bitzer, "The Rhetorical Situation," 1–14.

38. Bitzer, "The Rhetorical Situation," 3–4. He officially defined rhetorical situation as "a complex of persons, events, objects, and relations presenting an actual or potential exigence which can be completely or partially removed if discourse, introduced into the

exigence, an audience, and constraints. Exigence refers to the reason or occasion that prompted the writing. This occasion is characterized by urgency and the ability to be changed. The audience speaks of the recipients of the rhetorical discourse whom the author/speaker desire to persuade. The constraints are considered from two aspects: the communicator's own personal limitations (*ethos*, *pathos*, and *logos*— e.g., his character, the logic of his arguments, or his style) and the limitations of situation itself which can be varied (e.g., the physical constraints of communicating, laws, the audience's beliefs, mindset, interests, etc.). These constraints impact the communicator's ability to persuade the audience to change.[39]

Lloyd's discussion has been debated within the rhetorical studies community. The debated topics range in variety and include matters of the causal relationship of a piece of rhetorical discourse (i.e., if the rhetor is the one who creates the exigence),[40] the objective nature of Bitzer's proposed exigence being "objective" and "part of reality,"[41] or whether the rhetor and the exigence can even be separated.[42] Kennedy acknowledges the debates but concludes that attempting to find the rhetorical situation as "a useful tool of practical criticism."[43]

This book approaches the rhetorical situation with the following principles. First, the biblical prophets spoke from a contextualized perspective, attempting to address the conditions and circumstances of their audiences. The prophets were God's spokesmen, speaking out of a sense

---

situation, can so constrain human decision or action as to bring about the significant modification of exigence." Bitzer, "The Rhetorical Situation," 6. It is interesting to note, and it supports the need of this book, that Bitzer's definition omits any reference to spatiality. The social and temporal are included, but the third element of the trialectics of being is missing. Kennedy seemingly noticed this, adding time and place to items that should be examined. Kennedy, *New Testament Interpretation through Rhetorical Criticism*, 35.

39. Bitzer, "The Rhetorical Situation," 6–8.

40. Vatz, "The Myth of the Rhetorical Situation," 154–61.

41. Lyons, "Situations of a Certain Type," 154–63. See also Vatz, "The Myth of the Rhetorical Situation." Vatz highlights that the exigence does not stem from an objective reality but rather originates as the rhetor creates meaning that leads to salience.

42. Biesecker draws on Derrida and deconstructionism to argue that both Bitzer and Vatz approach the topic too linearly and that the process is more complex as sociological identities are articulated and shifting. Biesecker, "Rethinking the Rhetorical Situation," 110–30.

43. Kennedy, *New Testament Interpretation through Rhetorical Criticism*, 35. Vorster opposes Kennedy's approach as still being connected to an objectivistic philosophy that needs to be expanded into an interactional philosophy that aligns interpreters to different traditions. Vorster, "Reflecting on the Rhetoric of Biblical Critics," 293–320.

of compulsion and calling the people to covenant faithfulness (e.g., see Amos's report of his calling in Amos 7:14–15 and 2 Kgs 17:13). Second, as Kennedy points out, there is value in examining persons, events, objects, relations, time, and place to consider more about the situation that led the prophet to communicate (or that led the Lord to commission a prophet). Thirdly, as previously discussed, specific historic settings and thus exigencies are not often able to be depicted with certainty. As the interpreter is coming from an etic perspective, there is only so much that can be clearly determined.[44] It can be worthwhile to consider specific rhetorical situations, as seen for example with the previously mentioned work in Hosea by Kelle and others, yet it is best to approach many passages with humility and without dogmatism. As such, it is helpful to consider how various audiences would receive a prophet's message.

Rhetorical Situation in Hosea

When considering the rhetorical setting of Hosea, there are two emphases to be contemplated.[45] First, one can consider the rhetorical situation of the collection of messages that form the entire book. Historical-critical approaches to Hosea understand the book to be an amalgamated work, containing original speeches from Hosea and later redactions added to recontextualize Hosea's message to new audiences. The extent of redactions identified varies from scholar to scholar.[46] Even prior to the modern

---

44. For sure, some passages provide further details that assist the interpreter to pinpoint the situation more clearly (e.g., Isa 7 or Haggai). It is interesting to note that Bitzer does recognize that some rhetorical discourse (e.g., The Gettysburg Address) are "more than just historical documents, more than specimens for stylistic and logistical analysis. They exist as rhetorical responses *for us* (italics his) precisely because they speak to situations which persist—which are in some measure universal." Bitzer, "The Rhetorical Situation," 13. To this category, one can consider the Scriptures and even the Great Works of Literature.

45. The reference to two aspects is still rather broad, focusing in on the final composition and the recipients of the message of Hosea. Certainly, more is considered regarding the relationship of the composition of the messages themselves and the composition's relationship to rhetoric. There is a relationship, as will be seen below, between the 'how' a writer communicates and the 'what' he is communicating. This relationship is what helped lead to the rise of rhetorical criticism. For a sample of this relationship in Hosea, see Mazor, "Hosea 5.1–3," 115–26.

46. For example, Nissinen only dates the text according to his suggested times of redaction. Nissinen, *Prophetie, Redaktion und Fortschreibung im Hoseabuch*, 56.

historical-critical application, the Babylonian Talmud recorded that Jewish tradition attributed the writing of the Twelve to "the Men of the Great Assembly" who lived during the Persian period (B. Bat. 15a).

On the other hand, Hilber has shown that parallels from other ancient Near Eastern cultures confirm that oral messages from prophets were often written and collected at the time of the message or shortly thereafter.[47] Dictations from prophets were taken seriously, especially if they involved the king. The speeches were considered messages from the gods. While the speeches are sometimes paraphrased, "In each case . . . the illocution, if not the actual wording of the message, is faithfully transmitted."[48] Based on Neo-Assyrian prophecies from the seventh century (e.g., the Third Collection of Oracles: La-dagil-ili to Esarhaddon[49]), he proposes that individual speeches may have first been recorded on small horizontal tablets at the time the message was given, but then copied onto an archive vertical tablet shortly afterwards.[50] Since Hosea is a compilation of multiple messages that occurred over a long prophetic ministry, this proposal would suggest that the original messages were written during Hosea's lifetime, and that the compilation could have happened during Hosea's life or shortly afterwards.

Regarding the rhetorical situation, how one approaches the aspect of compilation impacts how one views the rhetorical message of the book. For example, Dearman proposes that Hosea's text could have been written shortly after Samaria had fallen in 720 BC, primarily as a warning to the people of Judah to learn from Israel's failures. He references the numerical growth in and around Jerusalem when Samaria was captured.[51]

---

47. Hilber, "The Culture of Prophecy and Writing in the Ancient Near East," 219–41.

48. Hilber, "The Culture of Prophecy and Writing in the Ancient Near East," 229.

49. These are found in the State Archives of Assyria (SAA) 9 3.1. For a translation and discussion, see Nissinen, Seow, and Ritner, *Prophets and Prophecy in the Ancient Near East*, 118–24.

50. Hilber, "The Culture of Prophecy and Writing in the Ancient Near East," 232–34.

51. Broshi attributes the main cause of the expansions of Jerusalem to the influx of refugees from the Assyrian invasion of Israel. He states, "L'agrandissement de Jérusalem à près de trois fois ses anciennes dimensions et le doublement du nombre des installations en Juda doit s'expliquer, croyons-nous, par l'arrivée de nombreux réfugiés israélites qui s'établirent en Juda après la chute de Samarie (721 av. J.-C.), et la migration vers l'Est de la population judéenne abandonnant les provinces de l'Ouest cédées par Sennachérib aux villes des Philistins (701 av. J.-C.)." Broshi, "La Population de l'ancienne Jerusalem," 9. For further discussion on the population growth in Jerusalem, see: Na'aman, "When and How Did Jerusalem Become a Great City?, 21–56; Finkelstein, "The Settlement History of Jerusalem," 499–515; Broshi and Finkelstein, "The Population of Palestine in the Iron

In this scenario, the book would then have been written when Hosea or his followers moved south to Judah. Thus, the book of Hosea in its final form would have been created and preserved in Judah, serving as a literary message to the people in Judah.[52]

Ben Zvi proposes that Hosea was written during post-monarchic times as an instructional text to the exilic community. He suggests that the original target audience lived centuries after the historical setting of the book of Hosea. Specifically, he pinpoints the audience as the highly literate, post-exilic community of Yehud. Trotter also proposes that the final redactions were made, and the book took its final form, within the context of Achaemenid Yehud.[53]

In this scenario, Hosea's message had two rhetorical functions. First, it was a message of hope. Since Hosea's messages of destruction were fulfilled historically, the audience could have confidence that his messages of salvation would soon be fulfilled. Secondly, it was a message of instruction to its post-monarchic readership. As the text was read and reread, the audience learned about that historic period and was directed by Hosea's messages.[54]

A third alternative suggests that Hosea was written over a period of time during his ministry and possibly edited later in Judah's monarchic history, serving as a message to both Israel and Judah. Hosean authorship of the book is naturally depicted in 1:1. Perhaps one could suggest authorship by an amanuensis or a faithful follower of Hosea. Either way, the text is clearly presented as Hosea's prophetic words. Sweeney proposes that Hosea left Israel to settle in Judah when kings who favored anti-Assyrian alliances were assassinated (Shallum or Pekah's assassinations by Menahem and Hoshea). This proposal would provide further explanation for references to Judah in the book. Thus, for its final composition, Sweeney proposes a Judean location during the time period of Hosea's ministry.[55]

Age II," 47–60; Broshi, "The Expansion of Jerusalem," 21–26.

52. Dearman, *The Book of Hosea*, 28.

53. See also, Trotter, "Reading Hosea in Achaemenid Yehud"; Trotter, *Reading Hosea in Achaemenid Yehud*.

54. Ben Zvi, *Hosea, The Forms of Old Testament Literature*, 12–19.

55. Sweeney, *The Twelve Prophets*, 4–6. Similarly, Dewrell posits a date after 720 BC from Judah with a southern audience. He states, "we should envision a prophet who has fled to Jerusalem, reflecting on the destruction of Samaria and its implications for the continued cult at Bethel." Dewrell, "Yareb, Shalman, and the Date of the Book of Hosea," 429. His argument stems from interpreting the mention of King Yareb as a reference to Sennacherib (Hos 5:13; 10:6) and Shalman as a reference to Shalmaneser V (Hos 10:14).

THE RHETORICAL SITUATION

This thesis will approach the rhetorical situation from the standpoint of the implied audience as depicted in the book's superscription, namely that of the eighth-century Israelites. While it does not discount that later edits may have been made, the rhetorical use of space and geography discussed below supports the concept that the persuasive effectiveness best fits an eight-century audience.[56]

One other aspect regarding the audience should be considered. Stuart briefly suggests that the audience could be those who were supportive of Hosea's message as opposed to those who were being corrected by him.[57] This idea would be similar to the Israelites being the audience when a prophet like Amos pronounced judgment against another nation. Although the message is against another nation, such as Edom, the audiences hearing the messages were Israelites (cf. Amos 1:3—2:5). This position appears to be less plausible given the function of the highly rhetorical messages of Hosea. If his messages were to the righteous only, then the direct addresses, emotionally charged accusations, and dire warnings lose rhetorical force. It seems most plausible to understand that his audience consisted of various groups of Israelites, such as the priests (Hos 4:4–10; 5:1), royalty (5:1), the general population of Israel, and those in Samaria specifically (Hos 2:1; 4:1–3, 11–19; 5:1). Hosea's cultic messages very well could have included audiences in Bethel and Gilgal. Wolff, using a form-critical approach, proposes that the messages that model court disputes were orally presented in the city gates (2:4; 4:1, 4; 12:3).[58] In addition, although Israel is the main recipient of his oral messages, Hosea also included the people of Judah, perhaps validating Sweeney's proposal.[59]

---

56. It should be noted that the principles of the methodology proposed in this book can be applied to any of the options. The answers to the questions would certainly change. For example, the postexilic community would certainly have some differences from the implied audience in the way they conceived of Jezreel. The recent history would be vastly different. From this perspective, the interpreter would consider the history in between Hosea's time and the postexilic community.

57. Stuart, *Hosea-Jonah*, 12–13.

58. Wolff, *Hosea*, xxii–xxx.

59. Bullock, *An Introduction to the Old Testament Prophetic Books*, 96–98. Judah is mentioned by name fifteen times in Hosea (1:1, 7; 2:2; 4:15; 5:5, 10, 12, 13, 14; 6:4, 11; 8:14; 10:11; 11:12; and 12:2). Bullock offers a summary perspective of the references to Judah and their message of hope.

The Dating of Hosea 1–3

As previously mentioned, references to specific times, places, people, and events are minimal throughout the book, making it difficult to be certain as to the specific setting of each rhetorical unit. However, the implied time and setting of chapter 1 is generally agreed upon.[60] The dating of chapter 2 is highly debated. Chapter 3's dating also varies, based on how one approaches the relationship of the dates of chapters 1 and 2.

The symbolic naming of Hosea's children provides a clear rationale for the implied dating of chapter 1. Hosea's naming of his son Jezreel is intended to provide a prophetic message that Yahweh would bring an end to the dynasty of Jehu. Thus, the threat to Jehu's dynasty sets the latest possible date for chapter 1 to the end of his dynasty, namely the assassination of Zechariah, the last royal descendant of Jehu's family, by Shallum in 752 BC. Stuart proposes that the events of Hosea 1:2–9 require at least five or six years, thus requiring that the events of chapter 1 occurred during the reign of Jeroboam II (cf. the superscription in Hos 1:1).[61]

Given the close thematic and verbal connections to chapter 1, specifically the references to prosperity and political rest (2:4–15), some date chapters 2 and 3 to this same time period.[62] Wolff dates Hos 2:4–17 and 3:1–5 with chapter 1, during the setting of Jeroboam II's later reign. However, he dates Hos 2:18–25 to the end of the Syro-Ephraimite war and Tiglath-pileser III's invasion of Israel.[63] Kelle argues that all of chapter 2 is a unified whole. Regarding its date, he states, "Hosea 2 can fruitfully be understood as the prophet Hosea's metaphorical and theological commentary on the political affairs of Samaria and their implications for both Israel and

---

60. Of course, those who approach the text from a redactional approach may differ, with even some who do not tie Hosea 1–3 to any historic period. Thus, "implied time and setting" is used. Davies, *Hosea*, Birch, *Hosea, Joel, and Amos*. Ben Zvi provides one example of such an argument. He argues that the use of the marriage metaphor is intended for the male literati who originally read the text and for those who would later read and reread it. In its final form, he considers Hosea to be postmonarchic, with its earliest dating to be during the times of either Hezekiah or Josiah. Ben Zvi, "Observations on the Marriage Metaphor," 363–84.

61. Stuart, *Hosea-Jonah*, 25.

62. Andersen and Freedman, *Hosea*, 33, 35; Mays, *Hosea*, 4.

63. Wolff, *Hosea*, 33, 48. Of Hos 2:18–25 he states, "Accordingly, the collection of sayings in vv 18–25 would not have existed until after the fall of Pekah; at the earliest, during the beginning of King Hoshea's reign." He argues, "Verses 18–25 presuppose that the judgment threatened in 1:2–6, 8f; 2:4–17; and 3:1–5 has already taken place."

Judah around the time of the close of the Syro-Ephraimite war (731–730 BCE)."[64] Similarly, Stuart proposes that this passage is a unified whole and acknowledges the feasibility of dating the chapter to Tiglath-pileser III's invasion of Israel around 733 BC.[65]

The dating of chapter 3 is also contended. As previously mentioned, some date this chapter to Hosea's early ministry years, during Jeroboam II's reign. Kelle suggests the possibility of a chronological paneling in which Hosea 1–3 sequentially panels Hosea 4–14. He states, "the book consists of two panels that are not identical but overlap on chronological endpoints: chapter 1 (ca. 750) begins earlier than chapter 4 (ca. 747), and chapter 3 (ca. 725) ends earlier than chapter 14 (ca. 720)."[66] Stuart also places chapter 3 in a later setting. He understands the chapter as describing a second marriage of Hosea in his later years. He states, "In chap. 3 not only is no evidence of prosperity forthcoming; vv 4 and 5 could be understood to imply that the North is about to or has already fallen, since they emphasize the long time that Israel will endure without its former institutions."[67] Thus, Stuart dates chapter 3 to the reign of Hoshea, as late as or shortly after Samaria's fall.

While it is difficult to be dogmatic on the dating of the individual rhetorical units in Hosea, this study supposes that chapters 1–3 were likely written during the latter part of the reign of Jeroboam II (prior to his death in 753 BC). However, when significant, the rhetorical usage of geographical and spatial references will be considered in light of the various major proposed times.

---

64. Kelle, *Hosea 2*, 20.

65. Stuart, *Hosea-Jonah*, 57. While Stuart appears to lean towards this position, he is uncommitted to the date, suggesting that it is "merely speculation."

66. Kelle, *Hosea 2*, 296.

67. Stuart, *Hosea-Jonah*, 64–65.

4

The Rhetorical Use of Jezreel

The Firstspace of Jezreel

Etymological Significance of Jezreel

THE TERM "JEZREEL" (יִזְרְעֶאל) has multiple nuances. Etymologically, the proper name is a compound word, composed of זָרַע ("to sow, plant" in an imperfect form) and אֵל ("God"), meaning "God sows/will sow" or "may God sow."[1] The etymological name is based on the physical aspects of Jezreel's Firstspace, being an agriculturally rich location. The Jezreel Valley's alluvial soil receives sixteen to twenty inches of rain per year and also water drainage from the Kishon River, causing the land to be extremely fertile.[2] For this reason, it was considered the "Bread Basket" of the northern tribes. It's agricultural bounty is attested in Egyptian annals.[3]

---

1. Ran Zadok provides a study of the place names of the Jezreel Valley and its surrounding towns throughout its historic periods, highlighting the role this area had in historical geopolitics. Zadok, "On the Toponomy of the Jezreel Valley," 345–71.

2. Thomas, *Atlas of the Bible Lands*, 6. Baly estimates that the alluvial soil is roughly 100 m. deep (330 ft.). Baly, "Jezreel, Valley of," 1060–61.

3. The Annals of Thutmose III, carved on the relief walls at the shrine of Amun in Karnak, refer to the rich agriculture of Jezreel as it relates to Megiddo. After describing the conquest of Megiddo and the booty gained, the inscriptions detail the harvesting of the fields: "Now the fields were divided into plots and assigned to royal agents in order to reap their harvest. A list of the harvest which was taken away for his majesty from the fields of Megiddo: 207,300 [+x] sacks of wheat, apart from the gleanings taken by the army of his majesty." (*COS* 2.2A). El Amarna tablet 365 also reflects the agricultural

Hosea used the etymology of "Jezreel" as wordplay in various parts of the book. The first two chapters (see below in discussion of Hosea 2:24–25) display a paronomastic play on the etymology of "Jezreel" (יִזְרְעֶאל) and "Israel" (יִשְׂרָאֵל).[4] This rhetorical use of the etymology of "Jezreel" reflects the oral nature of the ancient culture. Parunak, when comparing modern authors to those of the ancient times, comments, "Where we use signals specially tailored to the printed page, they employ a system of indicators that can function in either oral or written presentations."[5] In this case, Jezreel, as a geographical space, served as a visible object with significant associated meaning to those listening and was intended to serve as a teaching or memory aid, associating the space with the people. The paronomasia rhetorically served to grab the audience's attention and provided an aid for memory.[6]

Later in the book, Hosea also used the verb זָרַע metaphorically. Figuratively, Israel "sowed the wind" and would "reap the whirlwind" (8:7 NET). When calling the people to repentance, Hosea exhorts them to "sow righteousness" and consequently "reap unfailing love" (10:12 NET). While not in conjunction with "Jezreel" in the immediate context, Hosea's prior etymological usage of "Jezreel" with the verb זָרַע in Hosea 2:24–25 suggests that the initial rhetorical usage set the stage for his later usage of זָרַע.

---

prosperity of the Jezreel Valley. In this tablet, Biridiya, one of the local city rulers, made a plea to the Pharaoh (Amenhotep III or Akhenaten) in the fourteenth century BC that he was the only ruler cultivating the lands of Shunem. It was apparently the city rulers' responsibility to harvest the land for Egypt. He claims, "But look at the city rulers who are with me! They are not doing as I. They are not cultivating in Šunama and they are not furnishing corvée workers; but (it is) I, all by myself, (who) am furnishing corvée workers." Rainey, *El Amarna Tablets 359–379*, 28–31.

4. Lunn defines paronomasia as "all occasions in which two (or more) similar words are deliberately placed in the same environment, whether the intention is to amuse or otherwise." Lunn, "Paronomastic Constructions in Biblical Hebrew," 31.

5. Parunak, "Oral Typesetting: Some Uses of Biblical Structure," 154. Möller makes this point as well, arguing that in ancient Judaism, reading was a social event that was almost always done aloud. Möller, *A Prophet in Debate*, 50–56.

6. Lunn categorizes paronomastic constructions into two categories: rhetorical paronomasia and grammatical paronomasia. He further divides the chief rhetorical uses into ten types. Hosea's use of "Jezreel" best falls into Lunn's categorization of "as a teaching aid." While his examples emphasize objects (Jeremiah's "almond tree" or Amos's "summer fruit"), in Hosea's case, the geographical location serves as the object. Regarding the use of paronomasia, he notes, "Underlying both rhetorical and grammatical paronomasia there is arguably a unifying concept, that of emphasis." Lunn, "Paronomastic Constructions in Biblical Hebrew," 32–39, 51.

The City of Jezreel

Geographically, the proper name Jezreel has three referents: the valley, a city within the valley, and a spring (*'Ein*) in the lower portion of the city. The city of Jezreel was a fourteen-acre fortified city that benefited from its access to sufficient water from the *'Ein Jezreel*. Baly's division of the valley into two subregions, the central plain of Megiddo and the eastern Beth-shean corridor, is helpful (see map below).[7] In relation to these two subregions, the city of Jezreel is located at their intersection.[8] It is located at the foot of Mt. Gilboa, strategically located between the two major cities of Megiddo and Beth-Shean.

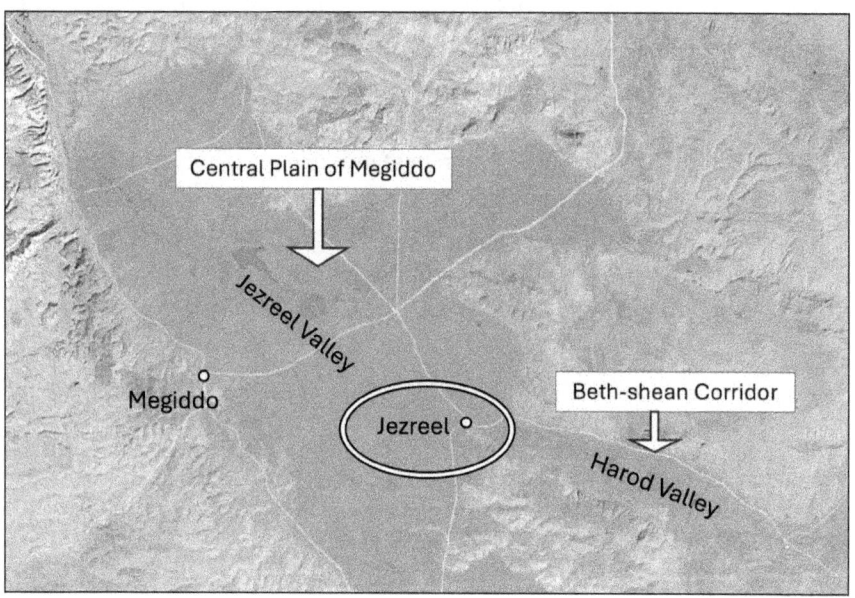

The city's location is significant and is an element of its Firstspace. When considering the physical aspects of the city, in addition to being at the intersection of the two subregions, it was also at the narrowest point of the Jezreel Valley. As such, the city could serve as a gateway for those traveling west towards Megiddo, east towards Beth-shean, and south through the Jezreel Valley towards Samaria. It was ideally situated as a

---

7. Baly, "Jezreel, Valley of," 1060.

8. This map reflects a portion of Schlegel's map of the Jezreel Valley. The labeled sections have been added to provide clarity with Baly's subregions. Used by permission of © W. Schlegel, *Satellite Bible Atlas*.

means to protect access to Samaria. From the west, Franklin calls Jezreel "the springboard to the east."[9] Travel through the valley for those coming from the East and for those traveling along the Way of the Patriarchs naturally passes the city of Jezreel.[10]

Furthermore, as previously mentioned, the city sits on a ridge near Mount Gilboa. Ussishkin notes, "Situated on a prominent summit, it dominates the valley below, where the highway from Megiddo to Beth-shean extended in ancient times."[11] Given its strategic location, it provided a tactical opportunity for Omri and Ahab during the ninth century BC. These Israelite kings fortified the city and made it their military headquarters, further contributing to the physical aspects of the city's Firstspace.

Archaeological excavations led by Ussishkin and Woodhead reflect that the Omride kings fortified the city in a manner that made it quite unique throughout all Israel.[12] The enclosed part of the city itself measured

---

9. Franklin, "Why Was Jezreel so Important to the Kingdom of Israel?"

10. The Road of the Patriarchs is the name given to the Hill Country watershed ridge, which is the only route that connects Israel and Judah in the Hill Country. The Way of the Patriarchs thus links the city of Jezreel with the major travel route to Shechem, Samaria, Bethel, and Jerusalem.

11. Ussishkin, "Jezreel, Samaria and Megiddo," 352. The site naturally only sits about 100 m above the valley. One might question Ussishkin's use of "dominates;" however, given the fortified structures present in the ninth and eighth centuries, the site would have certainly been impressive to those traveling by it.

12. These excavations lasted seven years and were a joint project of the Institute of Archaeology of Tel Aviv University and the British School of Archaeology in Jerusalem. There is some debate as to who actually fortified the city. Ussishkin and Woodhead concluded that the Omride kings were responsible for the fortifications. Norma Franklin proposes that while the Omride kings made significant use of the city, Jeroboam II was responsible for the fortifications in the eighth century. Franklin argues that Ussishkin and Woodhead made their conclusions based on limited stratigraphic evidence and ceramic material, and by relying on the biblical narrative. She argues that the pre-enclosure phase should be attributed to the Omride dynasty. However, she states that the enclosure phase is post-Omride dynasty, likely that of Jeroboam II. She bases her argument on a revision of the stratigraphy and by comparing the architecture to that of Samaria (IA phases of Samaria) and the courtyard enclosure and city type to that of Megiddo (Stratum IV). The latest publication from the archaeological research at Tel Jezreel comes from Charlotte Whiting and Gloria London. Regarding the stratigraphy of Area A, Whiting provides a caution regarding Ussishkin and Woodhead's earlier conclusions. She finds that "a more detailed Iron Age sequence cannot be established based on recorded evidence" in Area 1 of Area A. In Area 2, she concludes that one cannot be certain of the dating, but Ussishkin and Woodhead's conclusions are reasonable. In Area 3, she refutes some of the earlier conclusions regarding the corner tower evidence that is contemporary with the Iron Age gatehouse. Instead, she warns that the evidence in layer 3152 and wall 102 are

about eleven acres, more than doubling Samaria's five acres.[13] Furthermore, three sides of the city were surrounded by a moat cut out of the natural rock. (The northern side was omitted since it bordered a steep hill).[14] The city had either a four- or six-chambered gate and was surrounded by a casemate wall.[15] Two towers have been discovered, and excavators suggest that the southwest and northwest corners of the fortification also comprised towers.[16] The builders of the fortress made efforts to level the interior of the fortification, dumping large amounts of soil to balance the surface and build a podium.[17] While there is evidence of a public administrative building, and the biblical text references a royal palace (1 Kgs 21:1; 2 Kgs 9:30—10:3), the archaeological evidence suggests that ashlar masonry, commonly used in royal residences, was minimally used at Jezreel.[18]

Several of these characteristics have led Woodhead and Ussishkin to propose that Tel Jezreel "was the central military base for the royal

---

clearly dated to the Iron Age, but one must be cautious to assume that the tower that was constructed is from the Iron Age. London evaluated the pottery conclusions from Ussishkin and Woodhead. She concluded that, in light of the limited quantity of material from clean deposits, chronological significance from pottery "can be imperfect at best." Most of the pottery found was not from "well-defined loci or from floors" but mostly from disturbed construction fills or deposits from an area of the collapsed wall after it was burned. She concludes that Ussishkin and Woodhead's conclusions for the dating of the pottery are "not compelling." Thus, dating is left at a stalemate. However, the presence of "aesthetically pleasing red-slipped and burnished ceramics" that range in shapes and diversity, in conjunction with large amounts of storage jars and utilitarian pottery, points to an elite population present at Tel Jezreel during the Iron Age. Ussishkin, "Jezreel, Samaria and Megiddo"; Cantrell, "'Some Trust in Horses'"; Ussishkin and Woodhead, "Excavations at Tel Jezreel 1994–1996"; Ussishkin and Woodhead, "Excavations at Tel Jezreel 1992–1993"; Ussishkin and Woodhead, "Excavations at Tel Jezreel 1990–1991"; Na'aman, "Historical and Literary Notes"; Whiting and London, *Stratigraphy and Neolithic-Iron Age Pottery from Tel Jezreel*, 39, 90–91, 93.

13. Ussishkin and Woodhead, "Excavations at Tel Jezreel 1992–1993," 44.

14. Ussishkin and Woodhead measured the moat's length to be "c. 150 m. along the eastern side, 320 m. along the southern side, and c. 200 m. (or more) along the western side—altogether 670 m. Assuming that its width is 8 m. or more and its depth 5 m. or more, c. 26800 cubic metres of rock were quarried here." Ussishkin and Woodhead, "Excavations at Tel Jezreel 1992–1993," 45–46.

15. The gate structure was not well preserved, making it difficult to be certain as to the specific construction. Ussishkin and Woodhead, "Excavations at Tel Jezreel 1994–1996," 19–25.

16. Williamson, "Tel Jezreel and the Dynasty of Omri," 41–42.

17. Ussishkin and Woodhead, "Excavations at Tel Jezreel 1992–1993," 44–47.

18. Ussishkin and Woodhead, "Excavations at Tel Jezreel 1992–1993," 46–47.

THE RHETORICAL USE OF JEZREEL

Israelite army at the time of the Omride kings."[19] The size of the enclosure and the efforts made to level its surfaces required significant labor and point to a functional usage of the space. There were great efforts to make sure the enclosure was well fortified. Its towers, casemate walls, gate, and surrounding moat all point to an effort to defend the site. The minimal use of ashlar masonry also indicates that the enclosure was not intended to serve as a capital like Samaria. Furthermore, Aster strengthens the proposal by drawing a comparison between the site of Jezreel and the Assyrian Fort Shalmaneser at Calah.[20] By showing the similarities in the enclosed sizes, the similarities in the large courtyards at Calah and the podium at Jezreel, and the use of the Calah location for both a military training center and a royal residence (cf. the biblical references to Ahab's royal residence in Jezreel), Aster furthers the likelihood that Woodhead and Ussishkin's proposal is credible.[21] Similarly, Cantrell concludes that "Jezreel's strategic location, easy access to ample supplies of pasture and grain, the large spring at the base of the fortress, and the large open area inside the enclosure certainly made it the perfect place to prepare horses for war."[22] In fact, Cantrell suggests that the city of Jezreel was a prototype for how Megiddo developed in the eighth century.

According to Ussishkin and Woodhead, the military function of the city had been abandoned by the eighth century, despite evidence of only minor damage to the fortifications.[23] This was likely the result of Hazael's invasion (see below in "Jezreel in the Recent History").[24] Unlike Jezreel, Megiddo's usage as a chariot-training center was still prominent in the

---

19. Ussishkin and Woodhead, "Excavations at Tel Jezreel 1992–1993," 47. The Omride dynasty's possession and use of chariots is attested in the Assyrian records (see footnote 3 in chapter 3).

20. Aster, "The Function of the City of Jezreel," 38–39.

21. This interpretation contrasts earlier proposals that Israel had two capitals (Samaria to oversee the Canaanites and Jezreel to oversee the Israelites) or that, due to its mild climate, Jezreel served as the winter capital for Israel. It argues instead that, given the strategic location of Tel Jezreel, for a season of time, Israel's kings established the city as the place of training for the cavalry, and the horses and chariots were stationed there. Morgenstern, *Amos Studies*.

22. Cantrell, *The Horsemen of Israel*, 112.

23. As previously mentioned, Norma Franklin disagrees with their dating and suggests that the fortification actually dates to the eighth century. This dating does impact the rhetorical influence of Hosea's use of Jezreel. The differences will be discussed below in the discussions on the rhetorical influence of Jezreel in Hosea 1–2.

24. Aster, "The Function of the City of Jezreel," 40–41.

eighth century. Thus, while the city of Jezreel's military usage was now a memory of the people, the military connotations continued with other cities in the Jezreel Valley.

The city of Jezreel's location not only presented an ideal site to fortify for militaristic strategies, but it also served as an ideal location to communicate a message. The building of a city and its physical structures communicate messages. As Harmanşah notes, "building cities was envisioned as a social event that then became part and parcel of the policies of kingship and the shaping of social memory at the time."[25] The fortifications of Tel Jezreel and Megiddo reflect the decisions of royal families to build monumental architecture. The biblical text conveys that Tel Jezreel also housed a royal palace. As such, a royal presence impacted the surrounding life. Monumental architecture served propagandistic purposes.[26] The royal buildings provide an example of the aforementioned spatial tactics (creating space tactically to control social structures) and served to promote an ideology regarding social and political relations. While the fortress at Tel Jezreel was no longer in use by the time of Hosea, it was still a standing structure, and the former implications would still have been felt in the lives of the people. As Matthews states, "Memory is sparked by the senses (a sound, smell, a taste) or by movement into familiar or remarkably similar spaces."[27] The collective memory of former events associated with Tel Jezreel and of the manpower needed to create the fortress were sparked by the existence of this "memory site."[28] Thus, the site communicated both current and past meanings. Whitelam asserts, "Royal fortifications, temple-palace complexes, and public displays would have displayed before a wide audience, both internal and external, the might, power, and wealth of the king and his court."[29] During the Omride dynasty, the city's Firstspace fortifications

---

25. Harmanşah, *Cities and the Shaping of Memory*, 2.

26. Pollock, *Ancient Mesopotamia: The Eden that Never Was*; Whitelam, "The Symbols of Power"; Williamson, "Tel Jezreel and the Dynasty of Omri."

27. Matthews, "Remembered Space in Biblical Narrative," 74.

28. See previous discussion on memory and "memory sites" in Chapter 2. Hosea's use of Jezreel displays that Tel Jezreel's history had become part of the collective memory of the people. The fortress is an example of Flores's claim that "collective memory is semiotically grounded in geographic sites." Flores, "Memory-Place, Meaning, and the Alamo," 429.

29. Whitelam, "The Symbols of Power," 169.

communicated to a broad audience the strength of the Israelite kings and their commitment to protecting the area and its trade routes.[30]

Jehu and his dynasty serve as an example of Soja's principle of the social production of spatiality. Their decision no longer to use the city as the training center demonstrates how a space is the product of its society. No space is fixed, but its usage and meaning change and evolve. The city of Jezreel was likely abandoned due to the Aramean oppression at the hand of Hazael, which continued in Israel through the reigns of Jehu and Jehoahaz.[31] Bolen's proposal for Hazael's path of invasion en route to Gath shows how Megiddo was not invaded during Hazael's oppression, thus allowing its continued usage as a prominent location for training horses.[32]

The Valley of Jezreel

As mentioned above, Jezreel is also the name of the valley. The Jezreel Valley is a large triangular-shaped valley (ranging from nineteen miles to fourteen miles on each side) that lies north of Samaria and south of Galilee.[33] Topographically, the valley's significance was tied to its relation to the surrounding mountains, the physical attributes of its agricultural prosperity, and its relationship to major travel routes (the International Coastal Highway and the Way of the Patriarchs). Due to its ideal location and topography, it became the home of significant cities (e.g., Megiddo, Tel Jezreel, Beth Shean).

The valley is strategically located. Being surrounded by mountains (Mt. Carmel, Mt. Gilboa, the Hill of Moreh, Mt. Tabor, and the Nazareth Ridge), it provided a major travel route for east-to-west connections. The valley permits east/west access without any mountainous barriers. International travel avoided travel along the mountains in favor of the low valley (ranging from sea level to 200 feet above sea level). The following

---

30. The fortress and fortifications are discussed further below in "Royal Presence and Propaganda."

31. The biblical text portrays the Aramean oppression as a form of judgment against the Israelites for their Baal worship (1 Kgs 19:17–18). Furthermore, it mentions the reduction of territory that would begin during Jehu's reign (2 Kgs 10:32–33). Bolen, "The Aramean Oppression of Israel in the Reign of Jehu," 28.

32. Bolen, "The Aramean Oppression of Israel in the Reign of Jehu," 174–82.

33. Negenman, "Geography in Palestine," 6; Schlegel, *Satellite Bible Atlas*, 16. Schlegel provides a more general estimate of 20 x 15 x 15 miles.

slides reflect the ease of travel through the Jezreel Valley in contrast to its surrounding hills.³⁴

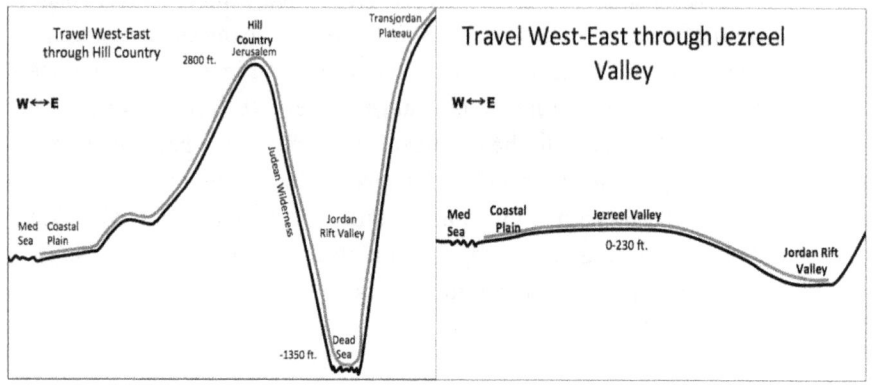

Topography of Travel through the Jezreel Valley

The International Coastal Highway (*Via Maris*), which provided access to Egypt and Damascus, cut inland north of the Sharon Plain and ran through the Jezreel Valley. Control of this highway enabled a nation to control trade. In light of this, the Jezreel Valley has been called the "hub of international routes."³⁵ The emphasis on controlling the trade routes in the eighth century is reflected in Tiglath Pileser III's campaigns against Syria and Palestine (Rezin and Pekah). He placed an emphasis on controlling the Coastal Plain, the Jezreel Valley, Galilee, and the King's Highway (Transjordan).³⁶ Its significance is also validated by its use by the dynasty of Omri as a secondary royal residence and militaristic training center (1 Kgs 21:1; cf. 1 Kgs 18:45; 21:23; 2 Kgs 8:29).

---

34. These slides were created by William Schlegel and shared with the current author.

35. Schlegel, *Satellite Bible Atlas*, 16.

36. Hallo and Younger, eds., *The Context of Scripture*, 285; Pritchard, *Ancient Near Eastern Texts*, 283–84. The Annals of Tiglath Pileser III record his conquests of these areas and the care he takes to establish governors over them. For a detailed explanation of these campaigns see Aharoni, *The Land of the Bible*, 372–74.

The Memory and Secondspace of Jezreel

Jezreel, a Historical Overview

Jezreel's history is rich in the significance of the history of Israel. Warfare, battles, and murder have characterized the Jezreel Valley throughout its history, even preceding Israelite occupation. Cline captures this well, stating, "The Jezreel Valley can be compared to the meeting place of two tectonic plates, where the stress and strain frequently result in cataclysmic, earth-shaking events of immense magnitude, whose reverberations are felt far away, both geographically and temporally."[37] Since the valley was rich in agriculture and control of this valley enabled a nation to control trade, it was considered highly valuable. Nations fought for its possession. Again, Cline notes, "Of the 34 battles which have been fought at Megiddo or in the Jezreel Valley during the past 4,000 years by Canaanite, Egyptian, Greek, Roman, Byzantine, Islamic, Crusader, Mongol, Mamluke, Ottoman, Palestinian, French, and Allied Forces, at least seventeen have been fought because this valuable and strategic area was in an unwelcome geographical predicament—a contested region situated on the periphery of two or more powerful world systems."[38]

Jezreel in the Recent History of Hosea's Audience

In the recent past of Jezreel at the time of Hosea's writing, Ahab and Jezebel murdered Naboth there to gain possession of his vineyard. Jehu's coup of Ahab's successor, Joram (Jehoram)—and the ensuing bloody massacre of Jezebel, Ahab's seventy sons, Joram's close acquaintances and priests, and forty-two relatives of Ahaziah—occurred in both the valley and the city (2 Kgs 9–10; discussed in greater detail below). During the reigns of Jehu and his descendants, Israel had experienced a period of defeat at the hands of Hazael (841–801 BC) and the Arameans, reducing their territory (2 Kgs 8:12; 10:32–33; 12:17–18; 13:3, 7). Bolen proposes that Hazael's campaign to Gath took a route through Jezreel (see below).[39]

---

37. Cline, "'Contested Peripheries' in World Systems Theory," 12.
38. Cline, "'Contested Peripheries' in World Systems Theory," 8–9.
39. Bolen, "The Aramean Oppression of Israel in the Reign of Jehu," 152–89.

Hazael's Campaign[40]

The Aramean oppression was unrelenting in Israel until the Assyrian king, Adad-nirari, subjugated Hazael (ca. 805 BC). While Hazael's son, Ben-Hadad III, sought to maintain Aramean dominance over Israel, Jehoahaz's son, Jehoash, recovered much of Israel's territories in major defeats of Ben-Hadad III (2 Kgs 13:25). Furthermore, Ben-Hadad III suffered defeat at the hands of Zakkur, King of Hamath.[41] These losses provided a reprieve for Israel, which enabled Israel's success against Syria to continue during the reign of Jeroboam II. Jeroboam II continued Jehoash's re-establishment of Israel's economic stability, expanding both the economy and the borders

40. Archaeology has revealed destruction layers from the ninth century at Beth Shean, Tel Rehov, Tel 'Amal (3 miles W of Beth Shean & 8 miles S/E of Jezreel), and Jezreel (ca. 813 BC). Bolen proposes that this is the result of Hazael's campaign to Gath. After conquering Jezreel, he avoided other locations (like Megiddo, Tanaach, and Jokneam) in the Jezreel Valley by taking the Dothan Valley Pass. Used by permission of © W. Schlegel, *Satellite Bible Atlas*. Map 1-3 from Schlegel's work has been modified to highlight Bolen's proposal.

41. Unger, *Israel and the Arameans of Damascus*. The inscription on the stele of Zakkur records that Ben-Hadad had unified multiple kings (7 or 17) against Zakkur, but Zakkur received assurance from his god, Ba'Ishamayn, that he would be successful (*COS* 2:155).

(2 Kgs 13:25; 14:28; Amos 6:13). As a result, the Gadites and the Reubenites resettled in the Transjordan (1 Chron 5:16–25). This provided an extra buffer of safety for those living in the area of Jezreel.

Such a history has a social impact on the people living during ancient times. Historical events create symbolic meanings and contribute to a collective memory of a people group. These recent events were still fresh in the memories of Hosea's audience. Additionally, the audience would have been familiar with Jezreel's comprehensive history. Furthermore, Israel's recent growth and military success contributed to its contemporary perception of Jezreel. While Jezreel had always been a place of agricultural prosperity, travel, and battle, it had now been impacted by the growth of the royal military and bureaucracy (see Social Structure below). Based on Jezreel's Firstspace, the area was vital to those in power, leading to Jezreel's symbolic value.

Ahab solidified Jezreel as a place of social injustice with the murder of Naboth. The violent coup of Jehu and the significant losses suffered at the hands of the Syrians certainly still resonated in the memory of the people. The social injustice that had its roots with Ahab grew under Jeroboam II and the expanding bureaucracy. Given the agricultural nature of this area, the people were certainly impacted by taxation.[42] When considering the city of Jezreel's recent history, the fortifications remained, even though the city was apparently unoccupied, leaving a visual reminder of the past efforts to fortify the city. Furthermore, military presence was still extant in the valley at Megiddo.[43] Symbolically, Jezreel was associated with military presence (e.g., horses, chariots, bows, soldiers). Jezreel was thus perceived as the place of agricultural abundance, social injustice, violent warfare, and military presence.

The Thirdspace of Jezreel

The "imagined representations" (Secondspace) of Hosea's audience was influenced by both its agricultural prosperity (Firstspace) and the events

---

42. Consider the implications of Megiddo's vast storage capabilities. The more crops produced, the greater the taxes. Large cities required military and administrative presence. This presence was supported by taxes.

43. Aster, "The Function of the City of Jezreel and the Symbolism of Jezreel in Hosea 1–2"; Cantrell, "'Some Trust in Horses'"; Cantrell, *The Horsemen of Israel*; Ussishkin, "Megiddo and Samaria: A Rejoinder to Norma Franklin."

of its history. Jezreel was symbolized as a place of bounty; yet, Jezreel also was a contested space and a space whose symbolic meaning and social practices were subject to change. Taking Israel's social structure, its military presence and life, its royal presence and the propaganda of royalty, and the life of the general public into account leads to a deeper understanding of the Thirdspace of Jezreel.

Social Structure

As a result of the reversal of prosperity brought about by Jeroboam II's reign, eighth-century Israel sustained a change in its social life.[44] With the prosperity, Israel experienced the rise in political power, the growth of both an elite class, and an expanded military.[45] These social changes led to the exploitation of the peasants and the land. The costs of providing for the needs of the military (see below for the size of Israel's military and the requirements to feed their horses), the ruling elite, and the judicial bureaucracy contributed to the oppression of the common people. Chaney notes, "Military measures to resist Assyrian incursions and payment of tribute when these measures failed both tapped the same agrarian economic base."[46] Dearman also points out that the season of Aramean domination

---

44. See chapter 3. Premnath, *Eighth Century Prophets*, 43–98. Chaney notes how Israel and Judah's freedom from military threat "coupled with the lengthy tenure in office of both kings . . . gave the elites of the two states unusual freedom to initiate change in their political economies." Chaney, "Micah—Models Matter," 146.

45. Franklin points out that Megiddo was listed among key locations of Assyrian trading posts. Franklin, "Megiddo and Jezreel Reflected," 191. It should be noted that Fales and Postgate note that this geographical list of provinces in K 1521 is among a "mixed bag" of tablets that have general geographic info. The purpose of the list is unknown, as is its dating. Historically, it would make sense that Megiddo's role as an Assyrian trading post would have followed Jeroboam II's reign, during the time when Israel was a vassal of Assyria. However, this does not suggest that Megiddo was not already a major trading post under the rule of the Israelite monarchy. Cantrell notes the trading of horses in Megiddo and Franklin notes that this is likely why Tiglath-pileser did not destroy Megiddo. It served him well as a trading station and a location to obtain horses. Fales and Postgate, *Imperial Administrative Records, Part II*, xiv; Cantrell, *The Horsemen of Israel*, 44–46.

46. Chaney, "The Political Economy of Peasant Poverty," 36. Chaney discusses the negative impact on eighth-century peasants in multiple categories. He traces the impacts of the growing military, the increases import/export trade, the regional specialization implemented by royal initiative required to satisfy the elite's luxurious tastes and forced production of oil and wine to meet the trade economy. These realities left the peasants

would have already left this same group, the average citizen, economically struggling.[47] Now, their property rights were being violated.

Dearman's work on property rights in the eighth century highlights the social and economic dilemma facing the poor in Israel.[48] Since the crown controlled the economic system, the exploitation of the peasantry led to a redistributed economic system to be used "at the direction and purpose" of the king and his officials.[49] Israel's elite became part of the government, and regular citizens were treated like peasants. Without power, the citizens were subject to both immovable property loss (land and houses) and exacting property loss (taxes, usury, and pledges) while members of the royal bureaucracy were granted land and tax privileges. Chaney notes, ". . . the ruling elite bore few of the costs of the import/export trade but enjoyed most of its benefits. The peasant majority, by contrast, bore most of the costs, but reaped few of the benefits."[50]

Military Life

Thirdspace considers a geographical space's social and spatial practices. It draws upon the physical (Firstpace) and the mental (Secondspace) and emphasizes life as it was actually practiced. As noted previously, Tel Jezreel was fortified under the dynasty of Omri to serve as a military fort and training ground. While unoccupied during Hosea's time period, the memory of its military usage continued to "live." While the training grounds in Tel Jezreel were no longer in use, Megiddo was still an active town that housed the military horses. When analyzing the intersection of life and power in

---

in vulnerable positions, forced to take greater risks and would have led to them being forced to borrow. As a result of what Chaney refers to as "survival loans," more peasants lost their land rights to foreclosure (thus the violation of property rights). Furthermore, with few safeguards in village courts, the elite could manipulate the system (cf. Amos 5). Chaney, "The Political Economy of Peasant Poverty," 34–60. For a succinct summarization of the impact on peasants during the eighth century, see Chaney, "Micah—Models Matter," 146–49.

47. Second Kings records that Israel's army was decimated by Hazael during his invasions. The army was reduced to fifty horsemen, ten chariots, and 10,000 foot soldiers. Dearman, *Property Rights in the Eighth-Century Prophets*, 140.

48. Dearman, *Property Rights in the Eighth-Century Prophets*, 132–35, 48–49.

49. Dearman, *Property Rights in the Eighth-Century Prophets*, 132–35, 48.

50. Chaney, "The Political Economy of Peasant Poverty," 37.

the Jezreel area, one must consider the nature of Israelite military in the monarchic and divided kingdom eras.

During the monarchic period, Israel's military became an organized army that was comprised of two different military units.[51] One unit was made up of the professional soldiers, who presumably trained at centers like Tel Jezreel and Megiddo. The second unit contained the local militia, who were not full time but were farmers and soldiers. Herzog and Gichon refer to them as Israel's general national levy. They also note that one would expect "a modicum of rivalry and friction between [the two units], especially between the household troops stationed at the capital and the general levy."[52] Given the abuse in property rights previously mentioned, one would expect this friction to be heightened in the eighth century.

During Jeroboam II's reign, Israel's army became an established force in the region. While the biblical data does not mention the specific size of his army, it does enumerate the size of Uzziah's army, Jeroboam II's Judean counterpart. Uzziah's army was organized and included scribes for counting. He had organized 307,500 "skilled and able" soldiers into ancestral houses with 2,600 leaders (2 Chron 25:11). Given that Israel's territory was larger than Judah's, one would suspect that Israel's military was larger or at least equal to the size of Judah's. As previously noted, the Kurkh Stele of Shalmaneser III noted that Ahab contributed 2,000 chariots and 10,000 foot soldiers to the western coalition of kings that opposed Shalmaneser III.[53] Even if these numbers were exaggerated, it is recognized that Jeroboam II's army exceeded that of Ahab. There were seventeen stables at Megiddo alone, and each stable could house twenty-four to thirty horses.[54] Thus, Megiddo could house somewhere between 408 and 510 horses. Such a large army, complete with chariots, required

---

51. Herzog and Gichon, *Battles of the Bible*, 146; Matthews, *Manners and Customs in the Bible*, 132.

52. Herzog and Gichon, *Battles of the Bible*, 147–48.

53. Again, this number may be exaggerated or a scribal error. Herzog and Gichon explain the logistics behind that many chariots and horses traveling to Qarqar. The transportation efforts would have been extravagant. The daily consumption would include 4 pounds of fodder per horse and 110,000 gallons of water for the soldiers, not to mention the fodder needed to take care of the bulls pulling carts. Herzog and Gichon, *Battles of the Bible*, 164. Cantrell notes a much greater amount of needed food as healthy horses would have needed 12–15 pounds of grain and 10 pounds of barley per day. Cantrell, *The Horsemen of Israel*, 95–96.

54. Cantrell, *The Horsemen of Israel*, 96. See footnote above about food requirements for the horses.

an enormous amount of effort and resources to manage. While the Jezreel Valley provided rich agriculture and nearby streams to sustain the horses and soldiers, the requirements certainly taxed the citizens (e.g., the cisterns and storehouses in Megiddo had to remain filled.)

The prophets Amos and Hosea both confronted the false sense of security Israel had in its military strength. Amos declared that even the most brave and fastest warriors would not escape the judgment (2:14–16). Their military would suffer losses that equaled ninety (5:3). The Lord hated their fortresses and would hand them over to their enemies (6:8). Similarly, Hosea declared that Israel's military strength would be broken in Jezreel, while Judah would be spared without the use of its military (see comments on Hos 1:5 below).

From a militaristic perspective, one could consider multiple nuances in Hosea's rhetoric.[55] The threat of an attack conjures different responses from different recipients of the message. The full-time soldiers may be inclined to mentally prepare for battle, but civilians and local militia might respond with anxieties and former memories of war. While Israel had been experiencing peace, albeit from a growing royal bureaucracy that was oppressive, the thought of an invading army entering the land certainly heightened fears and concerns. Additionally, the hardships of a siege would certainly be contemplated. Megiddo was established to withstand a siege. The threat of a siege would have conjured memories of the conditions the people had experienced in previous sieges. Of course, warfare is deadly, but the crowded nature of a siege leads to inferior sanitation, water contamination, and inadequate diets. As a result, famine, thirst, and disease are also experienced in a siege.[56] As food becomes scarce, prices become highly inflated. When Ben-Hadad attacked Samaria, a "donkey's head" sold for eighty shekels of silver, and two quarts of dove dung sold for five shekels of silver (2 Kgs 6:25).

---

55. One could do the same for Amos. For example, in Amos 5:3, the judgment includes 90 percent losses. If a city sent out 1000 soldiers, only one hundred would return. If a town sent out one hundred soldiers, only ten would return. In a military that has a unit comprised of soldiers who are called up when necessary to depart their agricultural jobs, it is likely that Amos is referring to local militia/general levy unit. Thus, it is not just the professional soldiers who will perish; the husbands and farmers who usually live in the towns and cities will also perish.

56. Eph'al, *The City Besieged*, 66–68.

Royal Presence and Propaganda

The decision of the king to expand the military presence not only impacted the social aspects of life in the area of Jezreel, but it also communicated a clear message from the king. No doubt, the presence of the military, with the multitude of its horses, chariots, and foot soldiers, highlighted the power of the king to his citizenry. The fortifications of Tel Jezreel and Megiddo and the royal palace in Tel Jezreeel, were examples of how monumental architecture displayed the power and presence of royalty. Furthermore, the archaeological evidence confirms that the area was used to train Israel's military. As such, a royal presence directly impacted life in this region. Again, monumental architectures served the propagandistic purposes of the king.[57]

The fortifications and royal buildings served to promote an ideology regarding social and political relations. Whitelam states, "The sheer size of the structures would have denoted assurance and power, and their visibility and simplicity would have communicated to all levels of society."[58] By recreating the landscape of a region, a king communicated his power and created a sense of awe.[59] As Williamson notes, "Buildings are capable of communicating awe, size, assurance, power, or dynamism, and if in a central or imposing position, can do this to a fairly large audience over a long period."[60] This was communicated to both the elite and non-elite members of Israel,[61] and to any outsiders that traveled through the region. Given Israel's revitalized control over the Jezreel Valley and the vast amount of trade in this region, the fortifications at Megiddo and Jezreel were certainly in central and opposing positions and thus represented power to the people in the land and to other traveling political entities.[62]

The massive city gate at Megiddo (19–20 meters long and 16–18 meters wide) served as the focal point of the royal fortifications.[63] In speaking

---

57. Whitelam defines propaganda as "the process by which a particular worldview (ideology) is disseminated to a specific audience." Whitelam, "The Symbols of Power," 166; Pollock, *Ancient Mesopotamia*, 173–95; Williamson, "Tel Jezreel and the Dynasty of Omri," 47.

58. Whitelam, "The Symbols of Power," 169.

59. Uziel, "Middle Bronze Age Ramparts," 25–26.

60. Williamson, "Tel Jezreel and the Dynasty of Omri," 49.

61. Williamson, "Tel Jezreel and the Dynasty of Omri," 47, 49.

62. Uziel, "Middle Bronze Age Ramparts," 27.

63. The archaeology of Megiddo is much debated. With some twenty levels of

of the gates at Megiddo and Gezer, Whitelam states, "the visual imagery is advanced by their skillful construction with finely worked ashlar blocks." This imagery was immediate to anyone who walked into the city. Additionally, the ashlar masonry, with its "elaborate and subtle iconography in the interior of the building, with its complex message, was directed to a restricted elite audience in much the same way as written propaganda."[64]

The fortifications at Megiddo were both functional and symbolic in nature. Finkelstein argues that the ramparts in the Middle Bronze Age served both functionally and symbolically. Functionally, they provided protection. Symbolically, they served as propaganda and a means to advance the bureaucracy. By the eighth century, the city was monumental. "Monumental palaces, ceremonial buildings and administrative structures occupied most of the internal space inside the cities, providing only limited space for residential quarters."[65] Socially, the city was likely inhabited by the military encampments and the growing bureaucracy needed to administratively manage the city, while the farmers lived in small villages and towns on the outskirts of the city. As such, the city was also a statement of the economic potential established by the king. The casemate walls, ramparts, gate, water system, storehouses, and governor's palace displayed to one entering the city that the king was legitimate, strong, wealthy, and capable of protecting what belonged to him.[66]

---

strata, archaeologists differ regarding the details of the dating of different strata of the city. In this case, the gates of the city are disputed. The biblical text describes Solomon as having fortified Megiddo (1 Kgs 9:15). Early biblical historians attributed the gate and stable complexes to Solomon. Yet, later archaeologists date the gates and stable complexes to a later time. There have been two gates unearthed at Megiddo, one built on top of the other at a later time (Gate 3165 to the time of Stratum VIA and Gate 2156 to the time of Stratum VA–IVB). Ussishkin provides a brief overview of the research on Megiddo and the bibliographic sources for each view. He then disagrees with Finkelstein's 2019 conclusions that there is a third gate, Gate 500b, that was a four-chambered gate that replaced the six-chambered gate (Gate 2156). Ussishkin, "The 'Solomonic,' Six-Chambered Gate 2156," 246–55.

64. Whitelam, "The Symbols of Power," 169.

65. Herzog estimates that 82 percent of Megiddo was allocated for administrative purposes. Mazar points out that at least 40 percent of that is allocated to the horse stables. Herzog, *Archaeology of the City*, 228–29, 34; Finkelstein and Mazar, *The Quest for the Historical Israel*, 171.

66. Finkelstein, "Middle Bronze Age 'Fortifications,'" 213. Uziel makes the same point. He likens the dual nature of the fortified city—protection and symbolic—to a modern-day automobile. One might have a more expensive vehicle that serves the same function as a less expensive automobile, but its value also communicates wealth and

The impact of the fortifications at Tel Jezreel need to be considered from both the time of the Omride dynasty and that of Jeroboam II. Like Megiddo, the fortification would have served dual purposes during the Omride dynasty. Williamson notes, "The amount of labour involved, particularly to quarry the moat and to pile up the ramparts, reminds us of the use of such grandiose public works as a means of social control and as a way of pressing claims to legitimacy."[67] The height and visibility of the fortifications would have proved intimidating for the local population and would have the same impact on travelers coming through the Jezreel Valley. Williamson also notes, "the very use of the site for military purposes would only have added to its effectiveness as a statement of complete domination to a potentially rebellious population."[68]

If Ussishkin and Woodhead (and others) are correct that the fortress at Tel Jezreel was no longer in use by the time of Hosea, then the propagandistic messages need also to be considered in light of an unoccupied structure that still stood.[69] While the former implications would still have been felt, what message would the House of Jehu have communicated? Perhaps the message has a greater symbolic effect. Jehu and his dynasty could have left the city fortified while empty as a polemic against the Omride dynasty and as a tribute to their power. In essence, the thought would be, "The Omrides fortified this city, even putting a moat around it, thinking they were indestructible. Yet, look how I (Jehu) was able to overthrow them (or perhaps look how YHWH gave them into my hand)." Additionally, at least initially, they could have attempted to appeal to the locals who had been under the "social control" of the Omride dynasty and were forced to provide the labor to build the fortification.

Israelite Life in Jezreel

Finkelstein proposed that during the Omride dynasty, Samaria contained a largely Israelite population, but Jezreel was comprised of a mostly Canaanite

---

status symbolically. Uziel, "Middle Bronze Age Ramparts," 27.

67. Williamson, "Tel Jezreel and the Dynasty of Omri," 49.

68. Williamson, "Tel Jezreel and the Dynasty of Omri," 49.

69. Of course, if Franklin is correct in associating Tel Jezreel's fortifications with Jeroboam II, then the previous argument for the dual function of the fortification would apply to Jeroboam's efforts.

population.⁷⁰ He argues that the fortifications at Jezreel and Megiddo were partially designed to control the Canaanite population (also furthering the propagandistic message of the legitimacy of the kingship north of them in Samaria).⁷¹ Certainly archaeological evidence could reflect some Canaanite life, as Canaanite deity figurines and, in some cases, pig bones have been found in these areas,⁷² but these artifacts could also simply be a reflection of the syncretistic worship and disobedient lifestyle practices of Israelite life during the eighth century. Mazar concludes that the "settlement history is still deficient" regarding the later period of the Iron Age IIB–C.⁷³ While the details of Canaanite life intermingled with Israelite life in the north may be undeterminable, archaeology has assisted in our understanding of other elements of settlement patterns and social life.

In 2001, Zertal organized the Iron Age II excavated sites by category.⁷⁴ Half of the settlement sites (131) were farms. He concludes that this reveals that "the small independent peasants played a central role in quantity and quality."⁷⁵ These sites reflect the agricultural nature of those living in small farm villages. Borowski estimates that 2/3 of all the people lived in these villages.⁷⁶ This certainly confirms the agricultural lifestyles for those living in this agricultural "bread basket" of Jezreel, especially when considering the aforementioned reality that Megiddo was largely an administrative city that housed mainly the administrative bureaucracy. Since such a large percentage of Israelites lived in these villages, it is worth summarizing the physical elements of a village.⁷⁷ The villages were typically built with the following characteristics:

---

70. Finkelstein and Neil Asher Silberman, *The Bible Unearthed*, 192.

71. Finkelstein and Mazar, *The Quest for the Historical Israel*, 150.

72. While the majority of the faunal remains from Tell Qiri reveal the predominant food to be sheep/goat, they also found fourteen pig/boar bones. Ben-Tor and Portugali, *Tell Qiri A Village in the Jezreel Valley*, 249.

73. Mazar, *Archaeology of the Land of the Bible*, 415.

74. Zertal, "The Heart of the Monarchy," 38–64. Stager provides helpful charts of the Iron Age I sites and their sizes. Stager, "Archaeology of the Family," 1–35.

75. Zertal, "The Heart of the Monarchy," 46.

76. Borowski, *Daily Life in Biblical Times*, 13.

77. For simplicity's sake, the list provided is a summary of Borowski's findings. Certainly, others point to a similar list (e.g., Zertal, Herzog, Mazar, etc.). Borowski goes on to categorize the villages into three types: ring-shaped villages, agglomerated villages, and farmsteads. Borowski, *Daily Life in Biblical Times*, 14–15.

- On rocky surfaces, so as not to occupy land that was agriculturally useful
- Close to the fields
- Near travel roads
- Without fortifications, although sometimes the terrain helped defensively (some villages were constructed in a circular structure, which assisted their defenses)
- Without clear planning (houses and street placements were irregular)
- Close to natural sources of water (if natural sources were not available, cisterns were built)

Within the village, families were centrally organized around the "house of the father" (בֵּית אָב). Unlike modern Western family structures, Ancient Israel's nuclear family unit fit into a broader social structure. This broader social structure connects the overall nation or people (עַם) to individual households through wider systems. Each individual household was part of a larger family unit, known as the "house of the father." This structure was comprised of "a single living male ancestor, his wife/wives, the man's sons and their wives, grandsons and their wives, and conceivably even great grandchildren; any unmarried male or female descendants (married female descendants were excluded, having left the household to live with the families of their husbands) and unrelated dependents; male and female hired servants and slaves, along with their families; resident laborers; and on occasion resident Levites (Judg 17:7–13)."[78] The house of the father is connected to yet a broader social structure: the extended family clan (מִשְׁפַּחַת). Each clan is then connected to one of the twelve tribes of Israel (שִׁבְטֵי יִשְׂרָאֵל), which then makes the nation as a whole. At the heart of the nation is the family.[79] Thus, when speaking of the nation, biblical writers often refer to them as the sons of Israel or the house of Israel.

In relation to the village, extended family units had houses built next to one another within the village.[80] Schloen notes that the typical home

78. Block, "Marriage and Family in Ancient Israel," 38.

79. Block notes that the tribal units were not emphasized as much from Solomon's administrative reforms onward. King and Stager, *Life in Biblical Israel*, 39; Block, "'Israel'-'Sons of Israel': Hebrew Eponymic Usage," 322; Block, "Marriage and Family in Ancient Israel."

80. Borowski describes the nature of these homes and how the prevalent form was a four-room house. Borowski, *Daily Life in Biblical Times*, 16–21.

housed ten people. In a home that had multiple families within the same house of the father, he proposes that three to four couples with their children would also stay in the same house.[81] If each family had its own home within the "house of the father," then one can see how the house of the father would expand into a family compound.[82]

Given the nature of an agrarian society, the entire family "invested most of its efforts in making a living, whether by tilling the land, herding, or a combination of the two."[83] Borowski's fictional representation of an eighth-century agrarian family paints a clear and reasonable picture of the roles of each member of the family.[84] Regarding the everyday life of the common civilian, the day was hard. The family arose before sunrise, worked most of the day, and retired for their evening meal. Afterwards, they continued to work to prepare for the next day. Living as an extended family unit assisted this laborious lifestyle.

The Rhetorical Significance of Jezreel in Hosea 1–2

Hosea 1:4–5

Having considered the historical context, the rhetorical situation, and the Firstspace, Secondspace, and Thirdspace of Jezreel, the interpreter can read the references to Jezreel in Hosea 1–2 within Hosea's intended rhetorical significance. The word Jezreel appears five times in the first two chapters of Hosea (twice in 1:4, and once in 1:5; 2:2 [Eng 1:11]; and 2:24 [Eng 2:22]).

The first usage of "Jezreel" occurs in chapter 1. The structure of the first chapter is relatively easy to follow. After the superscription (1:1–2a), there are four panels of divine speech and response (1:2b–3; 1:4–5; 1:6–7; and 1:8–9). Each one begins with a narrative introduction,[85] contains a

---

81. Schloen, *The House of the Father as Fact and Symbol*, 136.

82. Stager provides multiple figures and sketches of typical households in ancient Israel. Stager, "Archaeology of the Family," 1–35. Brody addresses this also from site work done at Tell En-Naṣbeh. Brody, "Archaeology of the Extended Family," 237–54.

83. Borowski, *Daily Life in Biblical Times*, 63.

84. Borowski, *Daily Life in Biblical Times*, 109–26.

85. Each of the four is introduced with an initiatory *wayyiqtol* form, and panels three and four provide further sequential *wayyiqtols*.

command[86] and is followed by a rationale for the command.[87] The first panel provides the initial setting when Yahweh shockingly commands Hosea to go and take ("marry") a wife of harlotries and bear children of harlotries to symbolically represent the nation's gross involvement in spiritual adultery.[88] It ends with a statement of Hosea's obedience to the command as he takes Gomer to be his wife, who bears him a son.[89] Each of the following three panels introduces the birth of a child and the command to name the child a specific symbolic name that rhetorically communicates God's judgment for the nation's unfaithfulness.

A Survey of Translations

Following the birth of Hosea's first child described at the end of the first panel, Hosea is instructed to name the child Jezreel. "Jezreel" is used twice in this verse, once as the name for Hosea's first child and once as a reference to the location of Jezreel (unspecified as to whether this is the valley or the city, although one assumes this refers to the city since עֵמֶק is not used). The second usage is found in the rationale given for the name. The following explanation is given for the choice of the name Jezreel:

כִּי־עוֹד מְעַט וּפָקַדְתִּי אֶת־דְּמֵי יִזְרְעֶאל עַל־בֵּית יֵהוּא וְהִשְׁבַּתִּי מַמְלְכוּת בֵּית יִשְׂרָאֵל:

---

86. Each of the four follows the introductory *wayyiqtols* with a quote of the Lord's commands to Hosea, all taking the Qal imperative form.

87. Each rationale is introduced by כִּי.

88. The word זְנוּנִים or its verb form is repeated for emphasis in Hosea to highlight the metaphor of Israel's unfaithfulness. When describing the nation, Hosea's use of the infinitive absolute followed by the imperative highlights the nation's involvement in a rhetorical manner. Dearman elaborates on the nature of Gomer's sexual infidelity. Dearman, *The Book of Hosea*, 363–68.

89. The announcement of the first child's birth specifically states that the child was born "to him" (לוֹ). The next two children's birth announcements omit the preposition and pronominal suffix. While it is tempting to conclude that the second and third child were not Hosea's but were born through prostitution, the omission may simply be stylistic. The introduction of Yahweh's words to Hosea shows similar variation. In the first (1:2), Hosea's personal name follows the preposition אֶל. The second time the Lord spoke to Hosea, the pronominal suffix is added to the preposition (1:4). The third statement switches the preposition and adds the pronominal suffix (1:6). The last time the Lord spoke to Hosea, the preposition and pronominal suffix are both omitted, but the context is clear that Hosea is still the recipient of Yahweh's words. Perhaps it is best to say that the lack of the preposition and pronominal suffix provides a sense of ambiguity and suspicion as to the nature of the births of Lo-Ruhamah and Lo-Ammi.

The translation and interpretation of these words have received much attention. A brief survey of translations demonstrates the interpretive challenge:

> RSV: for yet a little while, and I will *punish* the house of Jehu *for the blood* of Jezreel, and I will put an end to the kingdom of the house of Israel.
>
> NKJV: for in a little while I will *avenge the bloodshed* of Jezreel on the house of Jehu and bring an end to the kingdom of the house of Israel.
>
> NIV: because I will soon *punish* the house of Jehu *for the massacre* at Jezreel, and I will put an end to the kingdom of Israel.
>
> NASB: for yet a little while, and I will *punish* the house of Jehu for the *bloodshed* of Jezreel, and I will put an end to the kingdom of the house of Israel.
>
> NET: because in a little while I will *punish* the dynasty of Jehu on account of *the bloodshed* in the valley of Jezreel, and I will put an end to the kingdom of Israel.
>
> McComiskey: for yet a little while, and I will *visit the bloodshed* of Jezreel on the house of Jehu, and I will destroy the dominion of the house of Israel.
>
> Stuart: because it will not be long before I *apply the bloodshed* of Jezreel to the family of Jehu and then destroy the kingdom of the family of Israel.

The survey of these translations reflects that translators are differing on the nature of the verb פָּקַד and its relationship to אֶת־דְּמֵי יִזְרְעֶאל. The interpretation of this verse is best understood in light of Hosea's rhetoric, including his use of the geographic reference to Jezreel.

Comparing Hosea and 2 Kings

Most of the translations and most scholars interpret this verse as a reference to divine justice on account of Jehu's bloody coup of Jehoram that occurred in the Jezreel Valley and in the city of Jezreel (2 Kgs 9–10). A minority (e.g., McComiskey and Stuart) understands the verse in a manner that does not directly assign guilt to Jehu. It is clear that the child's name would symbolically send a message of judgment for the blood that was shed at

Jezreel. Warfare, battles, and murder have characterized the Jezreel Valley throughout its history, including Ahab's murder of Naboth (1 Kgs 21). Yet, this bloodshed is linked to the House of Jehu. The interpretation is complicated by the account in 2 Kings that portrays Jehu's actions as receiving divine approval. After reviewing the account in 2 Kings and surveying the attempts to interpret the passages, we will return to see that the rhetorical use of the space of Jezreel provides a more satisfying solution.

Second Kings 9–10 records Jehu's coup and assassination of Joram (a short form of Jehoram), Ahab's successor. Jehu was an officer in Joram's army. While partnering with his cousin, King Ahaziah of Judah, Joram was injured in battle against King Hazael and the Syrians at Ramoth Gilead (across the Jordan River on the northeast border of Gilead). His injury caused him to return to his residence in the city of Jezreel (2 Kgs 8:29; 9:15). Ahaziah also departed Ramoth Gilead to go to Jezreel to check on Joram (2 Kgs 8:29; 9:16). Upon their departure from Ramoth Gilead, Elisha sent a prophet to anoint Jehu as the new king of Israel (2 Kgs 9:1–10). When Joram's servants responded with their endorsement, Jehu quickly departed for Jezreel to carry out his coup (2 Kgs 9:11–16). Jehu's successful coup was filled with bloodshed. Just outside the walls of the town of Jezreel, on the property of Naboth, Jehu shot an arrow through Joram's heart, killing him (2 Kgs 9:24). Jehu then pursued Ahaziah, chasing him to Samaria. While Ahaziah was fleeing on the Ascent of Gur, Jehu shot Ahaziah, causing him to die when he reached Megiddo.[90]

The bloodshed continued as Jehu commanded Jezebel to be thrown out of the palace window. The text portrays this event in a manner that highlights its violent nature. Jezebel's blood splattered on the wall and on the horses, and then Jehu trampled over her body with horses (2 Kgs 9:33). He later gave instructions for Jezebel's burial, but dogs had already eaten her body (9:35–37). Jehu then had Ahab's seventy sons killed and their heads brought back to Jezreel to be displayed in piles at the city gates (2 Kgs 10:1–8). His violent coup later included killing Joram's close acquaintances, his priests, forty-two relatives of Ahaziah, and all the remaining descendants of Ahab (2 Kgs 10:11–17).

In light of the prophetic approval given by Elijah and Elisha of Jehu's actions in Kings, and Yahweh's direct statement of approval, one has to ask

---

90. Second Chronicles 22:9 states that Ahaziah actually made it to Samaria and hid there for a period of time. Since 2 Kgs 9:27 says that the Ascent of Gur was by Ibleam, it is most likely that Ahaziah was shot along the Dothan Pass. From Samaria, this is the direct path that passes Ibleam before entering the Jezreel Valley.

why the text in Hosea appears to suggest that Jehu's actions are the divine rationale for the fall of his dynasty. While the author of Kings condemns Jehu for not ridding Israel of the false cultic sites in Bethel and Dan (1 Kgs 10:29, 31), he praises Jehu for his actions regarding the coup.[91] Elijah told Elisha to anoint Jehu as king, including an allusion to the violent coup (1 Kgs 9:16–17). When Elisha carried this out, Jehu was instructed to entirely strike down Ahab's house as punishment from the Lord (2 Kgs 9:7–10). Jehu himself understood his actions as motivated by zeal for Yahweh (2 Kgs 10:16).[92] The narrator of Kings quoted Yahweh's divine approval: "because you have done well in doing what is right in My sight, and have done to the house of Ahab all that was in My heart, your sons shall sit on the throne of Israel to the fourth generation" (2 Kgs 10:30 ESV).

A Survey of Interpretations

Often, this seeming contradiction is interpreted as a discrepancy of views between prophets, with Hosea condemning Jehu's actions and Elijah and Elisha approving them. Wolff takes this interpretation, suggesting that Hosea was unaware of the ninth century prophetic tradition of Elijah and Elisha.[93] Sweeney argues further that disagreement was the norm amongst prophets from Israel and Judah. He added that Hananiah represents Isaiah's tradition with which Jeremiah was in disagreement (Jer 27–28).[94] Mays also backs the theory of contrary prophetic traditions, suggesting that the judgment is "on account of the blood crying out from Jezreel's soil for revenge."[95] Harper considers Hosea a moral reformist who, after a century, had been given "a better point of view."[96]

However, regarding Hosea's supposed evolution in morals, Irvine rightly observes that "the prophet generally does not appear squeamish about the use of violence in carrying out Yahweh's judgment upon sinful

---

91. Jehu removed the worship of Baal from the land but did not remove the golden images and cultic sites established by Jeroboam.

92. Interestingly, similar wording is used by Elijah after he killed the prophets of Baal in 1 Kgs 19:10. There, Elijah uses the Piel infinitive absolute and Piel perfect form of קנא plus ליהוה. In this passage, Jehu uses the nominative form of קנא plus ליהוה. Both passages describe one's zeal for Yahweh on the heels of bloody massacres.

93. Wolff, *Hosea*, 18.

94. Sweeney, *The Twelve Prophets*, 18.

95. Mays, *Hosea*, 27–28.

96. Harper, *A Critical and Exegetical Commentary on Amos and Hosea*, 211.

human beings."⁹⁷ Hosea includes violent images in his own announcements of judgment. God is portrayed as an attacking lion (5:14). As lions are born predators, so too will Ephraim bring their sons out to the murderer (9:13).⁹⁸ God promises to strike Israel with infertility. However, even if a couple were to have children, he claims he will "slay their precious offspring" (9:16 author's translation). Perhaps the most shocking image of violence is found in Hosea 14:1 (13:16 English Bible). Samaria would die by the sword, their infants would be dashed in pieces, and their pregnant women would have their wombs ripped open. While Jehu's violence seems excessive to a modern culture, it was common in the ancient Near East. Even the prophet Hosea has no qualms about using such imagery.

Irvine proposes an alternative theory for why the two traditions are in disagreement.⁹⁹ He dates the writing of the account in 2 Kings 9–10 to the reign of Jeroboam II. Jeroboam was facing threats, not only from Rezin in Syria but also from prophets like Hosea and Amos. In an effort to validate his reign, Irvine suggests that Jeroboam had the Kings account written as propaganda that would counter growing opposition. The Kings account would show that he had the rightful claim to the throne because Yahweh and his prophets rewarded his great-grandfather Jehu. Thus, when Hosea writes, he refutes the king's propaganda.¹⁰⁰ While the theory is interesting and creative, it leaves one considering its flaws. Was it not for the apparent discrepancy in Hosea 1:4–5, would such a theory ever be suggested? It is true that 1 Kings 17 through 2 Kings 10 is significantly different than the rest of Kings. It focuses on the northern kingdom and the narratives of Elijah and Elisha. However, if this were propaganda from Jeroboam, one wonders why the northern kings are portrayed in such a negative light. Judah's kings are presented with mixed endorsements, some good and some bad. Yet, the northern kings are all portrayed as bad, following the "sins of Jeroboam the son of Nebat." Even Jehu's positives are tainted by the emphasis on this same sin. Would Jeroboam portray his family's dynasty this way? If he really wanted to validate his kingship, why include Jehu's sins? By mentioning these, he would provide more ammunition for his opponents.

---

97. Irvine, "The Threat of Jezreel (Hosea 1:4–5)," 499.
98. This interpretation is based on the text in the LXX as opposed to the MT.
99. Irvine, "The Threat of Jezreel (Hosea 1:4–5)," 499–500, 502–3.
100. Similarly, Robker does not disagree with Irvine but prefers to see the Kings passage as being written in response to Hosea. Robker, *The Jehu Revolution*, 64.

Others suggest that Jehu was not instructed to assassinate Ahaziah, the king of Judah.[101] Andersen and Freedmen suggest that Jehu's violence was excessive, understanding verse four as speaking to both the coming judgment and the reason for the fall of the dynasty.[102] They liken God's use of Jehu as an instrument of judgment to his use of the Assyrians and Babylonians. Of Jehu they state, "In the act of carrying out the divine judgment against the house of Ahab, he overstepped the bounds of his mandate and showed that arrogance and self-righteousness which was the undoing of the preceding dynasty."[103] Yet, as previously mentioned, nothing in the Deuteronomistic history suggests that Jehu's dynasty was being judged for how Jehu treated Ahaziah and his family. In fact, Ahaziah's assassination is portrayed as divinely approved in Chronicles (2 Chr 22:7). Chisholm highlights this reality and shows how the Chronicler "portrays Ahaziah very negatively . . . like that of the house of Ahab . . . all but identifies Ahaziah with the house of Ahab."[104]

---

101. Dearman takes this approach. Dearman, *The Book of Hosea*, 93.

102. Andersen and Freedman, *Hosea*, 177. Chisholm, in his earlier writings, also argued this way in his early interpretation of the passage. Chisholm, *Interpreting the Minor Prophets*, 24.

103. Andersen and Freedman, *Hosea*, 180.

104. Chisholm, "'The Bloodshed of Jezreel,'" 435. Chisholm also argues that the references to Jezreel also make this solution problematic since Ahaziah died in Megiddo and his forty-two relatives in Beth Eked, not Jezreel (2 Kgs 10:12–14). He argues, ". . . only the house of Ahab was slaughtered in Jezreel *per se*." One could argue that Hos 1:4 does not specify which Jezreel, the city or the valley. Since Ahaziah died in Megiddo, he is still in a city in the Jezreel Valley. Additionally, the location of Beth Eked is unknown. As Hunt and Gray point out, it could refer to a town en route from Jezreel to Samaria or it could simply refer to a meeting place for the shepherds. While the biblical evidence points to the inclusion of עֵמֶק for references to the Valley of Jezreel, there are times when a valley or a plain of a location is alluded to when the town alone is named. For example, the author of 2 Kings claims that Josiah was killed in Megiddo (2 Kgs 23:29–30). Yet the writer of 2 Chronicles states that Josiah was killed in the plain/valley (בְּבִקְעַת) of Megiddo (2 Chr 35:22). It is also possible that the reference to Jezreel in 2 Samuel 4:4 is a broader reference to the battlefield at Mount Gilboa (i.e., when the news from the battlefield where Saul and Jonathan dies had reached Ish-Bosheth's nurse). Jezreel being situated at the foot of Mount Gilboa could have been used as a metonymy for the region or the news could have actually traveled to Jezreel first and then from Jezreel to where Ish-Bosheth was. The soldier that escaped the battlefield on Mount Gilboa went to David to share the news (2 Sam 1:1–16). It is certainly not unreasonable to think that a report straight from the battlefield would have also gone to Saul's son. Hunt, "Beth-Eked (Place)," 685; Gray, *I & II Kings*, 556.

In opposition to these views, an argument can be made that the Hebrew text should be translated differently. McComiskey's translation "for yet a little while, and I will visit the bloodshed of Jezreel on the house of Jehu"[105] does not imply punishment like most translations but renders פָּקַד with the more neutral "visit." The basis of his argument is that the collocation of פקד על does not convey punishment automatically but only means punish when the direct object of the verb clearly connotes wrongdoing by the context. Certainly, פָּקַד is used in contexts other than punishment.[106] McComiskey's argument finds some strength in his analysis of the syntax of פָּקַד collocated with עַל when it is followed by both a direct object and an indirect object. Although he admits that, in most instances, "punish" is implied, based on the same construction in Jeremiah 15:3, he interprets the direct object as being brought into the experience of the indirect object.[107] The key question then becomes, "Does the direct object, אֶת־דְּמֵי יִזְרְעֶאל, necessitate wrongdoing?"

McComiskey, Stuart, and Chisholm all clearly argue that דמים does not necessitate a reference to sinful actions.[108] McComiskey points out that

---

105. McComiskey, "Hosea," 18; McComiskey, "Prophetic Irony in Hosea 1:4," 93–101.

106. For example, it is used to grant blessings in GEN 21:1; 50:24-25. It should be noted that the LXX translates פָּקַד with ἐκδικέω ("to avenge"). The translators of the LXX clearly saw the judgment as penalty for wrongdoing.

107. JEREMIAH 15:3 has the same construction but clearly does not imply the people were guilty *for* four kinds of destroyers. Instead, they would be punished *by* the four destroyers. In essence, God is visiting the people *with* four destroyers not *for* the four destroyers. McComiskey, "Prophetic Irony in Hosea 1:4," 97–98. McComiskey further argues that "if פקד על has the function of bringing the direct object into the experience of the indirect object, then the assertion of Hosea 1:4 is that the blood shed by Jehu at Jezreel was to appear hauntingly in his dynasty to bring it to an end." McComiskey, "Prophetic Irony in Hosea 1:4," 100. He states that "this could only be true if Zechariah, the last of Jehu's dynastic succession met his end at Jezreel." To meet this requirement, he then makes a case, based on a defective Hebrew text in 2 Kgs 15:10, that Zechariah died in Ibleam, in the southern part of the Jezreel Valley. One could argue this on two points. First, one's hermeneutic of the prophetic genre needs to accommodate essential fulfillment of prophecies. Sandy, *Plowshares and Pruning Hooks*, 136–54; Chisholm, "Making Sense of Prophecy." Secondly, if "bringing the direct object into the experience of the indirect object" requires exact fulfillment, and the Jezreel of "bloodshed of Jezreel" in Hos 1:4 is in reference to the town and not the valley (however see n99 above), then Ibleam would still not be an exact fulfillment since it is a different town in the Jezreel Valley.

108. McComiskey, "Hosea," 20–22. McComiskey argues that the direct object "does not possess the intrinsic sense of bloodguilt." It need not refer to a sinful act. The use of "bloodshed" does not require blood shed from a wrongdoing. Stuart shows that דמי does not necessarily imply bloodguilt. He renders the term "massacre" as does the NIV. Stuart,

the word is used to refer to "blood emitted by cultic rite or physical function, blood shed in war, bloodguilt, and murder."[109] Chisholm elaborates on the usage of דמים in the context of shed human blood, showing that is not always considered wrong. He points out that while David condemns Joab's killing of Abner and Amasa during a time of peace (without cause דמי חנם), killing in a time of war can be justified (1 Kgs 2:5, 31). Furthermore, when David wanted to build the temple, the Lord expressed that David was not to build it for he was one who "spilled blood" (1 Chr 22:8; 28:3).[110] In the context of the story of David, this was certainly not a condemnation of David's wartime efforts. He was not condemned for being a warrior. In Hosea's context, the direct object, bloodshed (not necessarily bloodguilt), would become the experience of the indirect object, the house of Jehu. Hosea's point would thus be that bloodshed would become the instrument of God's punishment upon the house of Jehu.[111]

Chisholm attempts to strengthen McComiskey's view by looking at the immediate context of Hosea. He rightly acknowledges that there is strong evidence to support interpreting this verse as punishment for bloodshed that was sinful. However, he argues that both "context and parallel texts indicate that Jehu's actions are not the basis for the coming judgment of his dynasty."[112] As previously mentioned, the parallel text of 2 Kings argues against Jehu's guilt. Regarding the immediate context of Hosea, Chisholm argues that Hosea 1 functions like a judgment speech, with an accusation (1:2) and formal announcements of judgment (1:3–9).[113] He argues that the accusation lies with the metaphor of unfaithfulness to the covenant, thus the land is being punished for spiritual adultery.[114]

Hosea-Jonah, 29; Chisholm, "Bloodshed of Jezreel," 439–40.

109. McComiskey, "Prophetic Irony in Hosea 1:4," 99. McComiskey provides sample passages of each usage.

110. Chisholm, "The Bloodshed of Jezreel," 439–40.

111. This would then be similar to the collocation of פקד על in Jeremiah 51:27. There the imperative of the verb is used. Here the command is given to call upon a leader/commander (the object) to go against her (i.e., the commander will be the instrument of judgment). See also Chisholm, *Handbook on the Prophets*, 339–40.

112. Chisholm, "The Bloodshed of Jezreel," 440.

113. Chisholm is not arguing that Hosea 1 is taking the form of a judgment speech from a form-critical perspective. Rather, he is arguing that Hosea 1 is rhetorically functioning in a manner equivalent to a judgment speech.

114. Chisholm, "The Bloodshed of Jezreel," 440.

Chisholm clearly perceives the challenges of the parallel text and as discussed later, notes key rhetorical implications. However, one could question his emphasis on the passage having only one main accusation, that of covenant unfaithfulness in the form of idolatry.[115] Hosea 1 is written in a narrative discourse format but functions similar to a judgment speech in that it includes accusations and announcements of judgment.[116] As such, as previously mentioned, each paneling of divine speech in Hosea includes a rationale for the divine imperative. While covenant unfaithfulness/spiritual adultery is the main accusation against Israel that follows the first כִּי in verse two, it need not be the only accusation in this chapter. As will be discussed below, a more holistic consideration of the references to Jezreel carries an inferred accusation; namely, Israel trusted their military strength instead of Yahweh (1:5, 7). Thus, adding the accusation of bloodshed done in Jezreel does not necessarily militate against understanding it as a rationale for its punishment. Further accusations can be included within the rationale for the divine imperatives.

Jeremias argues that Hosea's focus is never on judgment for actions done in the distant past; rather, Hosea emphasizes that judgment is warranted for present wrongful actions.[117] If this guilt really lies in Jehu, then this judgment for distant past actions would be a unique instance in the entire book. Similarly, Stuart proposes a rhetorical nature of Hosea's words. He states, "Yahweh now announces that he will turn the tables on the house of Jehu because of the real issue, i.e., *what has happened in the meantime*. In the same way that Jehu in 842 had annihilated a dynasty famed for its long history of oppression and apostasy, so Yahweh himself will now put an end to the Jehu dynasty because it, in turn, has grown hopelessly corrupt."[118]

---

115. Chisholm, "'The Bloodshed of Jezreel,'" 440–42.

116. Later parts of Hosea contain form-critical judgment speeches. For example, Hosea 8 follows such a format with its call to alarm (8:1a), its accusations (8:1b–6, 9, 11–14), and its announcements of judgment (8:7–8, 10, 13b, 14b).

117. Jeremias states, "sie bliebe im ganzen Hoseabuch singulär, insofern der Prophet sonst nie die Strafe Gottes für weit (ein Jahrhundert!) zurückliegende Schuld ankündigt, sondern stets für gegenwärtige Vergehen. Wo er frühere Geschichtsereignisse nennt - ab 9, 10 in großer Zahl -, da tut er es, um gegenwärtige Schuld aufzudecken und zu beleuchten." Jeremias, *Der Prophet Hosea*, 30.

118. Stuart, *Hosea-Jonah*, 29. It should be noted that Jehu's annihilation of the Omride Dynasty is based on the text in 2 Kgs 9:16–29 in its final form. Critical scholarship debates the authenticity of this account. Those taking a redactional approach often conclude that the material in 2 Kings is from the time of Jeroboam II, written as an attempt to provide a positive view of Jehu's dynasty that contradicts the view of Hosea

A Twist on a Solution

The Deuteronomistic history supports the view that all of Jehu's descendants were viewed negatively: Jehoahaz (2 Kgs 13:1–9); Jehoash/Joash (2 Kgs 13:10–13); Jeroboam II (2 Kgs 14:23–29); and Zechariah (2 Kgs 15:8–12). Although few details are provided of the reign of Jeroboam II in 2 Kings, other sources reveal his negative reign. Hosea himself accuses the nation of murder, violence, and bloodshed (4:1–2; 12:2). Amos and Micah, Hosea's contemporaries, also spoke against the atrocities of Israel during Jeroboam II's reign and the reign of his successors. Amos's accusations included selling the righteous and needy (Amos 2:6); trampling on the heads of the poor (2:7); filling royal palaces with goods taken in violence (3:10); establishing winter and summer houses (3:15); perverting justice (5:7, 10); making the poor pay taxes on their crops (5:11); tormenting the innocent (5:12); and establishing a reign of violence (6:3). Micah, in his judgment speeches against Samaria and Judah, made similar accusations. Judah was guilty of following the ways of Samaria (1:9). They were guilty of seizing houses and fields (2:2); rising up against their own people as an enemy would (2:8); metaphorically treating people like food by tearing off their skin, ripping the flesh from the bones, and cooking them in a pot (3:2–3). Additionally, the rich were full of violence (6:12).

While the first chapter of Hosea lacks a direct reference to bloodshed done by Jeroboam II, it is important to remember that Hosea and his audience shared a cultural and rhetorical context. Hosea could assume that the audience is able to infer more than simply the propositions he stated. Given the nature of Jezreel's agricultural abundance, the rise of the royal bureaucracy and military, and the need to feed the growth of administration, military, and horses, the poor peasantry of Jezreel were certainly the

---

and Amos. The Tel Dan Inscription has also been at the center of this debate. Lines 7–9 of the inscription record what most scholars agree to be an Aramean king's claim to have killed Joram, son of Ahab, and Ahazyahu, son of Jehoram. This claim contradicts the Kings account that has Jehu killing them. Wesselius argues for a re-reading of the inscription and claims that Jehu is the one claiming to have killed the king. Wesselius, "The First Royal Inscription from Ancient Israel," 163–86. Becking refutes Wesselius's claim and considers it highly improbable that Jehu or Hazael is the one making the claim. Becking, "Did Jehu Write the Tel Dan Inscription?" 187–201. Robker disagrees with both Wesselius and Becking. He views the inscription's claim to be from Hazael. However, he considers the claim to be propaganda, "demonstrating the power of the king of Aram over Israel." While focusing on the redactional history of 2 Kings 9 in the first half of his book, Robker concludes that Jehu likely was the one who killed Joram and Ahaziah. Robker, *The Jehu Revolution*, 240–74, 246.

victims of the types of injustices against which the prophets cried out. The expanded growth experienced under Jeroboam's reign required land acquisition and materials. It is reasonable to suggest that Jeroboam committed violent actions in Jezreel. Josephus states that Jeroboam II "was the cause of ten thousand misfortunes to the people of Israel."[119] Andersen and Freedmen are thus correct in assessing that Hosea condemns Jeroboam for following in the footsteps of Ahab (as opposed to those of Jehu, his great-grandfather).[120]

Relevance Theory and the Meaning of Hosea 1:4

Judgment for more recent actions of Jeroboam II may be further supported by the superscription. As alluded to earlier, Hosea's introduction omits multiple Israelite kings who reigned during his prophetic ministry, only mentioning the reign of Jeroboam II. The rationale for this varies from commentator to commentator. Stuart suggests that this was purposeful from the book's final editor who compiled Hosea's messages after the fall of Samaria. As a result, the editor, while giving a token reference to one Israelite king (Jeroboam II), focused on the southern kings. He rationalizes that the Judean audience only recognized the Davidic line and had little interest in the northern kings. Furthermore, the mention of the rapidly shifting kings could confuse the southern readers. Chisholm acknowledges that the final editor's rationale is unclear, but he proposes that it could be a way for the editor to suggest that the other kings were insignificant or illegitimate (cf. Hos 8:4).[121] Wolff states, "The prominence given to Jeroboam's name may underline the intrinsic importance as well as the large extent of Hosea's preaching during his reign."[122]

Perhaps the sole mention of Jeroboam II, when connected to the punishment on the House of Jehu, led the recipients to focus on Jeroboam's more recent actions. Klingler highlights how an author's meaning is narrowed when additional utterances are provided and are relevant to the hearer's context.[123] When Hosea was compiled with the

---

119. Josephus, *The Jewish Antiquities, Books 1–19*, 9.10.1.
120. Andersen and Freedman, *Hosea*, 181.
121. Chisholm, *Handbook on the Prophets*, 336.
122. Wolff, *Hosea*, 6.
123. Klingler, "Validity in the Identification and Interpretation of a Literary Allusion in the Hebrew Bible," 152–53.

heading, Hosea's audience was drawn to the reign of Jeroboam II. This first utterance served as a stimulus for his audience to focus on Jeroboam II's reign. The second utterance to an Israelite king refers to the judgment on "the House of Jehu." This proclamation provided further context that is connected to the bloodshed in the Valley of Jezreel. This would lead to the conclusion that the mention of the House of Jehu is not intended to bring judgment for Jehu's bloody coup. Given the shared knowledge of Jeroboam's violent and oppressive reign, the two utterances suggested to the original recipients that the inferred referent of the cause of judgment on the dynasty of Jehu is Jeroboam II.

If understood as a direct reference to Jeroboam II, then Hosea is making a similar prophecy as his contemporary, Amos. Amos specifically mentioned Jeroboam's dynasty dying by the sword (Amos 7:9, 10). As was typical for Amos, the punishment was fitting to the crime committed (cf. Amos 5:7). As a result of his direct mention of Jeroboam II in his prophecy, the opposition he faced from Amaziah the priest focused on the threat made against the king (Amos 7:10–17). As Amos, Hosea brought a message of judgment against Jeroboam's dynasty.

The Rhetorical Use of Jezreel for Judgment on the House of Jehu

In light of this, a more common translation in verse 4 as "punish/avenge the bloodshed of Jezreel on the house of Jehu" could still be had without pitting the writer of Kings against Hosea. The text does not implicitly condemn Jehu's actions in that it mentions the "house of Jehu." As a result, the rhetoric is quite powerful and works on multiple levels. Like Dr. King, Hosea could simply mention the name of the place to conjure up in his audience memories and perceptions of atrocities done there. Certainly, Jezreel had a bloody past, including the violence Ahab had committed to attain land in Jezreel and the violent manner in which Jehu put an end to Ahab's dynasty. The memory of such actions certainly still lingered with the audience. Yet in the moment, given Amos's and Micah's references to the oppression of the poor, the accumulation of winter and summer houses, the exaction of grain taxes, the growth of fine vineyards, and violence, the audience of Hosea would infer the violent atrocities happening in Jezreel at that time. What better place to acquire land and supply the needs of the growing bureaucracy and military than the "breadbasket" of the land? The mere mention of Jezreel would ground Hosea's argument (i.e., achieve a mutual understanding with his audience) as it conjured up the collective memory of the past and the present.

Furthermore, by tapping into the collective memory of the audience with his mention of the House of Jehu, Hosea can focus on the current descendants of Jehu while still alluding to Jehu's past actions. Targum Jonathan supports a reading that includes both Jehu's past actions and his descendants' continued actions. Regarding Hosea 1:4, it reads, "for in a little while I will avenge the blood of the idolaters, which Jehu shed in Jezreel, when he put them to death because they worshipped Baal. Now they themselves have turned back to go astray after the calves at Bethel. Therefore, I will account it as innocent blood upon the house of Jehu, and I will abolish kingship from the house of Israel."[124] One can see an allusion to Jehu's act and a reference to his descendants without needing to accept the Targum's apologetic effort to harmonize Hosea and Kings by redefining the previous divinely commissioned act.

Ironically, as Stuart acknowledges, Hosea communicated that God would repeat the actions that Jehu did to Ahab, but on Jeroboam's family (Jehu's own great-grandson) for the same reasons for which Ahab's dynasty was judged. While Jehu zealously exterminated Ahab and his Baalism from the land, Jeroboam had allowed Ahab's paganism to be reestablished in the land (cf. 2:10, 15–19; 11:2; 13:1). The land was guilty of pagan adultery. As Ahab's dynasty was punished, so too would Jeroboam's be, and tragically for the same reasons. Jehu's own descendant had undone his zealous actions for Yahweh; therefore, there would be a new bloody coup. Yahweh would judge Jehu's dynasty, and they would suffer the same bloodshed as Ahab suffered. As Chisholm notes the underlying rhetoric, he states, "Yahweh will, as part of his judgment on Israel, cause the violence of Jezreel to reappear (as an instrument of judgment, as it were) in the house of Jehu, because Jehu's dynasty and the nation as a whole had perpetuated the sins of the house of Ahab."[125]

The Fulfillment of Hosea's Prophecy

Thus, Hosea's introduction to the first rhetorical usage of "Jezreel" established the coming fate of the dynasty of Jehu. Historically, the fulfillment of this judgment is easily traced. In 752 BC, Zechariah succeeded his father

---

124. Cathcart and Gordon, *The Targum of the Prophets*, 29–30.
125. Chisholm, "The 'Bloodshed of Jezreel,'" 12.

Jeroboam II (2 Kgs 15:8–10) but was assassinated after six months by Shallum. Zechariah's death officially ended the dynasty of Jehu (cf. 2 Kgs 10:30), "avenging the bloodshed of Jezreel on the house of Jehu." He continued with the judgment on the horizon for the nation of Israel by stating that he would put an end to the kingdom of Israel (1:4). This judgment is also tied into the significance of the geography of Jezreel. The "bow of Israel" would be broken in the Valley of Jezreel (Hos 1:5). The "bow of Israel" serves as a metonymy for the military strength of Israel (cf. 2:20; Jer 49:35; 51:56; Psa 46:10).[126] During Hosea's ministry, Assyria was the main threat and expanded its territory under the reign of Tiglath-pileser III (745–727). During his military campaigns against Phoenicia, Philistia, Syria, and Israel (733 BC), Tiglath-pileser III killed Rezin, "broke the bow of Israel," and took control of the Jezreel Valley (2 Kgs 15:29; Isa 9:1).[127]

The Rhetorical Use of the Memory of Jezreel

The rhetorical function of Israel's military strength ("the bow of Israel") being broken in the Valley of Jezreel is heightened when one considers Jezreel from a spatial perspective. Given the memory and perception of Israel's

126. For example, Wolff, *Hosea*, 19. First SamueL 2:4 provides a nice picture of the bow symbolizing military strength. For a detailed study in its ancient Near Eastern setting, see Waldman, "The Breaking of the Bow," 82–88. For a discussion of how the author of 1 Samuel uses the theme of the "fall" (נפל) of the proud juxtaposed to the exaltation of the humble, and how this theme contributes to the unity of 1 Samuel, see Jackson, "The Bows of the Mighty are Broken," 290–305. It is also possible that Hosea rhetorically intended another allusion in verse five. While "break the bow" (קשת ושברתי) is certainly a reference to breaking the military power of Israel, "the bow" was also the title of the lament sung over Saul and Jonathan's deaths (2 Sam 1:17–27). Saul and Jonathan battled the Philistines in the Jezreel Valley (1 Sam 31). Jonathan was killed in battle, and after being injured, Saul fell (נפל) on his own sword on Mount Gilboa (1 Sam 31:4). As discussed above, the city of Jezreel sits right at the foot of Mount Gilboa. Three times in this lament, David cries over how Saul and Jonathan had fallen (נפל: see 2 Sam 1:19, 25, and 27). The deaths of Saul and Jonathan marked the end of Saul's dynasty, an example of the costs of disobedience to Yahweh. On the heels of an announcement regarding the end of Jehu's dynasty, one wonders if Hosea intended to allude to this event. Later, Hosea references how the kings and leaders of Israel fall (נפל: Hos 7:7, 16; 14:1). Andersen and Freedman make a similar point. They point to references about sorcery, connecting Israel's sin to Saul seeking the witch of Endor. Andersen and Freedman, *Hosea*, 187. While a stronger argument would be made if there were more lexical links, the geography and circumstances (i.e., the fall of a king to mark the end of a dynasty) are intriguing.

127. For a map of the campaigns of Tiglath Pileser III and a brief history of the conquests, see Aharoni and Avi-Yonah, *The Macmillan Bible Atlas*, 94–95.

military strength in Jezreel, this spatial reference was a rhetorically effective way for Hosea to communicate with his northern audience. Without considering the social and historical background of this space, the rhetorical emphasis is missed. Specifically, Hosea mentions the "horses and chariots." Given the shared cognitive environment with his audience, this is certainly an allusion to the military training sites at Tel Jezreel and Megiddo. Israel had been guilty of building their military power and trusting it for protection. Yet, Hosea brought a functional message for the people to abandon this thinking. He challenged the people, including the military, the social elite, and royalty. As the people constantly saw Megiddo's over 400 horses training and feeding on the land, they were daily reminded of Hosea's message.[128] In this sense, given the daily operations of caring for those horses (see above), his message was inescapable.

The spatial use is even more effective when one considers how Hosea describes the Lord's mercy on Judah (1:7). Judah would be spared, but not by military power, for Judah's salvation would come by "Yahweh[129] their God" and not through their military. The training centers, which were the security of royalty and which contributed to the deprivation of the peasantry, were in vain. Hosea's message had an intentional function of calling the people to covenant faithfulness and allegiance to Yahweh. Perhaps he even intended to persuade the people to consider Judah as the place of safety.[130]

Rhetorical Implications of "Calling" Jezreel by Name

Consider the important role that "Jezreel" played for Hosea's implied audience. This child's name would serve as a prophetic message for the people. As the child grew, his name conjured perceptions and memories of events that occurred in Jezreel. It required explanation to family, friends, and all

---

128. Of course, if Franklin's interpretation of the archaeology is correct regarding Tel Jezreel being used during Jeroboam II's reign, then the daily reminders are even more prevalent.

129. Given the current state of Baalism, the mentioning of Yahweh was also polemical.

130. For further consideration, one could contemplate whether Hosea's words were intended to persuade his audience to relocate south to Judah. Perhaps this provides insight for the debate between Finkelstein and Na'aman regarding the population expansion on the western hill of Jerusalem in the eighth century. Finkelstein, "The Settlement History of Jerusalem," 499–515; Na'aman, "When and How Did Jerusalem Become a Great City?" 21–56.

those with whom he came in contact. In effect, every time his name was called, a prophetic message was given.

Furthermore, for the hearer or reader of Hosea, the symbolic use of Jezreel serves to prepare one for the future nuanced usages of "Jezreel" in these chapters.[131] Perhaps, given Hosea's paronomastic usage of "Jezreel" with "Israel" (see above), the hearers and readers would consider the judgment and future blessings (see below) of "Jezreel" every future instance of references to "Israel." In other words, when they hear the name "Israel" in later parts of the book, they reflect back on the judgment and future restoration of Israel associated with the use of "Jezreel."

Hosea 2:2 (1:11)

The use of Jezreel to signify judgment is reversed in the second chapter. Chapter 2 (Eng 1:10–11) begins with a glimpse of future hope. Despite the coming judgment, there would be a time when the Lord would restore favor and re-fulfill the Abrahamic covenant. This reversal of fortune is rhetorically symbolized by a reversal of Hosea's children's names. It was said of Israel that they were no longer God's people (Lo-Ammi), but they would later say to one another "my people" (Ammi). Although in Hosea's time, the Lord would no longer show pity on Israel (Lo-Ruhamah), in the future they would call to one another "pity" (Ruhamah). Though Jehu's dynasty would be judged, and Israel's strength broken (geographical use of Jezreel), later the "day of Jezreel will be great." There are multiple possibilities of understanding Hosea's words here.

It is possible that the "day of Jezreel" is a reference to a reversal of the military defeat mentioned in 1:5. Sometimes the phrase, "day of . . ." is used to refer to a former battle or destruction. Isaiah, a contemporary of Hosea, refers to Gideon's battle this way. "The day of Midian" looks back to Midian's defeat at the hands of Gideon (Isa 9:3; 9:4 Eng.).[132] Mays offers that in Gideon's situation, this highlights that the battle will be Yahweh's battle and not the people's battle.[133] Similarly, "the day of Jerusalem" looks back to Jerusalem's destruction at the hands of the Babylonians (Psa 137:7). While the

---

131. See Willis's discussion of Isaiah's symbolic naming of Shear-jashub and the root שאר in Isaiah. Willis, "Symbolic Names and Theological Themes in the Book of Isaiah," 74–81.

132. MacIntosh, *A Critical and Exegetical Commentary on Hosea*, 19–20.

133. Mays, *Hosea*, 33.

"bow of Israel" was broken in the Valley of Jezreel, in the future, the "day of Jezreel" will become great. In this sense, this passage would imply a reversal of the defeat suffered at the hands of the Assyrians in 733 BC

Moon interprets the mention of Jezreel in this light and highlights the theme of the reversal of fortunes. Two of Hosea's children's names are collocated with the negative particle לֹא (לֹא רֻחָמָה and לֹא עַמִּי). In the restoration of fortune, Hosea uses the same negative particle two times in a positive sense. The number of the children of Israel will not be able to be measured or counted (לֹא־יִמַּד and לֹא יִסָּפֵר). Moon thus connects the reversal of Jezreel with the "breaking of the bow" in the Valley of Jezreel. Alluding to the frequent military overtones associated with the "day of YHWH" in the prophets, he also suggests that "day of Jezreel" has militaristic tones. He furthers his argument, stating, "And to 'go up' commonly expresses military overtones (cf. Josh 10:9; 15:15; 1 Sam 13:15; 1 Kgs 15:19, etc.). In this context, such a use fits perfectly: the restoration of 'Jezreel' keeps the name's military significance."[134] Hence, Moon interprets Hosea's message as a future promise that the unified people of God will be re-established and go up in battle together in military strength.

Contextually, this interpretation has several strengths. Geographically, it certainly ties into the militaristic connotations and memories of Jezreel. Depending on the dating of Hosea 2, it could also reflect a reversal of the disunity of Israel and Judah during the Syro-Ephraimite war (see above). There is also ample validation from the usage of "go up" and "day of . . ." In contrast, Hosea's negative accusations of Israel falsely trusting in their military strength and fortresses contradicts a future promise of a great military force. However, as mentioned above, Mays suggests that this military strength would not come from the Israelite's efforts but would be the result of the presence of Yahweh.

Kelle attempts to identify the rhetorical situation and illocution of this reversal of imagery with a specific historical situation.[135] He suggests that this passage (2:1–3; Eng 1:10—2:1) is set within Hoshea's takeover of Pekah around 731 BC The Israelites from this period who supported Hoshea aligned themselves with Judeans. Others remained supportive of Pekah. Thus, from an illocutionary perspective, Hosea's rhetorical purpose is twofold: encouraging "the sanctioned cooperation between Israelites and Judeans"; and attempting to rescue "those 'brothers' and 'sisters'

---

134. Moon, *Hosea*, 46–47.
135. Austin, *How to Do Things with Words*.

who remain under the influence of Pekah and the rulers of Samaria."[136] If correct, Hosea's message had a strong perlocutionary intention. Those Israelites who were no longer God's people (Lo-Ammi) were now being welcomed back as "my people" (Ammi) and 'brothers' and 'sisters.' The intent would be clear: support Hoshea in his overthrow of Pekah and his rebellious ways.[137] For Kelle, Hosea was persuading his audience to "work toward the realization of Yahweh's goals among his people."[138]

More likely, it appears that Hosea is employing a reference to the etymology of the compound name "God sows/will sow." Two of the key elements described in this context are the numerical growth of the people of Israel in fulfillment of the Abrahamic covenant, and the reunification of the people of Israel and Judah.[139] When God sows the people back into the land, they will be like vegetation growing numerously and united in the fertile land of Jezreel. This imagery is certainly in alignment with the usage of Jezreel at the end of the chapter. Stuart even places this event into the distant future, as an eschatological hope.[140]

Hosea 2:24 (2:22)

This last usage of the term "Jezreel" is again found within a context of restoration: the betrothal between Yahweh and Israel. The judgment would be marked by the Lord's removal of grain, wine, wool, and flax (2:11; 2:9 English Bible).[141] In contrast, the restoration would be marked

---

136. Kelle, *Hosea 2*, 225–26. Kelle's view of Hosea as in favor of an Assyrian alliance takes the opposite view to that of Sweeney. Sweeney understands Hosea and his messages as reflecting an anti-Assyrian position. Sweeney, *The Twelve Prophets*, 5–6.

137. In terms of classical rhetoric, this function would be deliberative. Deliberative rhetoric invites the audience to make a deliberative assessment of actions that would be expedient or beneficial for future performance.

138. Kelle, *Hosea 2*, 228.

139. A third key component would be the appointment of one new leader. Later, Hosea will specify that this leader will come from the Davidic line (Hos 3:5).

140. Stuart, *Hosea-Jonah*, 39–40. The Targum of Hosea reads it eschatologically too. It reads, "After that, the people of Israel will return and seek the worship of the Lord their God and will obey the anointed One son of David their king. And they will follow eagerly the worship of the Lord, and great will be his goodness that will come to them in the end of days." Cathcart and Gordon, *The Targum of the Prophets*, 35–36. One could also consider the fulfillment of this passage from a conditional perspective. It conveyed the Lord's intentions, but those intentions were conditional upon repentance.

141. Hanley shows how the metaphoric language of this removal is connected to the

by agricultural prosperity. It is well noted that the complete agricultural cycle is presented in this passage. Yahweh speaks to the skies, which provide rain to the earth. The earth responds by providing vegetation in the form of grain, wine, and oil. Lastly, the agriculture responds to Jezreel.¹⁴² Initially the response "Jezreel" seems like an awkward way to say that the agriculture responds to the people. However, this usage of Jezreel forms a phonetic wordplay in Hebrew. The word יִזְרְעֶאל (*yizreʿeʾl* Jezreel) sounds like the word יִשְׂרָאֵל (*yiśraʾel* Israel), allowing Hosea to use "Jezreel" as another name for Israel. Thus, the agriculture responds to Israel, the people, completing the cycle (Yahweh-skies-ground-agriculture-people). The imagery is rhetorically powerful for the audience of ancient Israel. Their threshing floors would be filled with grain and their wine and oil presses would be full, too. The etymology of the compound name speaks to the new growth that will characterize the restoration.

Hosea continued the rhetorical use of "Jezreel" with the very next word. He created a wordplay using the term זָרַע ("to sow"). זָרַע is one of the root words in the compound proper name "Jezreel." In verse 25 (23 Eng), immediately following the word "Jezreel" in verse 24 (22), Hosea uses the verb form וּזְרַעְתִּיהָ (a *qal* perfect 1cs + *waw* conjunction + 3fs suffix from the root זרע). Through use of the shared root, Hosea solidifies the rhetorical meaning. Yahweh will sow Israel for himself in the land.¹⁴³ Israel's misfortunes will be reversed. The negative connotation of Jezreel resulted in the breaking of Israel's military strength (Hos 1:4–5). Assyria's conquest in 733 BC resulted in the people's exile from the land. In contrast, Israel is now portrayed as being replanted into the land. They have reentered into their marital relationship with Yahweh and have returned from the wilderness (exile) into the land.¹⁴⁴

---

stripping of the adulteress. In both cases, the language speaks of YHWH's enforcement of the covenant curses in Deuteronomy 28, 8:13, and 11:14. YHWH is removing every provision he had provided, leaving Israel empty and naked as they go into exile in the eyes of their "lovers." Hanley, "The Background and Purpose of Stripping the Adulteress in Hosea 2," 89–103.

142. For various explanations of the cycle, see: Stuart, *Hosea–Jonah*, 60; Wolff, *Hosea*, 53; Chisholm, *Handbook on the Prophets*, 345.

143. Contrary to Wolff, while Hosea's child Jezreel was a boy, the 3fs suffix is likely still in reference to Jezreel. Stuart proposes that the 3fs suffix is used because Jezreel, as the crop center of the north, stands as a synecdoche for all Israel agriculturally. Stuart, *Hosea–Jonah*, 61. Similarly, Kelle proposes that the 3fs suffix is used because the overarching metaphor is of Yahweh's bride, requiring a feminine suffix. Kelle, *Hosea 2*, 282.

144. MacIntosh, *A Critical and Exegetical Commentary on Hosea*, 89.

Ben Zvi proposes that Hosea used an inclusio based on the term "Jezreel." Jezreel is introduced in 1:4–5; is repeated as the center-point in 2:2; and concludes the inclusio in 2:24–25. The inclusio begins with judgment for the House of Jehu and all Israel as Israel's military strength is broken, and then the center shifts the focus to redemption in the "day of Jezreel." The use of the inclusio depicts Jezreel as encapsulating the "entire trajectory from punishment to ideal future."[145] Thus, Jezreel serves as an instrumental component in the arrangement and composition of the message of Hosea 1–2. While the threat of judgment was imminent, the promise of restoration in the magnitude similar to Jezreel's fertility, albeit a distant promise, highlights the intensity by which the Lord intends to bless Israel.

Hosea's Rhetorical Use of Space and the Various Social Groups

While some of the critical spatial questions (especially those dealing with Jezreel's Firstspace, Secondspace, and Thirdspace) described in the methodology were answered while working through Jezreel and the text of Hosea 1–2, it is beneficial to elaborate further and bring clarity to the proposed methodology. On the one hand, Hosea used the everyday practices to shape his prophetic poetry, providing the imagery and background for rhetoric (much of this has been elaborated on above). Yet, a more holistic approach will also consider how the geographical and spatial references impacted the different social groups within his audience. The answer to this question can be considered from the major social groups within Israel: the farmers, the military, the bureaucratic elite, and the royal household.

How Did Hosea's Rhetorical Use of Space Relate to the Peasants/Farmers?

Regarding the rhetorical impact on the farmers, consider the references to agriculture, warfare, Gomer's unfaithfulness, and Hosea's strategy to turn Gomer from unfaithful to faithful. Obviously, the references to the agricultural loss or bounty rhetorically impact this group. For extended families who spend their entire lives working the fields and leading herds, the imagery of having grain, wine, wool, and linen taken away and of their vines and fig trees rotting (2:9, 12) served to prosecute and persuade them. From

---

145. Ben Zvi, *Hosea*, 46. In support of Ben Zvi's proposal, one can see a repetition of the use of יוֹם ("day"). The end points of the inclusion use the phrase "in that day" (1:5; 2:21). The center-point uses "day" in a different phrase, the "day of Jezreel."

a prosecutorial perspective, the threat of the loss and coming famine was the result of being unfaithful to the covenant, committing adultery against Yahweh with Baal. From a persuasive perspective, the farmers were encouraged to return and honor their covenant with Yahweh in hopes that the prophetic announcement of God's intentions would be changed. Given that their livelihood was based on agriculture, and that Baal was considered by the Canaanites as the one responsible for agricultural fertility, this was a significant decision, one that would reflect in whom they trusted for the success of their crops.[146] Given the conditional nature of prophetic foretelling and the future promise of agricultural prosperity in Hosea 2, the farmers had the freedom and responsibility to return to faithfulness.

Hosea's messages of warfare in Jezreel also impacted the farmers on two levels. As previously noted, Israel's military included the farmers as the non-professional national levy. Thus, the threat of warfare carried with it the reality that farming would be put on hold, or that the wives and children would need to do the work, and many men would be called into battle. Furthermore, given the Firstspace of the farming villages (i.e., close to travel routes, water, without defenses, etc.), the threat of warfare carried drastic implications for their land, houses, and families. Matthews captures the impact on their environment well as he states of an invading army, "they trample fields of grain, destroy or strip fruit trees (Jer 7:20), and as they regularly destroy the houses in the villages in their path (COS 2.113C: 267). Sennacherib's account of his first campaign against Merodach-Baladan includes a boast that his army 'destroyed, devastated, and burned [their towns] and turned them into forgotten tells' (COS 2.119: 302)."[147] Furthermore, the peasants would consider that they would observe "their wells being destroyed or poisoned and their streams being filled with debris and muddied, making them undrinkable" by the invading armies.[148] The severity of the warfare could require—and, in the case of the Assyrian

---

146. The nature of the Baal references in Hosea is debated. For an overview of the issues and persuasive arguments for the Canaanite fertility god being the referent, see Day and Kató. Day, "Hosea and the Baal Cult," 202–24; Kató, "Baal and the Baals in the Book of Hosea," 35–54.

147. Matthews, "Spatial and Sensory Aspects of Battle in Biblical and Ancient Near Eastern Texts," 83. In this article, Matthews adds sensory analysis to the spatial so the interpreter considers new insights and considerations for new dimensions of research.

148. Matthews, "Spatial and Sensory Aspects of Battle in Biblical and Ancient Near Eastern Texts," 84.

invasion, did require—the local population's retreat into Megiddo or other strongholds to withstand the battle.

Regarding Gomer's unfaithfulness, the modern reader typically looks on Gomer's adultery mainly from the perspective of a broken relationship between a man and a woman. This is understandable, given that this is the primary emphasis of the metaphor. However, when considering critical spatial theory's broader contribution to spatial awareness, and considering relevance theory's emphasis on the relationship of the author and his audience, the modern interpreter needs to recognize that Hosea and the ancient readers shared a cognitive background that included the spatial concept of the "house of the father." Thus, the common farmer certainly would have also considered how Gomer's actions impacted the everyday practices of those within the "house of the father."

Depending on the age of Hosea and Gomer,[149] and his role in society,[150] it is possible that he was part of an extended family unit that included his father or even grandfather. It could be that Hosea and Gomer's dwelling was amidst the other members of the Beeri family, as part of the בֵּית אָב. As the family as a whole was responsible for farming its own patrimonial land (נַחֲלָה), Gomer's departure from the household directly impacted her role as a contributing member of the unit.[151] Furthermore, since marriage in ancient Israel included a corporate relationship between two families, an adulterous relationship had political, social, and economic impacts.[152]

Households in ancient Israel were patrilocal, and the man's social status in the community was at stake when a woman within his household was accused of infidelity. Matthews notes that the biblical teachings on adultery are not only tied to marital morals but also to "the social

---

149. Matthews stipulates the average ages of ancient Israelites at marriage. In pointing out the disparity in ages between the bride and the groom, he notes that the bride would typically be between twelve and fourteen years of age while the groom would be between twenty-five and thirty. Matthews, "Marriage and Family in the Ancient Near East," 9.

150. Outside of Hosea's role as a prophet, we know little about his background. Andersen and Freedman write, "Whatever his background, training, and circumstances, of his family and lineage, of his residence and locality we know next to nothing—only his patronymic: Hosea ben-Beeri. What sets him apart is his calling as a prophet: it places him in that select company of men and women who held this office, who were messengers of God to his people." Andersen and Freedman, *Hosea*, 44.

151. Block, "Marriage and Family in Ancient Israel," 73–75.

152. Matthews and Benjamin, *Social World of Ancient Israel 1250–587 BCE*, 13–16.

and economic relationships between the households in the village as a whole."¹⁵³ Every member in the household had social obligations to uphold the honor of the house.¹⁵⁴ Hence, family honor and stability were critical to both the house of the father and the whole village's economy. Again, Matthews states, "Swift action is necessary to prevent a complete loss of credibility and ultimately the extinction of the household when no other family will contract marriages or do business with it."¹⁵⁵

A holistic approach to understanding geography also considers how societies create places where their members can be considered "in place" or "out of place." As Cresswell notes, "spatial structures and the system of places provide historically contingent but durable 'schemes of perception' that have an ideological dimension. In particular, the place of an act is an active participant in our understanding of what is good, just, and appropriate."¹⁵⁶ In Israel's case, the house of the father had ideological dimensions and was not simply a place to sleep. In the Israelites' patrilineal, patrilocal, and patriarchal society, the community was built around the father.¹⁵⁷ Amongst many responsibilities, the father was liable for providing sustenance for the family, managing the land, defending the family from threats, representing the family as the elder at the gate, maintaining the well-being of everyone

---

153. Matthews, "Honor and Shame in Gender-Related Legal Situations in the Hebrew Bible," 97.

154. Matthews, "Honor and Shame in Gender-Related Legal Situations in the Hebrew Bible," 98.

155. Matthews, "Honor and Shame in Gender-Related Legal Situations in the Hebrew Bible," 112.

156. Cresswell, *In Place Out of Place: Geography, Ideology, and Transgression*, 16. Similarly, Richardson and Jensen seek to develop a "practice- and culture-oriented understanding of the spatiality of social life." Richardson and Jensen, "Linking Discourse and Space," 7. They recognize that "spaces are socially constructed, and that many spaces may co-exist within the same physical space . . ." Thus, based on the way that life was practiced and the way that the culture viewed spaces, individuals could be located "in place" or "out of place." Perhaps an easy analogy that Cresswell shares helps. Dirt is fine when it is in its proper place. However, dirt in the kitchen or the bedroom is "out of place" and must be remedied. Cresswell, *In Place Out of Place: Geography, Ideology, and Transgression*, 38.

157. In light of Israel's failures to carry out the responsibilities of fatherhood according to divine standards, Block prefers to use the term patricentrism as opposed to patriarchy. The term patrilineal refers to the reality that "official lines of descent were traced through the father's line." Patrilocal refers to the practice in which "married women joined the households of their husbands," and patriarchal speaks to the fact that "the father governed the household." Block, "Marriage and Family in Ancient Israel," 40.

in the household, and implementing decisions made by the broader clan. Specifically for the wife, he was responsible to provide peace, permanence, and security.[158] When a member of the family, in this case Gomer, left the "in place" and became "out of place" (i.e., removed from the house possibly by divorce due to adultery), the father was no longer responsible to make such provisions for her. As Kohn notes, "A woman out of place signifies disorder in the Israelite social fabric. On the other hand, her return to the perceived acceptable location restores not only her own social position in society but also the stability and health of society as a whole."[159] Based on her lack of connectedness to the בֵּית אָב, Gomer had disrupted the social fabric of the community and forfeited her rights to the privileges associated with it.[160] Keefe says it well when she states, "the trope used in Hosea is not really a *marriage* metaphor but rather a *family* metaphor; it is a parable of a בֵּית אָב that has been irrevocably disrupted. If Israelite identity was bound up with the symbolic centrality of the בֵּית אָב, then we can read Hosea's family metaphor about a fornicating wife and her illegitimate children as pointing to the disruption and dissolution of that identity."[161]

Hosea's calling upon the children to repudiate Gomer (Hos 2:4; Eng 2:2) makes sense in the context of the house of the father.[162] While the option to divorce Gomer was justified (Deut 24:1),[163] his efforts to win

158. Block, "Marriage and Family in Ancient Israel," 47–48.

159. Kohn, "In and Out of Place: Physical Space and Social Location in the Bible." Kohn goes on to show how biblical narratives reflect that Israelite women put themselves in danger when they are "out of place." For example, Dinah acts independently to go to see the daughters of the land, where Shechem takes her by force (Gen 34). In Kohn's words, "within one's family is safety, but outside, among the people of the land, lies social and status instability." Her stability declines in the rest of the story, and she ends with "no 'place' for her in society that could be deemed socially acceptable."

160. Leeb, *Away from the Father's House*; Kohn, "In and Out of Place"; Gudme, "Inside-Outside: Domestic Living Space in Biblical Memory."

161. Keefe, "Family Metaphors and Social Conflict in Hosea," 121.

162. Garrett and Macintosh show how the language used in 2:4 need not speak of an official divorce or a courtroom setting. MacIntosh, *A Critical and Exegetical Commentary on Hosea*, 40–42; Garrett, *Hosea, Joel*, 75–77.

163. While Leviticus 20:10 contains a casuistic law calling for the death of a man who commits adultery with his neighbor's wife, Deuteronomy 24 is often pointed to as the passage that permits divorce. The situation involves a man who had married a woman but later finds something "indecent" about her. The phrase "he finds something indecent about her" (מָצָא בָהּ עֶרְוַת דָּבָר) is interpreted variously. The use of מָצָא ("he found") suggests that the husband came to know something that he had not known prior to the marriage. While the use of this collocation does not always refer to some

Gomer back also provide a glimpse into a broader understanding of the spatial setting of Hosea's audience.[164] As a husband who loved his wife and was modeling Yahweh's love for Israel, he also desired her faithfulness. In this case, her well-being was best served by her remaining or being brought back into his house. Furthermore, in light of the aforementioned significance for the community's stability and health to have a woman's place in an acceptable position in the society, it seemed all the more important for Hosea to have Gomer stay or return to his house.

Of course, the reality behind the metaphor for Hosea's recipients is the relationship between Yahweh (the father) and Israel (the bride). Israel would find itself removed from God's House, the land, because of her unfaithfulness. The harsh judgment is prophesied in Hosea 9:15 (NET): "... on account of their evil deeds, I will drive them out of my house. I will no longer love them..." Yahweh would impede Israel's attempts to worship other deities.[165] This is communicated by the metaphor of Hosea's efforts to impede Gomer's attempts to visit her lovers.

Hosea's actions are to "fence her in with thorns; I will wall her in so that she cannot find her way/path" (Hos 2:8; Eng 2:6 NET). The imagery appears to reflect the archaeology of the house of the father. Thorns were used to keep animals out of land being used for agriculture. The stone wall

---

ethical conduct (e.g., Isa 51:3), within the context of a legal formula it suggests inappropriate actions (cf. 1 Kgs 1:52; 1 Sam 29:3, 6, 8; 2 Kgs 17:4). The phrase עֶרְוַת דָּבָר ("something indecent") is used only one other time in the OT. It is used in the prior chapter in the context of covering bodily excrement outside the camp (Deut 23:14). The word עֶרְוַת by itself is used to refer to the naked genital areas of a man or a woman (Gen 9:22; Exod 20:26; 28:42; Lev 18:6–19; 20:11, 17–21). This has led many to see the indecent behavior as having a sexual nature, namely adultery or something short of adultery. The rabbinic passage found in *Mishnah Gittin 9:10* reflects that the School of Shammai considered it unchastity. Isaiah 50:1 refers to this passage as a metaphor of the Lord's relationship with his people. In it, the certificate of divorce and the sale into slavery were the results of the wife's (Israel's) sins. Similarly, Jeremiah 3:8 refers to this passage as a metaphor and the Lord's divorce of his people for their adulteries with other pagan deities (cf. Jer 3:1). While the Law stated that adultery could be punishable by death (Lev 20:10; Deut 22:22), this passage allows for an alternative option for the husband. He could show leniency by providing a certificate of divorce (cf. the Code of Hammurabi §129). In this manner, the certificate provides a valuable possession for the wife. Instead of death, the certificate provided her proof of the leniency of her husband, allowing her to not only get remarried but to actually live.

164. Kelle argues that the three instances of לְכָה are to be taken as "a convoluted sequence of actions but a series of alternatives from which the wronged husband may choose." Kelle, *Hosea 2*, 239.

165. Or perhaps trust other nations for help.

(גָּדֵר) reflects a rampart of stone that was arranged to serve as a fence. The imagery of the security wall around the household compound is seen in Isaiah. Isaiah recorded a song that started with Israel described as Yahweh's lover using the analogy of a vineyard. However, the song quickly turned negative, and Yahweh spoke of his intentions to break the vineyard's wall so that it become a place trampled by animals (Isa 5:5). In Hosea's situation, he erected a fence to keep his wife in as opposed to keeping animals out.

It is also feasible to consider the wall within the context of the broader multiple family compound of a בֵּית אָב. Stager notes that compounds themselves could be separated "by streets, paths, or stone enclosure walls."[166] Perhaps Hosea is likening Gomer to a rebellious, dumb animal that kept wandering off and now could no longer find the path because it was blocked with thorns and a stone wall.[167] It is also possible that Hosea is referring to the creation of greater levels of separation that would make it more difficult for Gomer to leave the household compound to find her lovers in public places.

Kelle suggests that the wall has a stronger meaning with multiple referents.[168] On the one hand, it serves to reflect the wall serving as a boundary fence around a section of land or a vineyard. He also points to its imagery as a siege wall placed around a city's walls to "wall-in" the city, as גָּדֵר is used for city walls, too (Mic 7:11; Ezra 9:9). He concludes, "Yahweh's statement in Hos 2 similarly combines the metaphor of the adulterous wife with the imagery of the siege of a city and serves the purpose of prohibiting the wife from freely seeking out contact with others."[169]

Kruger reads the imagery in Hosea 2:8 (2:6 Eng) on four levels.[170] First, the actions Hosea took should be read as "an integral part of the marriage metaphor" in Hosea 2:4–17. The thorns and wall were intended to restrict the "adulterous movements of his wife." As "her paths" (נְתִיבָה) could allude to her course of life or plans,[171] Kruger likens Gomer to the adulteress

---

166. Stager, "Archaeology of the Family," 18.

167. Irvine, "The Threat of Jezreel (Hosea 1:4–5)," 49.

168. Kelle, *Hosea 2*, 240–41. Dearman also makes this point. Dearman, *The Book of Hosea*, 113.

169. Kelle, *Hosea 2*, 241.

170. Kruger, "'I Will Hedge Her Way with Thornbushes' (Hosea 2,8)," 92–99.

171. Garrett, *Hosea, Joel*, 82. Garrett points to the usage of גָּדֵר to describe God's blocking a person's alternatives in Job 19:8 and Lamentations 3:9. Thus, he suggests that this could "have been a stock metaphor for God's activity of frustrating human plans." Andersen and Freedman, *Hosea*, 238.

of Proverbs 7 (especially 7:25). As such, Hosea's actions were intended to restrict Gomer's ability to access the paths that enabled her to search out her prey.[172] Secondly, the actions should be read "as part of a political metaphor."[173] As such, "her paths" refers to the city of Samaria's attempts to seek political alliances. In this manner, the metaphor points to Yahweh's efforts to block Israel's alliances with political lovers. Thirdly, Hosea's actions are to be read "as part of the religious-mythological metaphor."[174] The actions are Yahweh's efforts to restrict the pagan cultic movements of the people. The thorns and stone fences inhibit Israel's ability to make pilgrimages to worship sites in high places. Lastly, the metaphor is to be "read intertextually."[175] The metaphor points to other metaphors throughout the book of Hosea that liken the Israelites to animals. For example, they are likened to a stubborn heifer (4:16), a wild donkey that wanders off (8:9), and a herd attacked by a lion, leopard, or bear (13:5–8).

The way one understands the rhetorical situation impacts how far the metaphor is pushed. For those reading the text as a reflection of Hosea's intentions to promote an anti-Assyrian king, Kruger's political interpretation of the wall metaphor makes sense of the context. However, without understanding Hosea's rhetorical motivation politically, the metaphor connects Hosea's actions in his own marriage with Yahweh's actions to prohibit the cultic worship of other deities. Given the siege imagery previously discussed, Kelle's multi-referent interpretation to include a reference to a siege wall is attractive.

While the broader biblical text reflects Yahweh's care for Israel, especially the peasants being oppressed, Hosea's prophecy is filled with emotion and judgment in extremes. It provided a way for Hosea to attempt to "wow" the people, showing them the harshness of God's judgment for the purpose of calling them to repentance. Relying on the shared cognitive environment, Hosea was able to paint a memorable picture with a simple reference to one city/valley. A simplistic propositional descriptive statement would not be remembered to the same degree as a rich word picture or a creatively crafted argument. Hosea's intent was to leave a vivid impression upon the audience.[176] Rhetorically, the use of such imagery equipped Hosea to

---

172. Kruger, "'I Will Hedge Her Way with Thornbushes' (Hosea 2,8)," 93–94.
173. Kruger, "'I Will Hedge Her Way with Thornbushes' (Hosea 2,8)," 95–97.
174. Kruger, "'I Will Hedge Her Way with Thornbushes' (Hosea 2,8)," 97–99.
175. Kruger, "'I Will Hedge Her Way with Thornbushes' (Hosea 2,8)," 99.
176. Sandy notes the power of prophetic literature and clearly shows how the

achieve his intended persuasive goals. By describing the area of Jezreel and the spatial concept of the house of the father in their most powerful terms, the prophet certainly would have stirred the audience's emotions.

How Did Hosea's Rhetorical Use of Space Relate to the Professional Military?

Having considered the rhetorical impact on the commoners (farmers), the interpreter can now consider the rhetorical impact on those in the professional military who heard Hosea's message. Of particular interest is the impact of Hosea's prophecy that the Lord would "break the bow of Israel" in the Valley of Jezreel (1:5), and that the Lord would deliver Judah but not by military strength (1:7). While the prophecy certainly had a desired illocutionary message to "stop trusting in your military strength," for the military, the threat was more severe. Their very lives were in danger if the military strength of Israel would be broken in the Jezreel. Despite all of their training and expertise in warfare, Hosea declared that they would be destroyed in the Valley in which they no doubt spent much time.

A prophetic message of doom should not be taken lightly within its ancient Israelite context. Prior to war, prophetic inquiry or input was often taken or received to determine the strategy and outcome of the battle (e.g., 1 Kgs 12:22–24; 1 Kgs 22:5–28; 2 Kgs 13:14–19). A negative prophetic word was not always trusted or followed, but kings and soldiers certainly sought and relied on divine words of assurance. Micaiah's prophetic announcement of doom stirred an emotional response from Zedekiah the prophet and King Ahab (1 Kgs 22:24–27).[177]

In Hosea's context, one would expect Israel's military to either respond in anger or fear to this prophecy of defeat. Furthermore, to hear that Judah would be spared but not through military might would potentially cause greater anger, especially if it were received in defiance. If Hosea's message was received as authoritative, one could imagine that a soldier would consider fleeing to Judah. This conclusion would be further supported by Hosea's later prophecy that, after Israel's demise, Israel will return to seek

---

prophets' use of imagery displays "God at the extreme limit of His attributes, humanity at the limits of disobedience, calamity that seems unlimited, and prosperity of peace and joy beyond limit." Sandy, *Plowshares and Pruning Hooks*, 19–23.

177. See also Schmitt's work on the role of prophets in war rituals. Schmitt, "War Rituals in the Old Testament," 149–61.

YHWH and their Davidic king (3:5), implying legitimacy to the Judaic throne over the Israelite king.

How Did Hosea's Rhetorical Use of Space Relate to the Bureaucratic Elite?

Beyond the farmers and military, one would also expect members of the bureaucratic elite to have heard or perhaps read Hosea's message. What impact would Hosea's rhetoric have on this social class? Hosea's messages of agricultural loss would have sent a different rhetorical message to this social elite. For them, agricultural prosperity was a means for their pleasure, often at the expense of the poor (see above and cf. Amos 4:1; 5:10–12). The reduction of grain, wine, wool, flax, and fig trees (2:9, 12) would mean the reduction or end of their lucrative export and trade business. Keefe interprets the references to the grain, wine, and olive oil (2:10; 2:8 in Eng) as a message for this elite class and not simply a message about adulterous cultic worship. She states, "The desire of the woman of fornications for the grain, wine, oil, linen, flax, and other commodities reflects critically upon the desire of Israel's powerful elites for the profits and pleasures that this trade produced."[178] The elite's way of life would be utterly destroyed. One would imagine that the response to Hosea's message, if taken as credible, would be one of fear. Their life of luxury and comfort would be traded for either their loss of life, a life in exile as vassals, or at best, a life that required them to manually work for their daily necessities.

How Did Hosea's Rhetorical Use of Space Relate to the King and His Household?

Lastly, Hosea's message likely made its way to the king and his royal household. Amos, Hosea's eighth-century contemporary, had similar messages of judgment against the Israelites, including the Lord's threat of attacking Jeroboam's house with a sword (Amos 7:9). His messages were sent to Jeroboam II, albeit in a twisted format,[179] by Amaziah the priest (Amos 7:10–11). It is worth considering the rhetorical impact on the royal household within three areas: the reversal of Jeroboam II's territorial expansions and economic success, the prophecy of punishment on the house of Jehu, and the future unification of Israel and Judah under one Davidic king.

---

178. Keefe, "Family Metaphors and Social Conflict in Hosea," 122.
179. Chisholm, *Handbook on the Prophets*, 398–99.

THE RHETORICAL USE OF JEZREEL

Given the success of Jeroboam II in expanding Israel's borders and building its defenses (see above), Hosea's prophecies of military defeat would undo the land expansions of Jeroboam II and be indirect opposition to his role as king of Israel. As king, Jeroboam II was known for his strength as a military warrior.[180] While not much is said of his acts in the biblical text, the author of Kings notes how YHWH used him to "deliver" Israel from their suffering (2 Kgs 14:26–27) and indicates that his military success resulted in the expansion of Israel's borders (2 Kgs 14:28). Furthermore, the fact that the military defeat would happen in Jezreel signified the loss of Jeroboam's military fortress,[181] which removed further protection for Samaria.

Defeat in Jezreel would also lead to a loss of agriculture, a primary source of wealth for the king. As Brettler notes, "The king's prestige in the ancient Near East was partially determined by his wealth."[182] Despite the prohibition against Israelite kings amassing much wealth (Deut 17:17), history proved that the kings often ignored this prohibition (e.g., 2 Kgs 14:14; 20:13). Much of the king's wealth came from either booty collected during victorious war or from taxes levied on his own people.[183] Certainly, Jeroboam taxed the poor (cf. Amos 5:11). With the military loss in Jezreel, the "breadbasket" of the north, the agricultural loss directly threatened the wealth of the king.

Specifically, the prophecies in 1:4–5 had a direct impact on Jeroboam's descendants. If the prior interpretive decision based on relevance theory is correct, then Hosea is bringing accusations against Jeroboam directly. It is the bloodshed that he brought that was being addressed. Hosea's prophecy of punishment against the House of Jehu was a direct threat against Jeroboam and his descendants. A recurrence of Jehu's bloody actions against his own descendants likely had an illocutionary intent for Jeroboam to consider his actions in light of his grandfather's zeal for YHWH. Hosea's rhetoric had the potential to awaken Jeroboam to see that his reign was more similar to Ahab's reign than to Jehu's. As a prophet intended to call the people back to covenant faithfulness, Hosea's message carried a perlocutionary intent

---

180. Brettler discusses the importance of "strength" for a king and his ability to reign. Brettler, *God Is King*, 57–68.

181. This at the least includes the fortress in Megiddo, and if Franklin's dating of Tel Jezreel is correct, also includes the fortress there, too.

182. Brettler, *God Is King*, 55.

183. Brettler provides a summary of how taxes were exacted by the king. Brettler, *God Is King*, 119–22.

to induce Jeroboam to repent. This would certainly be in line with other prophets who are recorded to have spoken directly to kings.[184]

Lastly, Hosea's prophecies of the future eliminate a future Israelite king, questioning the legitimacy of Israel's current king. In the future, both Israel and Judah will be reunited, but not under an Israelite king. First, Hosea foretells of a time when the people of Israel and Judah will be gathered together and will appoint one new head (רֹאשׁ). This will lead to a time of flourishing as the "day of Jezreel will be great!" (Hos 2:2; Eng 1:11) Later in his message, he elaborates that this new "head" will be a new Judahite king from the Davidic line (Hos 3:5).[185] This prophetic word would likely have had a hostile rhetorical impact for the royal Israelite household. Not only is the Israelite king removed from the future reunification, but the description of the future is celebrated as great—as great as the agricultural bounty of Jezreel. In this instance, the geography of Jezreel provided a picturesque agricultural understanding of this wordplay. Its fertile soil enabled it to be the breadbasket of the north and provided an opportunity for Hosea to leave his audience with a lasting image. For some, it provided a way for Hosea to attempt to "wow" them with the potential of God's future blessings. For the royal family, however, the "wow" furthers the sting of the message that they will be excluded from this time.

Concluding Thoughts on the Rhetorical Use of Jezreel

Jezreel played a significant part in Hosea's rhetoric in his first two chapters. When these chapters are read in light of their context and with a sensitivity to the principles of critical spatial theory, a more holistic view of how Jezreel's Firstspace, Secondspace, and Thirdspace rhetorically impacts Hosea's message emerges. By using Jezreel rhetorically, Hosea effectively communicated with his society's various social groups the need to return to covenant faithfulness.

---

184. For example, Elijah's prophecy of doom against Ahab resulted in Ahab's repentance. As a result, the Lord softened the judgment (1 Kgs 21:17–29). This does not imply that a prophet's message always persuaded the king towards repentance. Micaiah later spoke directly to King Ahab, who could have responded in repentance again but chose to ignore the prophetic word and imprison him (1 Kgs 22:10–40).

185. For an explanation as to why "David their king" fits the eighth century setting of Hosea and need not be a later Judean redaction, see Goswell, "'David Their King,'" 222–25.

5

The Rhetorical Reversal of Spatial images

THE PRINCIPLES OF THE ontological spatiality of being and the social production of spatiality[1] help the interpreter consider the nature of space that is changed or even transformed. The meaning of a space is centered on experiences that occurred there. These experiences lead to its symbolic aura; yet, the meanings associated with a space can change over time. Spaces are dynamic and can be transformed. As Matthews noted, a space can be a "newly designed product with new social possibilities."[2] Given the poetic nature of the prophets, one is not surprised that Hosea could take a space that was rich in symbolic meaning and reverse its situation, or that he took another space and transformed its meaning. Hosea did this when he prophesied that the fertility of the land will be reversed, that the Israelites would return to the wilderness, and that they would return to the promised land through the Valley of Achor.

---

1. Soja's principles were discussed above in chapter 2. The ontological spatiality of being principle refers to the reality that we are all spatial as well as social and temporal beings. The social production of spatiality principle recognizes that space is socially produced and can therefore be socially changed.

2. Matthews, "Remembered Space in Biblical Narrative," 67.

Reversing the Land of Fertility

The people of Israel and Judah entered a treaty with Yahweh as their suzerain.[3] As part of their covenant, Israel was to give their sole allegiance to Yahweh (Deut 6:4–5).[4] In Deuteronomy 6:10–15, Moses reminded the Israelites that, after the Lord brought them into the land, He was to be their sole recipient of worship. In the process, Moses described their entrance into the land as being given a land that was already intact (6:10–11). The Israelites would not have to build cities. Their houses would be filled already. They would not have to dig wells or plant vineyards. This description suggests that Israel's conquest generally would not involve destruction of property and land. At the end of the conquest, Joshua reminded the people of this same point (Josh 24:13). The materials gained were a gift from Yahweh. As a response to this gift, Moses reminded them that their responsibility was to give Yahweh their complete allegiance. Deuteronomy 6:15 provided further motivation for complete allegiance. God is described as a אֵל קַנָּא. Literally, this phrase is rendered "a jealous God." In light of the covenantal context, this description should be understood within the suzerain/vassal relationship. As part of the covenant, the stipulation was given that Israel not give allegiance to any other god (Deut 4:23–24; 5:6–7). Thus, the "jealous" description of God is in response to a

---

3. Israel's treaty with Yahweh was rooted in the ancient Near Eastern culture. It took the form of a grant treaty, a suzerain-vassal treaty based upon a previous grant. The Mosaic covenant reflected the democratization of the royal land grant given to Abraham. The domestic grant with Abraham had become an international treaty with the nation of Israel, comprised of his descendants (Exod 3:6–8; 9:3–6; Lev 26:9, cf. Gen 15:5–6; Deut 4:36–38). God used these ancient Near Eastern conventions as models to establish his relationship with his people, with Abraham first, and then, through Abraham, with the nation.

4. Deuteronomy 6:4, while one of the most familiar and significant passages in all of the OT, is full of translational and interpretive challenges. This reference is following the translation as reflected in the *NJPS, NRSV,* and by Abraham Ibn Ezra. It understands the first two words to form a verbless clause that identifies who the subject is (Yahweh). In this translation, יְהוָה אֶחָד is being understood as a nominal clause that functions adverbially, modifying the first verbless clause. The second clause serves to emphasize the relationship that Yahweh has with the people, that he alone is their God. The relational nature of the translation fits the context well. Yahweh, as the suzerain of the covenant, was to be the sole recipient of the vassal's (Israel's) allegiance. The next verse (6:5) emphasizes that Israel was to be completely loyal and obedient to Yahweh. The exclusivity of Yahweh worship was emphasized in the recounting of the Decalogue (5:8–9). Furthermore, Moses reminds them that when the Lord brings them into the land, He is to be their sole recipient of worship (6:1–15).

violation of a covenantal stipulation.[5] Violations of the covenant brought about God's intentions to judge their disobedience.

The curses and the blessings mentioned in the covenant as found in Leviticus 26 and in Deuteronomy 6–7 and 28–30 provided the basis for God's responses.[6] Although the blessings and the curses were intended to motivate the vassal (Israel) to future loyalty, Israel frequently ignored them.[7] Consequently, when prophets like Hosea announced their judgment speeches to the people, they were based on a rational argument from Israel's covenantal relationship with Yahweh. These speeches had an illocutionary force that was intended to remind the audience of their covenant with Yahweh. God expected obedience, allegiance, and ethical living to characterize Israel's relationship with Him. Hosea brought a message of God's intention to deal with His disobedient vassal.

---

5. Previously, the same terminology is used in Deuteronomy 5:9. In both contexts, the response came after Yahweh intervened for Israel, the vassal. In 5:6–10, the statement is made after Yahweh's acts to deliver them from the land of Egypt are mentioned. In 6:15, the warning comes after the mention of God's gifting of the land and its property. Furthermore, in 5:6–10, the negative consequences of God's קנא (i.e., punishment) are juxtaposed to the positive aspect of God's קנא, namely, his faithful blessings to those who obey the stipulations (5:10). Interestingly, קנא is used to speak of a husband's jealousy in response to his unfaithful wife. Jealousy is not used in the modern connotation of resentment of another because of success. Rather, it is righteous anger towards a covenant violation. This is clear as his "jealousy" is not towards the idols but with his people. "Jealousy" may not be the best translation. Alternatives include "impassioned God" (*JPS*, Weinfeld); "passionate God" (*CEB*); or "fervent lover" (*WYC*). Peels, "קנא," 937–40. Peels provides a lengthy discussion on the uses of this קנא.

6. The inclusion of curses are common in ANE treaties. This covenant is most like the form of Hittite treaties. The Hittite treaty is distinct from the Assyrian treaties in that the Hittite treaties include curses and blessings. Obedience to the Assyrian treaties was motivated by fear alone. The Hittite treaties added the dimension of rewards for faithfulness to the treaty. A sample of Hittite curses and blessings can be seen in Pritchard, *Ancient Near Eastern Texts Relating to the Old Testament*, 205. The Treaty between Mursilis and Duppi-Tessub of Amurru reflects the obligatory nature of the covenant in depicting the curses and blessings (Lines 20–21). A sample of an Assyrian curse list can be found in *ANE*, 537–41. The Vassal-Treaties of Esarhaddon reflect the long list of curses with which the Assyrians often threatened their vassals (lines 414–665 depict the curses). For the forms of these treaties, see Sparks, *Ancient Texts for the Study of the Hebrew Bible*, 438–41; Kitchen, *The Bible in Its World: The Bible & Archaeology Today*, 82.

7. Sandy acknowledges the illocutionary intent of the curses: "By imagining the worst possible consequences, kings sought to strike fear in the hearts of potential violators." Sandy, *Plowshares and Pruning Hooks: Rethinking the Language of Biblical Prophecy and Apocalyptic*, 84.

The reversal of fertility in the land was a consequence for the Israelites' disobedience to the covenant. Hosea identified Israel's adulterous lovers with Baal (2:10, 15; Eng 2:8, 13). They had attributed their agricultural provisions as blessings from "other lovers" rather than seeing Yahweh as their source of life (2:7, 10; Eng. 2:5, 8). Therefore, in judgment, Yahweh would take back his agricultural favor (2:11, 14; Eng 2:9, 12). They worshiped Baal to gain life and fertility but instead received destruction and death. Such destruction pointed Israel and its leadership to the reality of the curses of the covenant. This is clearly seen in verse 10 (Eng 8).[8] Israel is accused of not acknowledging Yahweh as their provider. He was the one who provided grain (דָּגָן), new wine (תִּירוֹשׁ), and oil (יִצְהָר). These same three agricultural blessings are linked to the covenant in Deuteronomy. The Israelites are told to keep the commandments, the statutes, and the ordinances. If they did, Yahweh would keep his covenant with them.[9] He would bless them with grain (דָּגָן), new wine (תִּירוֹשׁ), and oil (יִצְהָר), all mentioned in the same order (Deut 7:11–13). Furthermore, he would send them rain that would provide for them grain (דָּגָן), new wine (תִּירוֹשׁ), and oil (יִצְהָר) (Deut 11:14). In the covenantal curses, they are warned that disobedience would result in Yahweh raising up a distant nation who would swoop down like an eagle. That nation would devour their land, not leaving them with any grain (דָּגָן), new wine (תִּירוֹשׁ), or oil (יִצְהָר) (cf. Deut 28:49–51; cf. Hos 8:1).

As discussed in this book in chapter 4, the reversal of the agricultural prosperity had a rhetorical impact on the farmers, military, elite, and the king and royal household. By recognizing the dynamic nature of the conditions of the land, specifically that its agriculture depended on Israel's obedience, Hosea was able to prosecute the people for their disobedience.

---

8. Other elements also point to the reality of covenantal curses. The phrase וְאִישׁ לֹא־יַצִּילֶנָּה מִיָּדִי ("and no one will deliver her from my hand") likely alludes to the curse in Deut 32:39, וְאֵין מִיָּדִי מַצִּיל ("and there is no one who can deliver from my hand").

9. In Deuteronomy, Moses uses the three terms מִצְוָה, and חֹק, and מִשְׁפָּט repeatedly. All three terms are derived from verbs. מִצְוָה is derived from the verb צוה (to command); חֹק is derived from חקק (to engrave); and מִשְׁפָּט from שׁפט (to judge). Throughout Deuteronomy, Moses usually uses at least two terms to refer to the Lord's commands. It appears that the terms are most likely synonymous based on usage. In each instance, when these terms are used together in this order, they follow a covenantal context (5:31; 6:1; and 7:11). As the suzerain, the Lord is giving stipulations to his people, the vassal. The terms are used in conjunction with the verbs שׁמר and עשׂה, highlighting the importance of obedience to the stipulations of the covenant. As the vassal, the people committed to keep (שׁמר) his "statutes, commandments, and stipulations" (26:17). This covenantal context is also suggested when two of the three terms are used (i.e., 4:5, 8, 14, 45; 5:1).

THE RHETORICAL REVERSAL OF SPATIAL IMAGES

As a result, he proclaimed the impending judgement of this reversal of the land's prosperity. These proclamations had an illocutionary intention to call the people back to covenantal obedience.

Hosea's eighth-century counterpart, Amos, highlighted how the change in agricultural prosperity was God's means of calling the people to repentance. In his judgment speech in chapter 4, Amos declared that the Lord sent famine (4:6), withheld rain to impact the harvest (4:7), sent drought (4:8), and destroyed their crops (4:9). These actions were intended to drive the people back to covenant loyalty. Each announcement of land reversal is followed by "yet you did not come back to me."

As in Amos's case (cf. Amos 4:12–13; 7:1–9), the lack of a repentant response would lead to the impending judgment; however, that judgment would not be final. Continuing in the metaphor of the betrayed husband, the Lord would allure his bride back into a proper relationship. The language that Hosea used of this process continues to reflect his usage of spatial references. Israel had a history, and that history led to symbolic meanings of places. Such is the case when Hosea recorded God's words that include leading Israel back into the wilderness.

Returning to the Land of Wilderness

The judgment of a reversal in the land's fertility would not be the end of the story. Like a husband who refused to give up on his adulterous wife, the text shifts to Yahweh's efforts to heal and restore his relationship with his people. He would seduce[10] Israel and lead her back into the wilderness. When considering the wilderness as a place, it is important to recognize that Hosea shared a collective memory of the wilderness with the audience.[11] As Dearman notes, "There is a metaphorical geography in this verse associated with God's appeal to Israel."[12] In this and other verses

---

10. The term "allure" is the piel participle (plus the 3fs suffix) מְפַתֶּיהָ. It is used in seductive contexts in Exodus 22:15 (22:16 Eng), Judges 14:15; 16:5, and in Hos 7:11 to describe how a dove (Israel) is easily misled (in this context by Egypt and Assyria).

11. Much of biblical scholarship recognizes that Hosea is aware of various traditions regarding the wilderness, but do not see Hosea drawing upon Deuteronomy as they see Deuteronomy as a later source. For example, Dozeman argues that Hosea lays "the foundation for [Israel's] salvation history," not relying upon on the Pentateuchal histories. In contrast, Smith makes a convincing argument for Hosea's reappropriation of Deuteronomy (see n13 below). Dozeman, "Hosea and the Wilderness Wandering Tradition," 69.

12. Dearman, *The Book of Hosea*, 121.

in the book, Hosea used the wilderness as both a negative and positive metaphor as he alludes to the experiences of Israel.[13]

Earlier in the chapter, Hosea's marriage metaphor extended to the reality behind the metaphor and contains the Lord's threat to turn the land into a wilderness (2:5; Eng 2:3). In this case, the point is that the land would become a parched land, leading to death by thirst. Garrett provides a summary of the nature of a wilderness, emphasizing that it is a place of harsh conditions that are hostile to human as well as other forms of life.[14] While not evil in and of itself, its conditions are harsh and dangerous. These conditions led the Israelites to murmur in the wilderness during their exodus from Egypt. Hence, for much of the biblical text, references to the wilderness allude back to the negative aspects of their wilderness wanderings (e.g., Num 32:13). Hosea certainly was aware of this and mentions the idolatrous incidents of Baal-Peor (Num 25:1–5) in this negative light. However, in Hosea 2:16 (Eng 2:14), the negative connotations of the wilderness wanderings are absent.

Hosea presents the wilderness as part of a recapitulation of Israel's experiences. While Israel's past experience in the wilderness signified a time when they murmured and were not in the promised land yet, it also signified the place where Israel initially gained knowledge of Yahweh. Hosea portrayed the original wilderness as the place where Israel began its relationship with Yahweh, the honeymoon stage in Hosea's marriage metaphor. It was in the wilderness that Israel entered into the covenant with Yahweh as their God. Jeremiah, perhaps influenced by Hosea's imagery in this passage, made a similar but more idealized metaphor. In recalling Israel's past, he said, "This is what the Lord says: 'I remember for your sake how devoted you were to me in the early years. I remember how you loved me like a

---

13. Cooper Smith, providing an alternative view than that of Dozeman, argues that Hosea reappropriated Deuteronomy and used "wilderness" in a similar rhetorical manner as used in parts of Deuteronomy. Smith's categorization of the five instances of מִדְבָּר in Hosea are divided into three categories: those neutral that are referring to the ecological zone; those using "wilderness" in distinctly positive tones, highlighting Yahweh's provisions, protection, and self-revelation (248); and those using "wilderness" in distinctly negative tones, highlighting Israel's rebellion (249–51). Smith, "The 'Wilderness' in Hosea and Deuteronomy," 240–60. This book's reference to "negative and positive metaphors" is broader than Smith's categories. While the reference in Hos 2:5 does not speak of Israel's rebellion and does refer to Smith's category of ecological zone, the mood of the reference is negative. As noted, it does not speak to evil or sin, but it highlights the harsh nature of that ecological zone.

14. Garrett, *Hosea, Joel*, 88–91.

new bride and followed me through the wilderness, through a land that had never been planted" (Jer 2:2 NET).¹⁵ Jeremiah's words reflect a more nostalgic view, but Hosea does not emphasize such an idealized view of Israel's response as he alluded back to this event.

In fact, Hosea recalled Israel and Yahweh's past multiple times throughout the book, displaying the Lord's goodness to Israel and the people's disobedience. In Hosea 9:10, the people began as a delight to the Lord (like an early fig on a fig tree in its first season), but then they began to engage in idolatrous worship at Baal-Peor (cf. Num 25). A second recollection recalls the earlier times when the people were in the land of Canaan (Hos 10:1, 9, 11). There, they attributed their prosperity to Baal and added fertility pillars (cf. Deut 8:8–20). Hosea's rhetoric is extreme as he states, "Israel, you have sinned since the days of Gibeah." (NET) In doing so, he highlights the extreme sin against the Levite's concubine in Gibeah (cf. Judg 19, Hos 9:9). A third recollection of the past is recorded in Hosea 11:1. When Israel was a child (their beginnings in Egypt),¹⁶ the Lord loved him.¹⁷ His goodness to the nation was exemplified by his calling them "out of Egypt." He delivered them from the oppression of the Egyptians. His love is later displayed in terms of a parent training a child and a farmer being kind to his oxen. He

---

15. This certainly does not mean that Jeremiah considered Israel as perfect in the wilderness (cf. Jer 7:25–26, when Jeremiah points out their disobedience from the day they left Egypt). However, it could be that Jeremiah suggests that Israel's wilderness times expressed a level of devotion to YHWH that was relatively greater than that of the people of Jeremiah's time. Chisholm points out that Jeremiah is exploiting the people's nostalgic perspective, who looked back to this time, even if it was relatively more intimate, with an exaggerated sense of the early times. Chisholm, *Handbook on the Prophets*, 156.

16. No specific age is provided, for the Hebrew נַעַר simply refers to a young boy. Interestingly, the same word is used of Moses when Pharaoh's daughter found him in the basket (Exod 2:6).

17. There may be more involved here than the simple metaphor of the love of a father and a son. Inherent in the notion of "love" may be the concept of election. Yahweh, as the suzerain, had chosen Israel. "Love" (אהב) is used in the context of election. In Deuteronomy 4:37, in the context of discussing the Exodus, the verb is used in parallel to "chose." The Lord "loved" their ancestors and chose their descendants. It was not due to their large numbers but was his "love" and faithfulness to his promises that caused him to choose them (Deut 7:7–8). In light of his love, they were to express covenantal faithfulness to his commandments (Deut 7:11). Amos, Hosea's eighth-century contemporary expressed this same reality. Israel was in a special, prioritized relationship with Yahweh. In Amos's words, "you only have I chosen from all the peoples of the earth" (Amos 3:2). See Andersen and Freedman, *Hosea: A New Translation with Introduction and Commentary*, 576–77; Wolff, *Hosea: A Commentary on the Book of the Prophet Hosea*, 197–98; Eidevall, *Grapes in the Desert*, 168–69.

taught them to walk (v3) and removed the "yoke from their neck" to feed them (v4). Despite the Lord's abounding graciousness to the people, the nation turned from him (v2). The more he called them, the farther they departed from him.[18] A fourth recollection specifically mentions the time in the wilderness. The Lord declared that he cared for them in the wilderness, satisfying their needs (13:5). Yet, when they became satisfied, their hearts became exalted, and they forgot the Lord (13:6).

The main point of the Lord's leading Israel back into the wilderness was not to highlight a former time of modeled obedience. It was to recall a time when they entered into their "marriage" covenant with Yahweh. Chisholm states, "The 'desert' clearly has a positive connotation, for it is the site of a renewed romance between the Lord and his wife."[19] By pulling them back into the wilderness, the Israelites are removed from the voices of their other lovers. They could only hear the Lord's voice[20] and be forced to depend on him as their ancestors were (cf. Deut 29:5). As Moon states, "The 'place' is an idealized place, not the physical location of the wilderness between Egypt and Canaan but a rhetorical 'place' where the relationship can be reborn."[21]

While the imagery is positive in nature, there is an implied judgment included. If Israel is to be led back into the wilderness, then they will no

---

18. There is also a text-critical issue in verse 2. The MT reads the 3rd person plural form of the verb ("they called"). However, the LXX reads καθὼς μετεκάλεσα, the conjunction ("just as") plus the first-person aorist form ("I called"). The Syriac supports the LXX, while the Vulgate supports the MT. Wolff is probably right when he argues for the LXX reading. Wolff, *Hosea*, 190. If the MT is original, it likely refers to "the prophets" who speak on behalf of Yahweh. Hosea closely connects the prophetic role as intricately connected to and speaking for God (cf. Hos 9:8, 12:11 [Eng 10], 12:14 [Eng 13]). Hosea's contemporary, Amos, also relates this reality (Amos 3:7; 7:14–16). Thus, in the end, very little is distinguished between the two variant readings. Yet, this is not the only textual challenge in this verse. Similarly, the second colon in the MT reads כֵּן הָלְכוּ מִפְּנֵיהֶם ("So they went from them."). In contrast, the LXX reads οὕτως ἀπῴχοντο ἐκ προσώπου μου ("so they departed from my presence"). In this case, the distinction lies in the location of the word division [i.e., Is the third-person plural pronoun (הֶם) attached to a plural masculine noun in construct (פְּנֵי)? Or does the LXX presuppose the 3rd person plural pronoun unattached as a subject to a singular noun with a 1st person pronominal suffix (פָּנַי – "from before me" or "from my face")? The LXX best captures the context, but again, if the MT is maintained, the "them" probably refers to the prophets.

19. Chisholm, *Handbook on the Prophets*, 343.

20. Perhaps there is a wordplay involved here. Yahweh would lead them back into the מִדְבָּר (wilderness) where he would וְדִבַּרְתִּי (speak) to them. There is certainly a repetition of consonants.

21. Moon, *Hosea*, 63.

longer be in the land.²² Hosea projected to a time in the future when Israel would have been judged, but Yahweh would call them back into the wilderness from a place of exile. Thus, Hosea's recapitulation includes an exodus and a new time in the wilderness. The wilderness, however, will not be the final destination. The recapitulation looks forward to the time when Israel will reenter the land. Rhetorically, Hosea used this allusion to remind his audience of Israel's past, their present reality, and their future. While in the wilderness, the Lord will restore the agricultural prosperity and return the vineyard to Israel (2:17; Eng 2:15). Israel's return into the land would come through a surprising location, the Valley of Achor.

Returning to the Promised Land

Reversal of the Valley of Achor

Israel's return to the promised land would lead them on a journey through the Valley of Achor, transforming it into a doorway of hope. This geographical reference is rhetorically significant. Prior to considering this significance, it is helpful to consider its Firstspace. This is a challenge, as scholarship disagrees on its location.

The Geography of the Valley of Achor

The biblical text appears to locate the Valley of Achor among the territory of Judah. Joshua 15:1–12 describes the borders of the tribe of Judah. The northern border of Judah begins at the mouth of the Jordan, where it flows into the Dead Sea. From there, it ascends northwest, just south of Jericho, before descending southwest, just south of Jerusalem. While detailing Judah's northern boundary, the Valley of Achor is referred to in verse seven. The specific location of the Valley of Achor is debated. The main suggestions offered for its location include the Wadi Nueima, Wadi Qilt, the Buqeia Valley, and an unknown area or wadi located in the lower end of the Jordan Valley.

---

22. Macintosh provides discussion on rabbinical comments as to whether this actually referred to Israel's removal from the land or the land being made like a wilderness as a result of the oncoming calamities. MacIntosh, *A Critical and Exegetical Commentary on Hosea*, 70–71.

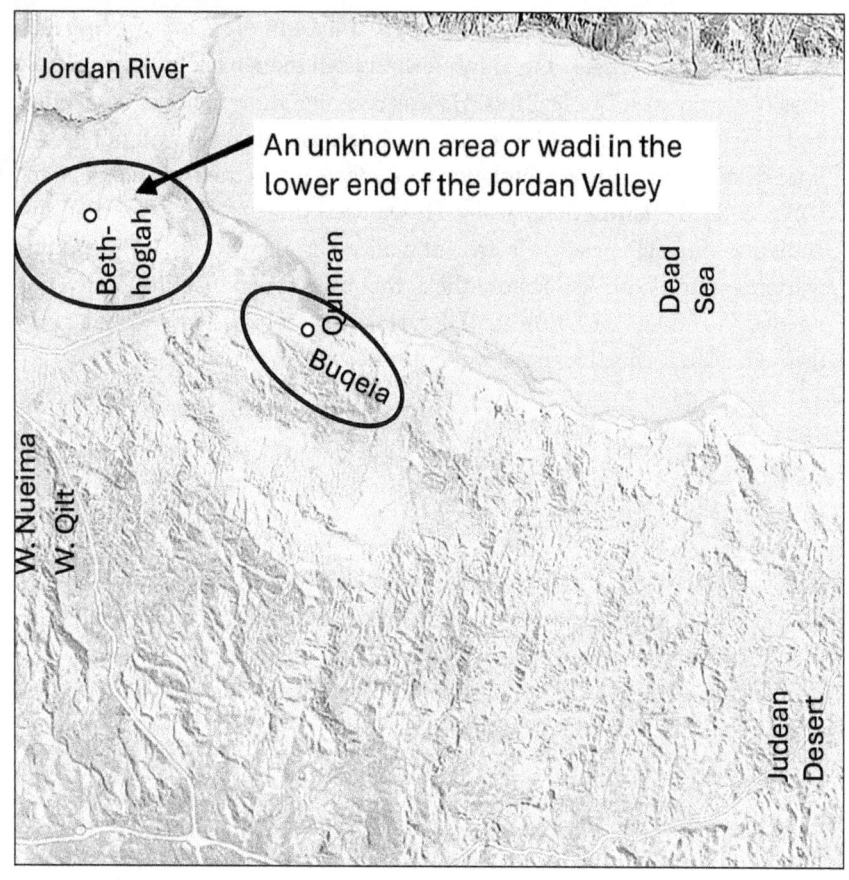

Optional Sites for the Valley of Achor.[23]

Noth proposed modern day El Buqeia as the site of the Valley of Achor.[24] El Buqeia means "little valley" and refers to a valley, about 12 miles south of Jericho (five miles long and two miles wide), which runs parallel to the Dead Sea. Noth argues that this is the only site close to Jericho

---

23. *Used by permission of* © W. Schlegel, Satellite Bible Atlas. *The map has been modified to highlight the optional sites.*

24. Noth, "Das Deutsche Evangelische Institut für Altertumswissenschaft des Heiligen Landes, Lehrkursus 1954," 42–55. Noth originally believed the site to be 'en-Nabi Musa but later changed his position to El Buqeia. Several others agree with Noth. Cross and Milik, "Explorations in the Judean Buqe'ah," 17. In this article, they identify three fortified settlements that date to Iron Age II and are proposed to be the ancient sites of Middin, Secacah, and Nibshan (Josh 15:61–62). Pressler, "Achor," 56; King, *Amos, Hosea, Micah*, 26–27; Stuart, *Hosea–Jonah*, 53.

that can accurately be called an עֵמֶק, arguing that an עֵמֶק is always "*von höheren Bergen begrenzt*" ("bordered by high mountains").[25] Cross also suggests that Hosea's reference to the Valley of Achor becoming "a doorway of hope" is a reference to an ancient route to Jerusalem.[26] Although Buqeia does fall within the territory of Judah, it has other geographical challenges. First, in the midst of laying out Judah's northern boundaries, it is difficult to conceive why the author of Joshua would include a site that is as far south as Buqeia. Having mentioned Beth Hoglah and Beth Arabah, the border would then have to dip drastically to Buqeia before it rose back up to Debir (Josh 15:6–7). Furthermore, the Valley of Achor is infamous for the stoning of Achan in Joshua 7:24–26. This event followed the Israelite retreat from Ai. It also included Achan's entire family and possessions, including his oxen, donkey, and flocks. Traveling roughly twelve miles south would be impractical and is not suggested in the text of Joshua 7.[27]

Alternatively, Wolff proposed Wadi Nueima, a valley roughly a half a mile wide and a mile long, as the site of the Valley of Achor.[28] There are several strengths to his proposal. Among the early Christian writings, Eusebius and Jerome regarded the Valley of Achor as lying north of Jericho. Eusebius writes, "It lies north of Jericho [territory], and is still so called by the inhabitants." Jerome likewise states, "It is north of Jericho, and even today it is called by that name by the inhabitants of that region. Hosea the Prophet mentions it."[29] Later, both writers locate it near Galagala/Galgal.[30]

Additionally, this valley is close to Jericho and Gilgal, allowing for a reasonable distance for the stoning of Achan, his family, and all of his possessions, including his livestock (Josh 7:24–26). It lies just in between the two ridges that ascend out of Jericho and are used for major travel: the Ephraim Route and the Zeboim Route. Hosea refers to the Valley of Achor in the context of Israel's entrance into the land (Hos 2:17; Eng. 2:15). Wadi Nueima falls along the path by which Israel entered Canaan.

25. See below for a response to this claim.

26. Cross, *Canaanite Myth and Hebrew Epic*, 109–10n57.

27. Kallai also questions Noth's interpretation of the words "And the border went up toward Debir from the Valley of Achor," suggesting that it should be understood as "And the border went up to the rear of the Valley of Achor." Noth's translation is the only means by which he is able to suggest that the northern end of the Buqeia is close enough to the border. Kallai, *Historical Geography of the Bible*, 119.

28. Wolff, *Hosea*, 42–43.

29. Eusebius, "Achor."

30. Eusebius, "Emekachor."

Lastly, this location provides a clear parallelism that completes the merism in Isaiah 65:10.[31] In this passage the Plain of Sharon, located on the western coast along the Mediterranean Sea, is placed in parallel with the Valley of Achor. If Wadi Nueima is the location, then Isaiah is emphasizing a location that is on the eastern side of the country, near the Jordan River. Thus, Isaiah employed this merism to make the point that the entire land will be available for the animals to graze in peace.

Two points have been argued against Wadi Nueima as the site of the Valley of Achor. First, it has been suggested that the Wadi Nueima does not fit the usage of the Hebrew term עֵמֶק, arguing that an עֵמֶק is always *"von höheren Bergen begrenzt"* ("bordered by high mountains").[32] However, both Wolff and Simons have shown that עֵמֶק is used for locations like Wadi Nueima, which is not surrounded by mountains. For example, Succoth is twice referred to as an עֵמֶק (Psa 60:8; 108:8).[33] A stronger challenge to Wadi Nueima is the reference to the Valley of Achor in Joshua 15:7. The author of Joshua lists the Valley of Achor as one of the sites that serve as the northern border of the territory of Judah, lying just south of the territory of Benjamin. Wadi Nueima, however, is not located within Judah's territory. It is actually in Benjamin, on the border of the territory of Ephraim. While this reality is challenging, it does not completely overturn the strengths of the position. Among the border sites mentioned in Joshua, Beth Hoglah and Beth Arabah are included (Josh 15:6), yet these two cities are listed among the cities that belonged to Benjamin (Josh 18:21–22). It is true that both of these locations are on the border between Benjamin and Judah, whereas Wadi Nueima is actually close to the border of Benjamin and Ephraim. Yet, when considering this part of the territory of Benjamin, it is evident that this section of Benjamin is extremely narrow, less than 5 kilometers wide. Wolff thus proposes that the author of Joshua mentions the Valley of Achor because it is well known, despite its location in Benjamin.[34]

---

31. Simons, *The Geographical and Topographical Texts of the Old Testament*, 271. Simons suggests that a location in this area makes a "more intelligible parallelism between the valley of Achor and the Plain of Sharon." While this may be true, one should be careful not to make too big a point of this. The other possible locations still leave the merism intelligible.

32. Noth, "Josua," 88.

33. Wolff, *Hosea*, 43; Simons, *The Geographical and Topographical Texts of the Old Testament*, 271.

34. Wolff, *Hosea*, 43.

The Wadi Qilt has also been proposed as a third option for the site of the Valley of Achor.³⁵ Jennings highlights that Joshua and the Israelites brought Achan, his family, and his possessions "up" to the Valley of Achor.³⁶ Having been encamped near Jericho at Gilgal, the climb from below sea level (Jericho is 800 feet below sea level) is quite drastic. Three main travel routes ascend out of Jericho along the ridges above the wadis: the Ephraim Route, the Zeboim Route, and the Ascent of Adummim. While Wadi Nueima falls in between the Ephraim and Zeboim routes, the Wadi Qilt runs just north of the Ascent of Adummim. Both of these valleys follow natural travel routes out of Jericho and make logical options for Achan's "last trip."

Perhaps the Wadi Qilt provides the clearest reference to the description provided in Joshua 15:5–7. The northern border of Judah is first described as coming from the northern part of the Dead Sea, where the mouth of the Jordan River enters (15:5). From there, three more locations are mentioned before it reaches the Valley of Achor: Beth Hoglah, Beth Arabah, and the Stone of Bohan, son of Reuben.³⁷ Verse seven not only mentions the Valley (עֵמֶק) of Achor, but when describing Gilgal's location, it also says that it (Gilgal) is "opposite the Ascent of Adummim south of the valley (נַחַל)." (NET) The Ascent of Adummim is described as being south of the valley. Despite the change of Hebrew terms used, the referent of נַחַל seems to be best understood as the Valley of Achor. At this point in the description, it is the only valley mentioned. עֵמֶק is frequently used in the context of specific place names.³⁸ It is feasible to suggest that the author freely used the Hebrew נַחַל when not specifically using the term "Achor." A similar occurrence is in 1 Samuel 17. When giving the proper name of the Valley of Elah, the author used עֵמֶק (1 Sam 17:2, 19). However, when speaking of the same valley more generically, he used גַיְא instead of עֵמֶק (1 Sam 17:3, 52).³⁹

---

35. Jennings, "Achor, Valley of," 5–6; Schlegel, *Satellite Bible Atlas: Historical Geography of the Bible*, map 3-5.

36. Joshua 7:24 uses the *hiphil* of עָלָה ("to lead up").

37. While the Stone of Bohan has yet to be located, Aharoni places Beth Hoglah as Deir Hajlah and Beth Arabah as Ain Gharabeh. Aharoni, *The Land of the Bible: A Historical Geography*, 255.

38. For example, within Joshua, it is used to speak of the Valley of Aijalon (10:12), the Valley of Rephaim (15:8; 18:16), the Valley of Jezreel (17:16), and the Valley of Jiphthah El (19:27).

39. It should be noted that the usage of גיא in 17:52 is possibly a corrupt reading. This possibility does not, however, impact the clear interchange of terms in 17:2 and 17:3.

Furthermore, the Wadi Qilt actually lies right on the border between Judah and Benjamin. While it does not fit the description given by Eusebius, lying south of Jericho, it does fit the biblical descriptions well. It, too, fits the merism with the Plain of Sharon employed by Isaiah (65:10). It also is located directly in the area of Israel's entrance into Canaan, thus fitting Hosea's recounting of the Israelite invasions (2:17; Eng 2:15).

Given the lack of unity regarding the specific location of the Valley of Achor, a few scholars have opted to maintain a broad indication of its location. Simons identifies it as "a place in the Jordan Valley, close to and within easy reach of already conquered Jericho."[40] MacIntosh states, "It is likely that Hosea refers here quite generally to the lower end of the Jordan Valley."[41] Likewise, Kallai writes, "the Valley of Achor, too, denotes a specific part of the Arabah, perhaps one of the wadis that go into it, from which the border ascends to Debir."[42] Those who take such a position all suggest that it must be within the vicinity of Jericho. Such a stance keeps the options open, even allowing for the Wadi Qilt. While it is rather difficult to argue against such an open-ended conclusion, it does appear that this site was quite prominent and should be well known. The Valley of Achor helped determine the northern boundaries of Judah and was used as an eastern parallel to the western Plain of Sharon. While one cannot be absolutely certain as to its specific location, given the biblical and geographical data, the Wadi Qilt appears to be the best option for its location.

The Valley of Achor in the Book of Hosea

Hosea mentioned the Valley of Achor in the context of a prophetic speech regarding the mercy of God and the restoration of his people (Hos 2:17). Due to the unfaithfulness of the people, the Lord would bring about drastic discipline (2:4–15; 2:2–13 Eng.). However, using romantic language, the Lord declared his intentions to woo Israel back into a relationship with him while they were in exile (2:16, Eng. 2:14). The agriculture, whose

---

40. Simons, *The Geographical and Topographical Texts of the Old Testament*, 271. He rejects Wolff's proposal of Wadi Nueima but does not address the possibility of Wadi Qilt.

41. MacIntosh, *A Critical and Exegetical Commentary on Hosea*, 74.

42. MacIntosh suggests that Kallai proposes Nebi Musa. However, after rejecting Buqeia, he simply states that Nebi Musa (referring to Noth's early position) should be taken into account among other possibilities. He does not argue for Nebi Musa as the location. Kallai, *Historical Geography of the Bible*, 120.

destruction was previously threatened (2:11, 14, Eng. 2:9, 12), would now be restored (2:17, Eng. 2:15). At this point, Hosea stated that the Lord would "turn the Valley of Achor into a door of hope."

Hosea's reference to the Valley of Achor is rhetorically significant.[43] Geographically, the allusion serves to refer to the Israelites' first entrance into the land.[44] After leaving the wilderness, they entered the land from the Plains of Moab. Their first victory at Jericho was tainted by the disobedience of one man, Achan. As a result of his disobedience, thirty-six Israelites lost their lives in the next battle, the Battle of Ai. Consequently, Achan, his family, and all of his possessions were taken to the Valley of Achor and stoned. The verb עָכַר means "to bring disaster or trouble." Thus, the valley highlighted the trouble that came upon Israel as a result of Achan's sin. It was the people's first recorded sin and God's first recorded judgment in the land. This valley will be transformed in the day when Israel repossesses the land.[45] Rather than being a hindrance to the possession of the land, it will later become a "door of hope." Hosea portrays a future time when Israel would reenter the land the same way it had the first time.[46]

Sweeney offers an interesting proposal regarding the rhetorical purpose of this passage. He suggests that the reference to the Valley of Achor goes beyond the historical allusion. By juxtaposing the Valley of Achor with a "door of hope," he submits that Hosea intended to use geographical features to teach Israel that their future hope is in Jerusalem. While he holds to El Buqeia as the site, his proposal is not limited to this location.

---

43. The Valley of Achor is also rhetorically significant in Isaiah 65:10 and the Copper Scroll (3Q15). In Isaiah 65:10, Isaiah, another eighth-century prophet, prophesied that the Valley of Achor would be transformed into a place where cattle rest. For Isaiah, the valley of trouble would become a valley of rest. The place that was barren would now become a place where cattle could graze (implied in the context of rest). The Copper Scroll contains a listing of geographical locations with treasures. The first line starts with "In the Valley of Achor under" and continues with directions and locations with treasures. Fidler sees an internal inclusion in the Copper Scroll, with the bookends of the Valley of Achor and Mount Gerizim. Rhetorically, it begins with a place of cursing (Josh 7) and ends with a place of blessing (Josh 8:33). Fidler, "Inclusio and Symbolic Geography in the Copper Scroll," 214–23.

44. Later in the verse, Hosea even mentions "as in the day when she came up from the land of Egypt."

45. Kelle understands the Valley of Achor reference to be a bridal gift that Yahweh gives to Israel at the initiation of a new marriage. Kelle, *Hosea 2*, 272.

46. Building on a new marriage metaphor, Andersen and Freedman suggest that the "door of hope" may be a promise of fruitfulness in the new marriage. Andersen and Freedman, *Hosea*, 276.

The south end of El Buqeia is bound by the Wadi Kidron, which eventually leads to the Kidron Valley and Jerusalem.[47] Perhaps this point would be stronger if one holds to the Wadi Qilt as the location of the Valley of Achor. As previously mentioned, the Wadi Qilt lies just north of the Ascent of Adummim, the major route taken from Jericho to Jerusalem. Such a theory certainly depends upon anti-Assyrian alliance themes in Hosea and a Judean setting for at least parts of the book. While intriguing, the immediate context of chapter 2 lacks any significant allusion to a pro-Jerusalem theme. The key emphasis is rather on the reversal of circumstances in the restoration, even including the infamous Valley of Achor.

Due to the content of Hosea's message—namely judgment and condemnation of royalty, cultic leaders, and the general public—he faced ridicule and rejection (cf. 9:7). The creation of his arguments required significant imagination and boldness.[48] While this is often seen in his judgment speeches, in this passage, it is reflected in a message of restoration and hope. Hosea's style reflects creativity and mastery.[49] The allusion to Achan's disobedience brought them back to one of the earliest signs of disobedience in the history of their nation. From a perlocutionary perspective, the mention of it should have conjured thoughts of the serious consequences of sin.[50] Furthermore, having remembered such an event, the audience should now be left in awe of God and the potential for a future restoration. This restoration would even include taking the worst of the nation's past and transforming it into future hope.

Renewed Fertility of the Land

The reversal of judgment to restoration continues throughout the rest of chapter 2. While the land of fertility was reversed due to covenant unfaithfulness (see above), that judgment could be undone. As discussed in chapter

---

47. Sweeney, *The Twelve Prophets*, 34–35.

48. In classical rhetoric, the term *inventio* entails the discovery of arguments that the speaker must create in an effort to persuade an audience.

49. In classical rhetoric, the speaker's persuasive power relied on his style (*elocutio*). Style was viewed as a vital element and not simply the "sprinkles on the icing." *Elocutio* included clarity and mastery of language. The use of a multitude of figures of speech became the rhetorical tools of the orator and writer, figures such as metaphors, irony, synecdoche, and allusion.

50. In speech act theory, the term "perlocution" is used to express the desired effect the speech is intended to have upon the audience.

THE RHETORICAL REVERSAL OF SPATIAL IMAGES

4 of this book, the judgment was marked by the Lord's removal of grain (דָּגָן), new wine (תִּירוֹשׁ), and oil (2:11) (יִצְהָר; Eng. 2:9). The restoration would be marked by a reversal in agricultural prosperity (2:24; Eng. 22).[51] Using the imagery of the complete agricultural cycle, Yahweh spoke to the skies, which provided the rain to the earth. The earth responded by providing vegetation in the form of grain (דָּגָן), new wine (תִּירוֹשׁ), and oil (יִצְהָר) (cf. Deut 7:11–13; 11:14). The cycle culminated with the agriculture's response to Jezreel. With the use of phonetic wordplay (see chapter 4), Hosea used "Jezreel" as another name for Israel. Thus, the agriculture responded to Israel, the people, completing the cycle (Yahweh-skies-ground-agriculture-people). The imagery is rhetorically powerful and worth considering for the different social groups within Hosea's implied audience.

For the farming community of ancient Israel, the message is positive of a future time when their threshing floors would be filled with grain and their wine and oil presses would be full, reflecting the extremes of God's blessings. For the professional military community, the bureaucratic elite, and the royal household, the message is stinging, as they will not be a part of the future blessings. The military will be broken. The royal household in Israel will come to an end, and the elite will no longer be in service to the king of Israel.

This aspect of Hosea's message is also similar to Amos's message. While Amos referred to agricultural loss as a result of judgment, he also foretold of a time when that loss would be undone. The future restoration of the Davidic dynasty would be characterized by military success (conquering Edom) and agricultural abundance. This bounty is described hyperbolically. It will be a time when the harvesting calendar will overlap as the reapers would still be in the process of gathering the harvest when the plowman were ready to start preparing the land to sow. The harvest will be so large that wine from the grapes will flow down the hills (Amos 9:13).

---

51. Bergant sees this as "an oracle of salvation which employs but reverses the meaning of some of the prominent imagery from the Exodus tradition: the wilderness; the valley of Achor, through which people entered Canaan; and the response of each of the covenant partners." Bergant, "Restoration as Re-Creation in Hosea 2," 10. In the reversal, Bergant sees more than a restoration; it is a new creation, recalling allusions to the primordial covenant with all of creation. Bergant, "Restoration as Re-Creation in Hosea 2," 10–12.

6

Conclusion

Accomplishing the Objectives

As explained in the introduction, space and geography have often been ignored amidst the rise of social and historical studies. A balanced approach must look at history, sociality, and spatiality together as a trialectic methodology. This volume set out to accomplish four objectives:

1. To consider how modern critical spatial theories provide the reader with further instruments to comprehend the shared cognitive and cultural environment of Hosea and his original implied audience;
2. To demonstrate the multidimensional aspects of Hosea's geographic and spatial references given the shared cultural context;
3. To consider how these references contribute to the overall rhetoric of Hosea's message, enabling him to effectively persuade his audience; and
4. To provide a methodology for utilizing critical spatial theory as a hermeneutical tool.

To accomplish these objectives, chapter 1 provided the rationale for why the study is needed. It also provided the thesis. Hosea 1–3 reflects the rhetorical usage of space and geography to effectively communicate with the eighth-century, original implied audience, that they must return to covenantal faithfulness to experience the blessings of God, or else they

CONCLUSION

would experience His wrath. In light of this, the modern interpreter's hermeneutic will be enhanced by applying a methodology that engages the principles of critical spatial theory. Chapter 1 included this methodology and a list of questions an interpreter should ask when approaching a prophetic passage that has spatial references.

Chapter 2 then provided an overview of three key disciplines that, when integrated, enable an interpreter to meet the objectives. Overviews of prophetic hermeneutics, rhetorical criticism, and critical spatial theory were all provided. The next chapter (chapter 3) placed Hosea 1–3 within its rhetorical situation. To do this, it considered the general historical setting of eighth-century Israel, the religious setting of that time, the rhetorical situation of the book of Hosea as a whole, and the rhetorical situation of Hosea 1–3 in particular.

Chapters 4 and 5 then focused specifically on spatial references in Hosea 1–3. Chapter 4 considered the rhetorical use of Jezreel throughout the first chapters of Hosea. It considered Jezreel's etymology as well as its Firstspace, Secondspace, and Thirdspace. It then considered the rhetorical use of Jezreel as it arose in the first two chapters. Chapter 5 continued looking at spatial references, specifically when spaces are reversed or transformed. It looked at the broad spatial reference to the land of fertility and the wilderness. The chapter ended with considering Hosea's promising future predictions of the transformation of the Valley of Achor and the renewed fertility of the land.

As this book just considered Hosea 1–3, it is helpful to consider recommendations for studying further spatial references in the book.

Approaching New Spaces in Hosea

As mentioned in chapter 3, identifying the historical and rhetorical situation of units within Hosea is a complex task. Since scholarship shows little unity and is divided on several major textual issues, and the speeches in Hosea contain few significant specific references to the times, places, people, and events, it is difficult to be certain as to the specific setting of each rhetorical unit. One must proceed with humility and openness when placing a specific unit within a specific rhetorical setting. With many units, it may be impossible to be certain that one situation is definitely the historical setting.

With that said, approaching the rest of Hosea with this methodology will provide fruit for the interpreter. It is well known that Hosea 1–3 is more tightly connected than the rest of the book, providing the story of Hosea and Gomer as the metaphor for Yahweh's relationship with Israel. The rest of the book contains individual judgment speeches. Given the long span of Hosea's prophetic ministry (1:1), it is most probable that these speeches came at different times throughout that ministry. So, on one level, one can approach each speech individually. Of course, it will be helpful to consider how the speech contributes to the rest of the book and to consider intertextual insights. This accounts for Hosea's individual rhetorical purposes and any literary and rhetorical intentions from the editor(s) who completed the book's final compilation.

When proceeding into each speech in Hosea 4–14, further historical setting should be laid. While the broad historical setting and the religious setting has already been set, this book read Hosea 1–3 in the context of Jeroboam II's reign. It would therefore be helpful to lay out further historical details regarding the constant shifting of political power in Israel. Geographic and spatial references are common throughout the book. The references in Hosea 4 will be briefly discussed as a sample of approaching a judgment speech with this methodology.

Cultic Sites, Gilgal, and Bethel in Hosea 4

Hosea provides a generic spatial reference to the pagan cultic sites in this chapter. Having already brought accusations and announcements of judgement against the religious leadership (4:4–10), he then brings an accusation against the people for engaging in pagan practices (4:11–14). Included in these accusations is a reference to the mountaintops and hills where they offered sacrifices (4:13). Hosea specifically mentions three types of trees and the shade they provide. Is this detail rhetorically significant? This reference also included mentions of cultic prostitutes as "daughters." Implied in this reference is the participation of the men, presumably fathers. Thus, when approaching this passage with the proposed methodology, the interpreter should elaborate on the pagan fertility rites.[1] When considering the intended rhetorical impact on various so-

---

1. Perhaps one could also consider this in light of the reference to Jehu in chapter 1. Jehu is said to have eradicated Baalism from Israel (2 Kgs 10:28). Is Hosea drawing on this shared cognition with parts of his audience? Similar to the irony of the judgment in

cial groups, consider the religious leadership as well. The prior judgment speech indicts them for leading the people astray. Furthermore, the fact that the prostitutes are referred to as daughters suggests that one should also consider this from the shared cultural environment of the house of the father, specifically the expectations for the father and the cultural norms of "proper places" for the safety of women/daughters.[2]

Hosea mentioned two specific locations that were rich in symbolic meaning and shared memories for the audience. In Hosea 4:15, he made the commands, "Do not come to Gilgal! Do not go up to Beth-Aven!" Gilgal was prominent in Israel's history when they renewed the covenant after they entered the promised land (cf. Josh 5:1–9). Beth-Aven was an insulting way to refer to Beth-El. The House of God had become the House of Wickedness. For each location, the interpreter should consider the Firstspace, Secondspace, and Thirdspace, taking into account the contested nature of the sites and the intended rhetorical impact for various social groups.[3] Certainly, these negative commands carry polemical value. By looking at the sites holistically, the interpreter can unpack this value.

Concluding Thought

Places are multivalent in character. Places and spaces are not simply physical or topographical locations; they encompass cognitive associations that include historical events and sociality. The modern interpreter's hermeneutic will be enhanced by applying a methodology that engages the principles of critical spatial theory.

Hos 1:4–5, the irony here is that Jehu's descendants allowed the practice to return to the land, and the people were grossly engaged in what Jehu eradicated.

2. Krispenz points out that the reference to daughters could also include a threat to military threat and destruction. Krispenz, "Idolatry, Apostasy, Prostitution: Hosea's Struggle Against the Cult," 21.

3. Matthews provides a detailed consideration of Bethel and how it went through a process of what he calls "geographic reiteration." He shows how Bethel was used and reused throughout Israel's history, including memories of high times and low times. Specifically in Hosea, Matthews argues that Hosea (and Amos) sought to "desacralize Bethel and to invalidate it as a place where Yahweh dwells or speaks." He notes, "Hosea draws this theme full circle in his prophetic indictment of Israel. He notes how God had chosen to appear to Jacob at Bethel and had offered him and his descendants the covenant. However, just as Jacob had been a contentious member of his family and a man willing to wrestle with God, the people of Israel have striven against God as well . . . 'the House of God' has been transformed by the people's unfaithfulness in Beth-aven, 'the House of Wickedness' (Hos 4:15; 5:8; 10:5, 8)." Matthews, "Back to Bethel," 163–65.

APPENDIX

Structure of Hosea 1:2–9

THIS SECTION OF HOSEA is written in narrative form. The following analyzes the narrative framework using Chisholm's model found in *From Exegesis to Exposition: A Practical Guide to Using Biblical Hebrew*.[1] It focuses on the main elements of a narrative: mainline (*wayyiqtol*) clauses and offline clauses (*waw* + nonverb, *weqatal* clauses, negated perfects, and asyndetic perfects). Both mainline and offline clauses will be classified using Chisholm's categories. Offline clauses will also be highlighted in bold. Quotations will not be classified but will be italicized.

Translation and narrative structure:[2]

2a When the LORD first spoke through Hosea (introductory)

2b The LORD said to Hosea (initiatory)

2c *"Go, marry a wife of harlotry, and have children of harlotry, because the land has certainly committed harlotry away from the LORD."*

3a So Hosea went (*consequential*)

3b and married Gomer, daughter of Diblaim (*sequential*)

3c Then she conceived (*sequential*)

3d and bore him a son (*sequential*)

4a Then the LORD said to him (*sequential*)

---

1. Chisholm, *From Exegesis to Exposition*.
2. The translation is the author's own translation.

APPENDIX: STRUCTURE OF HOSEA 1:2–9

4b "Name him Jezreel, because soon, I will punish the House of Jehu for the bloodshed in Jezreel, and I will put an end to the kingdom of the House of Israel.

5 At that time, I will break Israel's bow in the Valley of Jezreel."

6a She conceived again (*sequential*)

6b and bore a daughter (*sequential*)

6c Then He said to him (*sequential*)[3]

6d "Name her Lo-ruhamah, because I will no longer have compassion on the House of Israel for I have completely deceived them.[4]

7a But I will have compassion on the House of Judah. I will deliver them by the LORD their God; I will not deliver them by bow, by sword, by battle, by horses, or by horsemen."

8a When she had weaned Lo-ruhamah (*sequential*)[5]

---

3. If translating for a broader audience, translating these clauses in a clearer manner would be helpful (e.g., "Gomer conceived again and bore a daughter. Then the LORD said to Hosea...").

4. Most translations emend the text to reflect YHWH's unwillingness to pardon or forgive the Israelites. This translation is based on Kuhnigk's work on this passage. He notes that Dahood proposes that the MT's כִּי־נָשֹׂא אֶשָּׂא should read כִּי־נָשֹׁא אֶשָּׁא. In so doing, the proposal suggests that the Masoretic scribes mispointed the verb and that the root is actually נשׁא II ("to beguile or deceive"). Kuhnigk does suggest that the form could be a Qal passive instead. Stuart also follows Kuhnigk but translates the clause differently than above ("since I have been utterly betrayed by them"). The current translation takes into account the use of the same root (in its hiphil form, also with an infinitive absolute) in Jer 4:10. There, Yahweh is the subject, deceiving the people in judgment. The prophet cries out, "Surely you have utterly deceived this people and Jerusalem." Such a translation requires a repointing of the text while limiting the need to emend the text. It also aligns with the context. Yahweh will no longer have pity on them but will deceive them in judgment. As in Jeremiah, this is likely a reference to priests and prophets who promised prosperity and success (cf. Hos 4:5; 9:7). Hosea's contemporary, Amos, specifically notes Amaziah, the priest at Bethel, who sent lying words to Jeroboam II (Amos 7). Stuart, *Hosea–Jonah*, 23; Kuhnigk, *Northwestsemitische Studien zum Hoseabuch*, 4.

5. Chisholm's sequential designation describes events that occur in temporal order. This clause differentiates from the previous birth statement by highlighting that the third conception occurred after the weaning process.

Bibliography

"Churchill and the Commons Chamber." Accessed March 29, 2016. http://www.parliament.uk/about/living-heritage/building/palace/architecture/palacestructure/churchill/.

Extracts from the Book of Jasher: Mentioned in Joshua 10:13 and 2 Samuel 1:18. Los Angeles: Danhoff, 1916.

Aaron, David H. "Reflections on a Cognitive Theory of Culture and a Theory of Formalized Language for Late Biblical Studies." In *Remembering Biblical Figures in the Late Persian and Early Hellenistic Periods: Social Memory and Imagination*, edited by Diana V. Edelman and Ehud Ben Zvi, 451–73. Oxford: Oxford University Press, 2013.

Aharoni, Yohanan. *The Land of the Bible: A Historical Geography*. Translated by Anson F. Rainey. 2nd ed. Philadelphia: Westminster, 1980.

Aharoni, Yohanan, and Michael Avi-Yonah. *The Macmillan Bible Atlas*. Rev. ed. New York: Macmillan, 1977.

Aharoni, Yohanan, Michael Avi-Yonah, R. Steven Notley, Anson F. Rainey, and Ze'ev Safrai. *The Carta Bible Atlas*. 5th ed. Jerusalem: Carta, 2011.

Aḥituv, Shmuel. *Echoes from the Past: Hebrew and Cognate Inscriptions from the Biblical Period*. Translated and edited by Anson F. Rainey. Jerusalem: Carta, 2008.

Allen, Leslie C. *The Books of Joel, Obadiah, Jonah, and Micah*. New International Commentary on the Old Testament. Grand Rapids: Eerdmans, 1976.

Allen, Ricky Lee. "The Socio-Spatial Making and Marking of 'Us': Toward a Critical Postmodern Spatial Theory of Difference and Community." *Social Identities* 5 (1999) 249–77.

Alonso, Ana Maria. "The Politics of Space, Time and Substance: State Formation, Nationalism, and Ethnicity." *Annual Review of Anthropology* 23 (1994) 379–405.

Alt, Albrecht. "Der Stadtstaat Samaria." In *Kleine Schriften zur Geschichte des Volkes Israel*, vol. III, 258–302. Munich: Akademie Verlag, 1959.

———. *Essays on Old Testament History and Religion*. Translated by R. A. Wilson. Oxford: Basil Blackwell, 1966.

Alter, Robert. *The Art of Biblical Narrative*. New York: Basic, 1981.

———. *The Art of Biblical Poetry*. New York: Basic, 1981.

BIBLIOGRAPHY

Andersen, Francis I., and David Noel Freedman. *Hosea: A New Translation with Introduction and Commentary*. Anchor Bible 24. Garden City, NY: Doubleday, 1980.

Aristotle. *The "Art" of Rhetoric*. Translated by John Henry Freese. Loeb Classical Library 193. Cambridge: Harvard University Press, 2006.

Arnold, Patrick M. *Gibeah: The Search for a Biblical City*. Journal for the Study of the Old Testament Supplements 79. Sheffield: Sheffield Academic, 1990.

Assmann, Aleida. *Erinnerungsräume: Formen und Wandlungen des Kulturellen Gedächtnisses*. Munich: Beck, 1999.

———. "Transformations between History and Memory." *Social Research* 75 (2008) 49–72.

Assmann, Jan. *Religion and Cultural Memory*. Translated by Rodney Livingston. Stanford: Stanford University Press, 2006.

———. *Religion Und Kulturelles Gedächtnis*. 3rd ed. Munich: Beck, 2000.

Aster, Shawn Zelig. "The Function of the City of Jezreel and the Symbolism of Jezreel in Hosea 1–2." *Journal of Near Eastern Studies* 71 (2012) 31–46.

Austin, John L. *How to Do Things with Words*. Edited by J. O. Urmson and Marina Sbisa. Oxford: Oxford University Press, 1975.

Baly, Denis. *The Geography of the Bible: A Study in Historical Geography*. Rev. ed. New York: Harper & Row, 1974.

———. *The International Standard Bible Encyclopedia*. Grand Rapids: Eerdmans, 1982.

Barker, Joel. *Joel: Despair and Deliverance in the Day of the Lord*. Exegetical Commentary on the Old Testament: A Discourse Analysis of the Hebrew Bible 25. Grand Rapids: Zondervan, 2020.

Barnett, Richard D. *Ancient Ivories in the Middle East*. Qedem 14. Jerusalem: Hebrew University of Jerusalem, 1982.

Barstad, Hans M. "Hosea and the Assyrians." In *"Thus Speaks Ishtar of Arbela": Prophecy in Israel, Assyria, and Egypt in the Neo-Assyrian Period*, edited by Robert P. Gordon and Hans M. Barstad, 91–110. Winona Lake, IN: Eisenbrauns, 2013.

Barton, John. "History and Rhetoric in the Prophets." In *The Bible as Rhetoric: Studies in Biblical Persuasion and Credibility*, edited by Martin Warner, 51–64. Warwick Studies in Philosophy and Literature. London: Routledge, 1990.

———. *Reading the Old Testament: Method in Biblical Study*. 2nd ed. Louisville: Westminster John Knox, 1996.

Beck, John. "Geography as Irony: The Narrative-Geological Shaping of Elijah's Duel with the Prophets of Baal (1 Kings 18)." *Scandinavian Journal of the Old Testament* 17 (2003) 291–301.

Ben Zvi, Ehud. *Hosea*. Forms of Old Testament Literature 21A/1. Grand Rapids: Eerdmans, 2010.

———. "Observations on the Marital Metaphor of YHWH and Israel in Its Ancient Israelite Context: General Considerations and Particular Images in Hosea 1.2." *Journal for the Study of the Old Testament* 28 (2004) 363–84.

Ben-Tor, Amnon. "Hazor and the Chronology of Northern Israel: A Reply to Israel Finkelstein." *Bulletin of the American Schools of Oriental Research* 317 (2000) 9–15.

Ben-Tor, Amnon, and Y. Portugali. *Tell Qiri a Village in the Jezreel Valley: Report of the Archaeological Excavations 1975–1977*. Qedem 24. Jerusalem: Hebrew University of Jerusalem, 1987.

BIBLIOGRAPHY

Bendor, S. *The Social Structure of Ancient Israel: The Institution of the Family (Beit 'Ab) from the Settlement to the End of the Monarchy*. Jerusalem Biblical Studies 7. Jerusalem: Simor, 1996.

Bergant, Diane. "Restoration as Re-Creation in Hosea 2." In *The Ecological Challenge: Ethical, Liturgical, and Spiritual Responses*, edited by Richard N. Fragomeni and John T. Pawlikoski, 3–15. Collegville, MN: Liturgical, 1994.

Berlin, Adele. *Poetics and Interpretation of Biblical Narrative*. Bible and Literature Series 9. Sheffield: Almond, 1983.

Berquist, Jon L. "Critical Spatiality and the Construction of the Ancient World." In *'Imagining' Biblical Worlds: Studies in Spatial, Social and Historical Constructs in Honor of James W. Flanagan*, edited by David M. Gunn and Paula M. McNutt, 14–29. Journal for the Studies of the Old Testament Supplement Series 359. New York: Sheffield Academic, 2002.

Berquist, Jon L., and Claudia V. Camp, eds. *Constructions of Space I: Theory, Geography, and Narrative*. Library of Hebrew Bible/Old Testament Studies 481. New York: T. & T. Clark, 2007.

———. *Constructions of Space II: The Biblical City and Other Imagined Spaces*. Library of Hebrew Bible/Old Testament Studies 490. New York: T. & T. Clark, 2008.

Biesecker, Barbara A. "Rethinking the Rhetorical Situation from within the Thematic of 'Différance.'" *Philosophy and Rhetoric* 22 (1989) 110–30.

Birch, Bruce C. *Hosea, Joel, and Amos*. Westminster Bible Companion. Louisville: Westminster John Knox, 1997.

Bitzer, Lloyd. "The Rhetorical Situation." *Philosophy and Rhetoric* 1 (1968) 1–14.

Blake, Emma. "Spatiality Past and Present: An Interview with Edward Soja, Los Angeles, 12 April 2001." *Journal of Social Archaeology* 2 (2002) 139–58.

Blenkinsopp, Joseph. "The Family in First Temple Israel." In *Families in Ancient Israel*, 48–103. The Family, Religion, and Culture. Louisville: Westminster John Knox, 1997.

———. "Remembering Josiah." In *Remembering Biblical Figures in the Late Persian and Early Hellenistic Periods: Social Memory and Imagination*, edited by Diana V. Edelman and Ehud Ben Zvi, 236–56. Oxford: Oxford University Press, 2013.

Block, Daniel I. "'Israel'—'Sons of Israel': Hebrew Eponymic Usage." *Studies in Religion* 13.3 (1984) 301–26.

———. "Marriage and Family in Ancient Israel." In *Marriage and Family in the Biblical World*, edited by Ken M. Campbell, 33–101. Downers Grove, IL: InterVarsity, 2003.

Bolen, Todd. "The Aramean Oppression of Israel in the Reign of Jehu." PhD diss., Dallas Theological Seminary, 2013.

Bommas, Martin, ed. *Cultural Memory and Identity in Ancient Societies*. Cultural Memory and History in Antiquity. New York: Bloomsbury Academic, 2011.

Booth, Wayne C. "Metaphor as Rhetoric: The Problem of Evaluation." *Critical Inquiry* 5 (1978) 49–72.

Borowski, Oded. *Daily Life in Biblical Times*. Society of Biblical Literature Archaeology and Biblical Studies 5. Atlanta: Society of Biblical Literature, 2003.

Bos, James M. "Reconsidering the Date and Provenance of the Book of Hosea: The Case for Persian-Period Yehud." PhD diss., University of Michigan, 2011.

Botha, Eugene. "Speech Act Theory and Biblical Interpretation." *Neotestamentica* 41 (2007) 274–94.

Bourdieu, Pierre. "Social Space and Symbolic Power." *Sociological Theory* 7 (1989) 14–25.

Brayford, Susan A. "To Shame or Not to Shame: Sexuality in the Mediterranean Diaspora." *Semeia* 87 (1999) 163–76.
Brenner-Idan, Athalya. *The Israelite Woman: Social Role and Literary Type in Biblical Narrative.* 2nd ed. Cornerstone Series. New York: Bloomsbury, 2015.
Brettler, Marc Zvi. "Memory in Ancient Israel." In *Memory and History in Christianity and Judaism*, edited by Michael Singer, 1–17. Notre Dame, IN: University of Notre Dame Press, 2001.
———. *God Is King: Understanding an Israelite Metaphor.* Journal for the Study of the Old Testament Supplement Series 76. Sheffield: Sheffield Academic, 1989.
Brody, Aaron J. "The Archaeology of the Extended Family: A Household Compound from Iron Ii Tell En-Naṣbeh." In *Hosehold Archaeolgy in Ancient Isreal and Beyond*, edited by Assaf Yasur-Landau, Jennie R. Ebeling, and Laura B. Mazow, 237–54. Culture and History of the Ancient Near East 50. Leiden: Brill, 2011.
Broshi, Magen. "The Expansion of Jerusalem in the Reigns of Hezekiah and Manasseh." *Israel Exploration Journal* 24 (1974) 21–26.
———. "La Population De L'ancienne Jerusalem." *Revue biblique* 82 (1975) 5–14.
Broshi, Magen and Israel Finkelstein. "The Population of Palestine in the Iron Age II." *Bulletin of American Schools of Oriental Research* 287 (1992) 47–60.
Brown, Jeannine K. *Scripture as Communication: Introducing Biblical Hermeneutics.* Grand Rapids: Baker, 2007.
Brueggemann, Walter *The Land: Place as Gift, Promise, and Challenge in Biblical Faith.* 2nd ed. Overtures to Biblical Theology. Minneapolis: Fortress, 2002.
Bullinger, E. W. *Figures of Speech Used in the Bible: Explained and Illustrated.* London: Eyre and Spottiswoode, 1898. Reprint, Grand Rapids: Baker, 1968.
Buss, Martin J. *The Prophetic Word of Hosea: A Morphological Study.* Beihefte zur Zeitschrift für die alttestamentliche Wissenschaft 111. Berlin: Töpelmann, 1969.
Caird, G. B. *The Language and Imagery of the Bible.* Duckworth: London, 1980. Reprint, Grand Rapids: Eerdmans, 1997.
Campbell, Edward F., Jr. "A Land Divided: Judah and Israel from the Death of Solomon to the Fall of Samaria." In *The Oxford History of the Biblical World*, edited by Michael D. Coogan, 273–319. New York: Oxford University Press, 1998.
Cantrell, Deborah O'Daniel. *The Horsemen of Israel: Horses and Chariotry in Monarchic Israel (Ninth—Eighth Centuries B.C.E.).* History, Archaeology, and Culture of the Levant 1. Winona Lake, IN: Eisenbrauns, 2011.
———. "'Some Trust in Horses': Horses as Symbols of Power in Rhetoric and Reality." In *Warfare, Ritual, and Symbol in Biblical and Modern Contexts*, edited by Brad E. Kelle, Frank Ritchel Ames, and Jacob L. Wright, 131–48. Ancient Israel and Its Literature 18. Atlanta: Society of Biblical Literature, 2014.
Cathcart, Kevin J., and Robert P. Gordon. *The Targum of the Prophets: Translated, with a Critical Introduction, Apparatus, and Notes.* The Aramaic Bible: The Targums 14. Wilmington, DE: Glazier, 1989.
Catlett, Michael Lee. "Reversals in Hosea: A Literary Analysis." PhD diss., Emory University, 1988.
Chalmers, R. Scott. *The Struggle of Yahweh and El for Hosea's Israel.* Hebrew Bible Monographs 11. Sheffield: Sheffield Phoenix, 2008.
Chaney, Marvin L. "Bitter Bounty: The Dynamics of Political Economy Critiqued by the Eighth-Century Prophets." In *Reformed Faith and Economics*, edited by Robert L. Stivers, 15–30. Lanham, MD: University Press of America, 1989.

———. "Micah—Models Matter: Political Economy and Micah 6:9-15." In *Ancient Israel: The Old Testament and Its Social Context*, edited by Philip F. Esler, 145-60. Minneapolis: Fortress, 2006.

———. "The Political Economy of Peasant Poverty: What the Eighth-Century Prophets Presued but Did Not State." *Journal of Religion and Society* 10 (2014) 34-61.

Chang, Peter M. "The Significance of Jehu's Revolution in the Literary and Theological Development of the Deuteronomic/Deuteronomistic History." PhD diss., Union Theological Seminary and Presbyterian School of Christian Education, 2000.

Childs, Brevard S. "Speech-Act Theory and Biblical Interpretation." *Scottish Journal of Theology* 58 (2005) 375-92.

Chisholm, Robert B., Jr. *A Commentary of Judges and Ruth*. Kregel Exegetical Library. Grand Rapids: Kregel Academic, 2103.

———. *From Exegesis to Exposition: A Practical Guide to Using Biblical Hebrew*. Grand Rapids: Baker, 1998.

———. *Handbook on the Prophets*. Grand Rapids: Baker Academic, 2002.

———. *Interpreting the Historical Books: An Exegetical Handbook*. Handbooks for Old Testament Exegesis, edited by David M. Jr. Howard. Grand Rapids: Kregel, 2006.

———. *Interpreting the Minor Prophets*. Grand Rapids: Zondervan, 1990.

———. "When Prophecy Appears to Fail, Check Your Hermeneutic." *Journal of the Evangelical Theological Society* 53 (2010) 561-77.

———. "Wordplay in the Eighth-Cenury Prophets." *Bibliotheca Sacra* 144 (1987) 44-52.

———. "'The Bloodshed of Jezreel': Harmonizing Hosea 1:4 and 2 Kings 10:30." *Bibliotheca Sacra* 176 (2019) 429-43.

Cleave, Richard. *The Holy Land Atlas: Terrain Recognition*. Vol. 1. Nicosia, Cyprus: Røhr Productions, 1999.

Clendenen, E. Ray. "Textlinguistics and Prophecy in the Book of the Twelve." *Journal of the Evangelical Theological Society* 46 (2003) 385-99.

Clifford, Richard J. *Fair Spoken and Persuading: An Interpretation of Second Isaiah*. New York: Paulist, 1984.

Cline, Eric H. *The Battles of Armageddon: Megiddo and the Jezreel Valley from the Bronze Age to the Nuclear Age*. Ann Arbor: University of Michigan Press, 2000.

———. "'Contested Peripheries' in World Systems Theory: Megiddo and the Jezreel Valley as a Test Case." *Journal of World-Systems Research* 6 (2000) 7-16.

Cogan, Mordechai, and Hayim Tadmor. *II Kings: A New Translation with Introduction and Commmentary*. Anchor Bible 11. New York: Doubleday, 1988.

Cohen, Harry. *The Commentary of Rabbi David Kimhi on Hosea: Edited with Critical Notes Showing His Sources, on the Basis of Manuscripts and Early Editions*. New York: AMS, 1966.

Collins, John J. "Marriage, Divorce, and Family in Second Temple Judaism." In *Families in Ancient Israel*. The Family, Religion, and Culture, 104-62. Louisville: Westminster John Knox, 1997.

Coote, Robert B. *Amos among the Prophets: Composition and Theology*. 1981. Reprint, Eugene, OR: Wipf & Stock, 2005.

Corbett, Edward P. J., and Robert J. Connors. *Classical Rhetoric for the Modern Student*. 4th ed. New York: Oxford University Press, 1999.

Cresswell, Tim. *In Place Out of Place: Geography, Ideology, and Transgression*. Minneapolis: University of Minnesota Press, 1996.

BIBLIOGRAPHY

Cross, Frank M. *Canaanite Myth and Hebrew Epic: Essays in the History of the Religion of Israel*. Cambridge: Harvard University Press, 1973.

Cross, Frank M., and Jozef T. Milik. "Explorations in the Judean Buqeʿah." *Bulletin of the American Schools of Oriental Research* 142 (1956) 5–17.

Daniels, Dwight R. *Hosea and Salvation History: The Early Traditions of Israel in the Prophecy of Hosea*. Translated by Peter T. Daniels. Beihefte zur Zeitschrift für die alttestamentliche Wissenschaft 191. Berlin: de Gruyter, 1990.

Davies, G. I. *Hosea*. New Century Bible. Grand Rapids: Eerdmans, 1992.

Davies, Philip R. *Memories of Ancient Israel: An Introduction to Biblical History—Ancient and Modern*. Louisville: Westminster John Knox, 2008.

Day, John. "Hosea and the Baal Cult." In *Prophecy and Prophets in Ancient Israel: Proceedings of the Oxford Old Testament Seminar*, edited by John Day, 202–24. Library of Hebrew Bible/Old Testament Studies 531. New York: T. & T. Clark, 2010.

———. *Yahweh and the God and Goddesses of Canaan*. Journal for the Study of the Old Testament 265. Sheffield: Sheffield Academic, 2000.

de Vaux, Roland. *Ancient Israel: Its Life and Institutions*. Translated by John McHugh. 1961. Reprint, Biblical Resource Series. Grand Rapids: Eerdmans, 1997.

Dearman, J. Andrew. *The Book of Hosea*. New International Commentary on the Old Testament. Grand Rapids: Eerdmans, 2010.

———. *Property Rights in the Eighth-Century Prophets: The Conflict and Its Background*. Society of Biblical Literature Dissertation Series 106. Atlanta: Scholars, 1988.

Dever, William G. "Archaeology and the Fall of the Northern Kingdom: What Really Happened?" In *Up to the Gates of Ekron: Essays on Archaeology and History of the Eastern Mediterranean in Honor of Seymour Gitin*, edited by S. White Crawford et al., 78–92. Jerusalem: W. F. Albright Institute of Archaeological Research, the Israel Exploration Society, 2007.

———. "Archaeology and the Social World of Isaiah." In *To Break Every Yoke: Essays in Honor of Marvin L. Chaney*, edited by Robert B. Coote and Norman K. Gottwald, 82–96. The Social World of Biblical Antiquity 3. Sheffield: Sheffield Phoenix, 2007.

———. *Did God Have a Wife?: Archaeology and Folk Religion in Ancient Israel*. Grand Rapids: Eerdmans, 2005.

DeVries, LaMoine F. *Cities of the Biblical World*. Peabody, MA: Hendrickson, 1997.

Dewrell, Heath D. "Yareb, Shalman, and the Date of Hosea." *Catholic Biblical Quarterly* 78 (2016) 413–29.

Diop, A. G. "The Name 'Israel' and Related Expressions in the Books of Amos and Hosea." PhD diss., Andrews University, 1995.

Dornemann, Rudolph H. "The Iron Age Remains at Tell Qarqur in the Orontes Valley." In *Essays on Syria in the Iron Age*, edited by Guy Bunnens, 459–85. Ancient Near Eastern Studies Supplement 7. Louvain: Peeters, 2000.

Dorsey, David A. *The Roads and Highways of Ancient Israel*. Baltimore: Johns Hopkins University Press, 1991.

Dozeman, Thomas B. "Biblical Geography and Critical Spatial Studies." In *Constructions of Space I: Theory, Geography, and Narrative*, edited by Jon L. Berquist and Claudia V. Camp, 77–108. Library of Hebrew Bible/Old Testament Studies 481. New York: T. & T. Clark, 2007.

———. "Hosea and the Wilderness Wandering Tradition." In *Rethinking the Foundations: Historiography in the Ancient World and in the Bible Essays in Honour of John Van*

Seters, edited by John Van Seters et al., 55–70. Beihefte zur Zeitschrift für die alttestamentliche Wissenschaft 294. Berlin: de Gruyter, 2000.

Dutcher-Walls, Patricia. "The Clarity of Double Vision: Seeing the Family in Sociological and Archaeological Perspective." In *The Family in Life and in Death: The Family in Ancient Israel: Sociological and Archaeological Perspectives*, edited by Patricia Dutcher-Walls, 1–15. Library of Hebrew Bible/Old Testament Studies 504. New York: T. & T. Clark, 2009.

Ebeling, Jennie, Norma Franklin, and Ian Cipin. "Jezreel Revealed in Laser Scans: A Preliminary Report of the 2012 Survey Season." *Near Eastern Archaeology* 75 (2012) 232–39.

Edelman, Diana. "Cultic Sites and Complexes Beyond the Jerusalem Temple." In *Religious Diversity in Ancient Israel and Judah*, edited by Francesca Stavrakopoulou and John Barton, 82–103. New York: T. & T. Clark, 2010.

Eidevall, Göran. *Grapes in the Desert: Metaphors, Models, and Themes in Hosea 4–14.* Coniectanea Biblica: Old Testament Series 43. Stockholm: Almqvist & Wiksell, 1996.

Elitzur, Yoel. *Ancient Place Names in the Holy Land: Preservation and History.* Winona Lake, IN: Eisenbrauns, 2004.

Emmerson, Grace I. *Hosea: An Israelite Prophet in Judean Perspective.* Journal for the Study of the Old Testament Supplement Series 28. Sheffield: JSOT Press, 1984.

Eph'al, Israel. *The City Besieged: Siege and Its Manifestations in the Ancient Near East.* Culture and History of the Ancient Near East 36. Leiden: Brill, 2009.

Erll, Astrid, and Ansgar Nünning, eds. *A Companion to Cultural Memory Studies.* Berlin: de Gruyter, 2010.

Eusebius. *The Onomasticon: Palestine in the Fourth Century A.D. with Jerome's Latin Translation and Expansion in Parallel.* Edited by Joan E. Taylor. Translated by G. S. P. Freeman-Greenville. Jerusalem: Carta, 2003.

Fales, Frederick M., and John N. Postgate. *Imperial Administrative Records, Part II: Provincial and Military Administration.* State Archives of Assyria 11. Helinski: University of Helinski Press, 1995.

Faust, Avraham. *The Archaeology of Israelite Society in Iron Age II.* Translated by Ruth Ludlum. Winona Lake, IN: Eisenbrauns, 2012.

———. "Household Economies in the Kingdoms of Israel and Judah." In *Household Archaeology in Ancient Israel and Beyond*, edited by Assaf Yasur-Landau et al., 255–74. Culture and History in the Ancient Near East 50. Leiden: Brill, 2011.

Fernandez, James. "Emergence and Convergence in Some African Sacred Places." In *The Anthropology of Space and Place: Locating Culture*, edited by Setha M. Low and Denise Lawrence-Zúñiga, 187–203. Blackwell Readers in Anthropology 4. Malden, MA: Blackwell, 2003.

Fidler, Ruth. "Inclusio and Symbolic Geography in the Copper Scroll." In *Copper Scroll Studies*, edited by George J. Brooke and Philip R. Davies, 210–25. London: T. & T. Clark, 2002.

Finkelstein, Israel. "Hazor and the North in the Iron Age: A Low Chronology Perspective." *Bulletin of the American Schools of Oriental Research* 314 (1999) 55–70.

———. "Middle Bronze Age 'Fortifications': A Reflection of Social Organization and Political Formations." *Tel Aviv* 19 (1992) 201–20.

———. "The Settlement History of Jerusalem in the Eighth and Seventh Centuries BC." *Revue Biblique* 115 (2008) 499–515.

Finkelstein, Israel, and Amihai Mazar. *The Quest for the Historical Israel: Debating Archaeology and the History of Early Israel.* Edited by Brian B. Schmidt. Society of Biblical Literature Archaeology and Biblical Studies 17. Atlanta: Society of Biblical Literature, 2007.

Finkelstein, Israel, and Neil Asher Silberman. *The Bible Unearthed: Archaeology's New Vision of Ancient Israel and the Origin of Its Sacred Texts.* New York: Free Press, 2001.

Flanagan, James W. "Ancient Perceptions of Space/Perceptions of Ancient Space." *Semeia* 87 (1999) 15–43.

Fleming, Daniel E. *The Legacy of Israel in Judah's Bible: History, Politics, and the Reinscribing of Tradition.* New York: Cambridge University Press, 2012.

Flores, Richard R. "Memory-Place, Meaning, and the Alamo." *American Literature History* 10 (1998) 428–45.

Fokkelman, Jan P. *Reading Biblical Narrative: An Introductory Guide.* Translated by Ineke Smit. Louisville: Westminster John Knox, 1999.

———. *Narrative Art in Genesis: Specimens of Stylistic and Structural Analysis.* 2nd ed. 1991. Reprint, Eugene, OR: Wipf & Stock, 2004.

Fox, Michael V. "The Rhetoric of Ezekiel's Vision of the Valley of Dry Bones." *Hebrew Union College Annual* 51 (1980) 1–15.

Frankel, David. *The Land of Canaan and the Destiny of Israel: Theologies of Territory in the Hebrew Bible.* Siphrut: Literature and Theology of the Hebrew Scriptures. Winona Lake, IN: Eisenbrauns, 2011.

Franklin, Norma. "Jezreel: Before and after Jezebel." In *Israel in Transition: From Late Bronze II to Iron IIA (C. 1250–850 B.C.E.)*, vol. 1, *The Archaeology*, edited by Lester L. Grabbe, 45–53. Library of Hebrew Bible/Old Testament Studies 491. New York: T. & T. Clark, 2008.

———. "Megiddo and Jezreel Reflected in the Dying Embers of the Northern Kingdom of Israel." In *The Last Days of the Kingdom of Israel*, edited by Shuichi Hasegawa, Christopher Levin, and Karen Radner, 189–208. Beihefte zur Zeitschrift für die alttestamentliche Wissenschaft 511. Berlin: de Gruyter, 2018.

———. "Response to David Ussishkin." *Bulletin of the American Schools of Oriental Research* 348 (2007) 71–73.

———. "Why Was Jezreel So Important to the Kingdom of Israel?" 2013. Accessed December 29, 2016. http://www.bibleinterp.com/opeds/2013/11/fra378006.shtml.

Freshwater, Dawn. "The Poetics of Space: Researching the Concept of Spatiality through Relationality." *Psychodynamic Practice* 11 (2005) 177–87.

Frick, Frank S. "The Political and Ideological Interests of Female Sexual Imagery in Hosea 1–3." In *To Break Every Yoke: Essays in Honor of Marvin L. Chaney*, edited by Robert B. Coote and Norman K. Gottwald, 200–208. The Social World of Biblical Antiquity 3. Sheffield: Sheffield Phoenix, 2007.

Frishman, Judith. "Why Would a Man Want to Be Anyone's Wife? A Response to Satlow." In *Families and Family Relations: As Represented in Early Judaisms and Early Christianities: Texts and Fictions*, edited by Jan Willem van Henten and Athalya Brenner, 43–48. Studies in Theology and Religion 2. Leiden: Deo, 2000.

Fritz, Volkmar. *The City in Ancient Israel.* Biblical Seminar 29. Sheffield: Sheffield Academic, 1995.

Galil, Gershon. "The Last Years of the Kingdom of Israel and the Fall of Israel." *Catholic Biblical Quarterly* 57 (1995) 52–65.

Garr, W. Randall. *Dialect Geography of Syria-Palestine, 1000–586 B.C.E.* Philadelphia: University of Pennsylvania Press, 1985.

Garrett, Duane A. *Hosea, Joel.* New American Commentary 19a. Nashville: Broadman & Holman, 1997.

Geller, Markham J. "The Elephantine Papyri and Hosea 2, 3: Evidence for the Form of the Early Jewish Divorce Writ." *Journal for the Study of Judaism in the Persian, Hellenistic, and Roman Period* 8 (1977) 139–48.

George, Mark K., ed., *Constructions of Space IV: Further Developments in Examining Ancient Israel's Social Space.* Library of Hebrew Bible/Old Testament Studies 569. New York: T. & T. Clark, 2013.

———. "Space and History: Siting Critical Space for Biblical Studies." In *Constructions of Space I: Theory, Geography, and Narrative*, edited by Jon L. Berquist and Claudia V. Camp, 15–31. Library of Hebrew Bible/Old Testament Studies 481. New York: T. & T. Clark, 2007.

Gitay, Yehoshua. *Prophecy and Persuasion: A Study of Isaiah 40–48.* Bonn: Linguistica Biblica, 1981.

———. "The Realm of Prophetic Rhetoric." In *Rhetoric, Scripture and Theology: Essays from the 1994 Pretoria Conference*, edited by Stanley E. Porter and Thomas H. Olbricht, 218–29. Journal for the Study of the New Testament Supplement Series 131. Sheffield: Sheffield Academic, 1994.

———. "A Study of Amos's Art of Speech: A Rhetorical Analysis of Amos 3:1–15." *Catholic Biblical Quarterly* 42 (1980) 293–309.

Gomes, Jules Francis. *The Sanctuary of Bethel and the Configuration of Israelite Identity.* Beihefte zur Zeitschrift für die alttestamentliche Wissenschaft 368. Berlin: de Gruyter, 2006.

Gordis, Robert. "Love, Marriage, and Business in the Book of Ruth." In *A Light Unto My Path: Old Testament Studies in Honor of Jacob M. Myers*, edited by Howard N. Bream et al., 241–64. Gettysburg Theological Studies 4. Philadelphia: Temple University Press, 1974.

Gossai, Hemchand. *Justice, Righteousness and the Social Critique of the Eighth-Century Prophets.* American University Studies: Series 7, Theology and Religion 141. New York: Lang, 1993.

Goswell, Gregory. "'David Their King': Kingship in the Prophecy of Hosea." *Journal for the Study of the Old Testament* 42 (2017) 213–31.

Grabbe, Lester L. "The Kingdom of Israel from Omri to the Fall of Samaria: If We Had Only the Bible..." In *Ahab Agonistes: The Rise and Fall of the Omri Dynasty*, edited by Lester L. Grabbe, 54–99. Library of Hebrew Bible/Old Testament Studies 421. New York: T. & T. Clark, 2007.

Gray, John. *I & II Kings: A Commentary.* 3rd ed. London: SCM, 1977.

Grayson, A. Kirk. *Assyrian Rulers of the First Millenium BC.* Vol. 2, *(858–745 BC).* Royal Inscriptions of Mesopotamia, Assyrian Periods 3. Toronto: University of Toronto Press, 1996.

———. "Shalmaneser III and the Levantine States: The 'Damascus Coalition Rebellion.'" *Journal of Hebrew Scriptures* 5: article 4 (2005).

Gudme, Anne Katrine. "Inside-Outside: Domestic Living Space in Biblical Memory." In *Memory and the City in Ancient Israel*, edited by Diana V. Edelman and Ehud Ben Zvi, 61–78. Winona Lake, IN: Eisenbrauns, 2014.

BIBLIOGRAPHY

Guillaume, Philippe. "The Chronological Limits of Reshaping Social Memory in the Presence of Written Sources: The Case of Ezekiel in Late Persian and Early Hellenistic Yehud." In *History, Memory, Hebrew Scriptures: A Festschrift for Ehud Ben Zvi*, edited by Ian Douglas Wilson and Diana Edelman, 187–96. Winona Lake, IN: Eisenbrauns, 2015.

Gupta, Akhil, and James Ferguson. "Beyond 'Culture': Space, Identity, and the Politics of Difference." *Cultural Anthropology* 7 (1992) 6–23.

Gutt, Ernst-August. *Relevance Theory: A Guide to Successful Communication in Translation.* Dallas: Summer Institute of Linguistics and United Bible Societies, 1992.

Hagedorn, Anselm C. "Place and Space in the Song of Songs." *Zeitschrift für die alttestamentliche Wissenschaft* 127 (2015) 207–23.

Hall, Edward T. "Proxemics." In *The Anthropology of Space and Place: Locating Culture*, edited by Setha M. Low and Denise Lawrence-Zúñiga, 51–73. Blackwell Readers in Anthropology, vol. 4. Malden, MA: Blackwell, 2003.

Hallo, William W., and William Kelly Simpson. *The Ancient Near East: A History.* 2nd ed. Orlando: Harcourt Brace, 1998.

Hallo, William W., and K. Lawson Younger, Jr., eds. *The Context of Scripture: Monumental Inscriptions from the Biblical World.* Vol. 2, *The Context of Scripture: Canonical Compositions, Monumental Inscriptions, and Archival Documents from the Biblical World.* Leiden: Brill, 2000.

Halloran, Richard R. "Qarqar." In *Lexham Bible Dictionary.* Bellingham, WA: Lexham, 2013.

Hanley, Ryan C. "The Background and Purpose of Stripping the Adulteress in Hosea 2." *Journal of the Evangelical Theological Society* 60 (2017) 89–103.

Har-El, Menashe. *Landscape, Nature and Man in the Bible: Sites and Events in the Old Testament.* Jerusalem: Carta, 2003.

Hardin, James W. "Understanding Houses, Households, and the Levantine Archaeological Record." In *Household Archaeology in Ancient Israel and Beyond*, edited by Assaf Yasur-Landau, Jennie R. Ebeling, and Laura B. Mazow, 9–25. Culture and History of the Ancient Near East 50. Leiden: Brill, 2011.

Harmanşah, Ömür. *Cities and the Shaping of Memory in the Ancient Near East.* New York: Cambridge University Press, 2013.

Harper, William R. *A Critical and Exegetical Commentary on Amos and Hosea.* International Critical Commentary. Edinburgh: T. & T. Clark, 1905.

Hartmann, Angelika. "Mental Maps, Cognitive Mapping and Mental Space in Contexts of Near and Middle Eastern Societies." In *Authority, Privacy and Public Order in Islam: Proceedings of the 22nd Congress of L'union Europeennedes Arabisants Et Islamisants*, edited by Barbara Michalak-Pinulska and Andrzej Pinulski, 329–39. Orientalia Lovaniensia analecta 148. Leuven: Peeters, 2006.

Hasegawa, Shuichi. *Aram and Israel During the Jehuite Dynasty.* Beihefte zur Zeitschrift für die alttestamentliche Wissenschaft 434. Berlin: de Gruyter, 2012.

Häusl, Maria. "Jerusalem, the Holy City: The Meaning of the City of Jerusalem in the Books of Ezra–Nehemiah." In *Constructions of Space V: Place, Space and Identity in the Ancient Mediterranean World*, edited by Gert T. M. Prinsloo and Christl M. Maier, 87–106. Library of Hebrew Bible/Old Testament Studies 576. New York: T. & T. Clark, 2013.

Hayes, John H., and Jeffrey K. Kuan. "The Final Years of Samaria (730–720 BC)." *Biblica* 72 (1991) 153–81.

BIBLIOGRAPHY

Heaton, E. W. *Everyday Life in Old Testament Times*. London: Batsford, 1961.

Heidegger, Martin. "Being and Time (Sections 31–34)." In *The Hermeneutic Tradition: From Ast to Ricoeur*, edited by Gayle L. Ormiston and Alan D. Schrift, 115–44. Suny Series, Intersections: Philosophy and Critical Theory. Albany: State University of New York Press, 1990.

Heintz, Jean Georges, and Lison Millot. *Le Livre Prophétique d'Osee: Texto-Bibliographie du XXeme Siecle*. Travaux du Groupe de Recherches et d'Études Sémitiques Anciennes [G.R.E.S.A.] de l'Université des Sciences Humaines de Strasbourg 3. Wiesbaden: Harrassowitz, 1999.

Hendel, Ronald. "Culture, Memory, and History: Reflections on Method in Biblical Studies." In *Historical Biblical Archaeology and the Future: The New Pragmatism*, edited by Thomas E. Levy, 250–61. London: Equinox, 2010.

Herzog, Chaim and Mordecai Gichon. *Battles of the Bible*. London: Greenhill, 1997.

Herzog, Ze'ev. *Archaeology of the City: Urban Planning in Ancient Israel and Its Social Implications*. Monograph series / Sonia and Marco Nadler Institute of Archaeology 13. Tel Aviv: Emery and Claire Yass Archaeology Press, 1997.

Hess, Richard S. *Israelite Religions: An Archaeological and Biblical Survey*. Grand Rapids: Baker Academic, 2007.

———. "Achan and Achor: Names and Wordplay in Joshua 7." *Hebrew Annual Review* 14 (1994) 89–98.

Hilber, John W. "The Culture of Prophecy and Writing in the Ancient Near East." In *Do Historical Matters Matter to Faith?: A Critical Appraisal of Modern and Postmodern Approaches to Scripture*, edited by James K. Hoffmeier and Dennis R. Magary, 219–41. Wheaton, IL: Crossway, 2012.

———. "Royal Cultic Prophecy in Assyria, Judah, and Egypt." In *"Thus Speaks Ishtar of Arbela": Prophecy in Israel, Assyria, and Egypt in the Neo-Assyrian Period*, edited by Robert P. Gordon and Hans M. Barstad, 161–86. Winona Lake, IN: Eisenbrauns, 2013.

Høgenhaven, Jesper. "Geography and Ideology in the Copper Scroll (3Q15) from Qumran." In *Northern Lights on the Dead Sea Scrolls: Proceedings of the Nordic Qumran Network 2003–2006*, edited by Anders K. Petersen et al., 83–106. Studies on the Texts of the Desert of Judah 80. Leiden: Brill, 2009.

Holloway, Steven A. *Aššur Is King! Aššur Is King!: Religion in the Exercise of Power in the Neo-Assyrian Empire*. Culture and History of the Ancient Near East 10. Leiden: Brill, 2002.

Hornsby, Teresa J. "Israel Has Become a 'Worthless Thing': Re-reading Gomer in Hosea 1–3." *Journal for the Study of the Old Testament* 24 (1999) 115–28.

Houston, Walter. "Was There a Social Crisis in the Eighth Century?" In *In Search of Pre-Exilic Israel: Proceedings of the Oxford Old Testament Seminar*, edited by John Day, 130–49. London: T. & T. Clark, 2004.

———. "What Did the Prophets Think They Were Doing? Speech Acts and Prophetic Discourse in the Old Testament." *Biblical Interpretation* 1 (1993) 167–88.

Hubbard, David Allan. *Hosea: An Introduction and Commentary*. Downers Grove, IL: InterVarsity, 1989.

Hull, William E. "Woman in Her Place: Biblical Perspectives." *Review and Expositor* 72 (1975) 5–17.

Hunt, Melvin. "Beth-Eked (Place)." In *The Anchor Bible Dictionary*, edited by David Noel Freedman, 1:685. New York: Doubleday, 1992.

Hynniewta, Maksal Jones. "The Integrity of Hosea's Future Hope: A Study of the Oracles of Hope in the Book of Hosea." PhD diss., Union Theological Seminary, 1996.

Irvine, Stuart A. "The Threat of Jezreel (Hosea 1:4-5)." *Catholic Biblical Quarterly* 57 (1995) 494-503.

Isserlin, B. S. J. *The Israelites*. 1998. Reprint, Minneapolis: Fortress, 2001.

Jackson, Justin. "The Bows of the Mighty Are Broken: The 'Fall' of the Proud and the Exaltation of the Humble in 1 Samuel." *Themelios* 46 (2021) 290-305.

Japhet, Sara. "Some Biblical Concepts of Sacred Place." In *Sacred Space: Shrine, City, Land*, edited by Bejamin Z. Kedar and R. J. Zwi Werblowsky, 55-72. Jerusalem: Macmillan and the Israel Academy of Sciences and Humanities, 1998.

Jasinski, James. *Sourcebook on Rhetoric: Key Concepts in Contemporary Rhetorical Studies*. Rhetoric & Society. Thousand Oaks, CA: Sage, 2001.

Jennings, James E. "Achor, Valley Of." In *The New International Dictionary of Biblical Archaeology*, edited by Edward M. Blaiklock and R. K. Harrison, 5-6. Grand Rapids: Zondervan, 1983.

Jeremias, Jörg. *Der Prophet Hosea*. Das Alte Testament Deutsch 24/1. Göttingen: Vandenhoeck & Ruprecht, 1983.

Joüon, Paul. *Grammaire De L'hébreu Biblique*. Rome: Institut biblique pontifical, 1923.

Joüon, Paul and T. Muraoka. *A Grammar of Biblical Hebrew*. Vol. 1. Translated by T. Muraoka. Subsidia Biblica 14/1. Rome: Editrice Pontificio Istituto Biblico, 1993.

———. *A Grammar of Biblical Hebrew*. Vol. 2. Translated by T. Muraoka. Subsidia Biblica 14/2. Rome: Editrice Pontificio Istituto Biblico, 1993.

Kallai, Zecharia. *Historical Geography of the Bible: The Tribal Territories of Israel*. Jerusalem: Magnes, 1986.

Kató, Szabolcs-Ferencz. "Baal and the Baals in the Book of Hosea: A Comparative Study." *Journal of Northwest Semitic Languages* 49 (2023) 35-54.

Kautzsch, E., ed., *Gesenius' Hebrew Grammar*. Translated by A. E. Cowley. 2nd English ed. Oxford: Clarendon, 1910.

Keefe, Alice A. "Family Metaphors and Social Conflict in Hosea." In *Writing and Reading War: Rhetoric, Gender, and Ethics in Biblical and Modern Contexts*, edited by Brad E. Kelle and Frank Ritchel Ames, 113-28. Society of Biblical Literature Symposium Series 42. Leiden: Brill, 2008.

———. "Hosea's (In)Fertility God." *Horizons in Biblical Theology* 30 (2008) 21-41.

Keita, Katrin. *Gottes Land: Exegetische Studien Zur Land-Thematik Im Hoseabuch in Kanonischer Perspektive*. Theologische Texte und Studien 13. Hildesheim: Olms, 2007.

Kelber, Werner H. *Imprints, Voiceprints, and Footprints of Memory: Collected Essays of Werner H. Kelber*. Resources for Biblical Study 74. Atlanta: Society of Biblical Literature, 2013.

Kelle, Brad E. "Hosea 1-3 in Twentieth-Century Scholarship." *Currents in Biblical Research* 7 (2009) 179-216.

———. *Hosea 2: Metaphor and Rhetoric in Historical Perspective*. Academia Biblica 20. Atlanta: Society of Biblical Literature, 2005.

———. "Postwar Rituals of Return and Reintegration." In *Warfare, Ritual, and Symbol in Biblical and Modern Contexts*, edited by Brad E. Kelle et al., 205-42. Ancient Israel and Its Literature 18. Atlanta: Society of Biblical Literature, 2014.

Kelso, James L. *The Excavation of Bethel (1934-1960), William F. Albright, Director 1934; James L. Kelso, Director 1954, 1957, 1960 [by] James L. Kelso. With Chapters by*

BIBLIOGRAPHY

William F. Albright, et al. *Annual of the American Schools of Oriental Research 39.* Cambridge, MA: American Schools of Oriental Research, 1968.

Kennedy, George A. *New Testament Interpretation through Rhetorical Criticism.* Chapel Hill: University of North Carolina Press, 1984.

Kim, Sunhee. "The Concepts of Sacred Space in the Hebrew Bible: Meanings, Significance, and Functions." PhD diss., Boston University, 2014.

King, Philip J. *Amos, Hosea, Micah: An Archaeological Commentary.* Philadelphia: Westminster, 1988.

———. "The Great Eighth Century." *Bible Review* 5.4 (1989) 22–33, 44.

King, Philip J., and Lawrence E. Stager. *Life in Biblical Israel.* Library of Ancient Israel. Louisville: Westminster John Knox, 2001.

Kletter, Raz. "Clay Figurines and Scale Weights from Tel Jezreel." *Tel Aviv* 24 (1997) 110–21.

Klingler, David Ryan. "Validity in the Identification and Interpretation of a Literary Allusion in the Hebrew Bible." PhD diss., Dallas Theological Seminary, 2010.

Koehler, Ludwig, and Walter Baumgartner. *The Hebrew and Aramaic Lexicon of the Old Testament.* Translated and edited under the supervision of M. E. J. Richardson. Revised by Walter Baumgartner and Johann Jakob Stamm. Vol. 1. Study ed. Leiden: Brill, 2001.

Kofoed, Jens Bruun. "The Old Testament as Cultural Memory." In *Do Historical Matters Matter to Faith?: A Critical Appraisal of Modern and Postmodern Approaches to Scripture*, edited by Dennis R. Magary James K. Hoffmeier, 303–23. Wheaton, IL: Crossway, 2012.

Kohn, Risa Levitt. "In and Out of Place: Physical Space and Social Location in the Bible." In *From Babel to Babylon: Essays on Biblical History and Literature in Honour of Brian Peckham*, edited by Joyce Rilett Wood, John E. Harvey, and Mark Leuchter, 253–62. Library of Hibrew Bible/Old Testament Studies 455. New York: T. & T. Clark, 2006.

Kosal, Umur. "Society, Spatiality, and the Sacred: A Methodological Proposal." *Bulletin for the Study of Religion* 50 (2021) 53–60.

Kottsieper, Ingo. "'We Have a Little Sister': Aspects of Brother-Sister Relationship in Ancient Israel." In *Families and Family Relations: As Represented in Early Judaisms and Early Christianities: Texts and Fictions*, edited by Jan Willem van Henten and Athalya Brenner, 49–80. Studies in Theology and Religion 2. Leiden: Deo, 2000.

Krispenz, Jutta. "Idolatry, Apostasy, Prostition: Hosea's Struggle against the Cult." In *Priests and Cults in the Book of the Twelve*, edited by Lena-Sofia Tiemeyer, 9–29. Ancient Near Eastern Monographs 14. Atlanta: SBL, 2016.

Kruger, Paul A. "'I Will Hedge Her Way with Thornbushes' (Hosea 2,8): Another Example of Literary Multiplicity?" *Biblische Zeitschrift* 43 (1999) 92–99.

———. "The Marriage Metaphor in Hosea 2:4–17 Against Its Ancient Near Eastern Background." *Old Testament Essays* 5 (1992) 7–25.

Kuhnigk, Willibald. *Northwestsemitische Studien Zum Hoseabuch.* Biblica et Orientala 27. Rome: Pontifical Biblical Institute, 1974.

Kuper, Hilda. "The Language of Sites in the Politics of Space." In *The Anthropology of Space and Place: Locating Culture*, edited by Setha M. Low and Denise Lawrence-Zúñiga, 247–63. Blackwell Readers in Anthropology 4. Malden, MA: Blackwell, 2003.

Kwakkel, Gert. "Exile in Hosea 9:3–6: Where and for What Purpose?" In *Exile and Suffering: A Selection of Papers Read at the 50th Anniversary Meeting of the Old Testament Society of South Africa Otwsa/Otssa Pretoria August 2007*, edited by Bob Becking and Dirk Human, 123–46. Old Testament Studies 50. Leiden: Brill, 2009.

BIBLIOGRAPHY

Kwakkel, Gert. "The Land in the Book of Hosea." In *The Land of Israel in Bible, History, and Theology: Studies in Honour of Ed Noort*, edited by Jacques van Ruiten and J. Cornelis de Vos, 167–82. Supplements to Vetus Testamentum 124. Leiden: Brill, 2009.

Lakoff, George and Mark Johnson. *Metaphors We Live By*. Chicago: University of Chicago Press, 1980.

Lamb, David T. *Righteous Jehu and His Evil Heirs: The Deuteronomist's Negative Perspective on Dynastic Succession*. Oxford Theological Monographs. Oxford Oxford University Press, 2007.

Landy, Francis. "In the Wilderness of Speech: Problems of Metaphor in Hosea." *Biblical Interpretation* 3 (1995) 35–59.

Larsen, David W. "The Use of Critical Spatial Theory in a Canonical Reading of Genesis 1:1–2:25 and Revelation 21:1–22:5." PhD diss., St. Mary's University, 2020.

Leeb, Carolyn S. *Away from the Father's House: The Social Location of the Na'ar and Na'arah in Ancient Israel*. Journal for the Study of the Old Testament 301. Sheffield: Sheffield Academic, 2000.

Lefebvre, Henri. *The Production of Space*. Translated by Donald Nicholson-Smith. Democracy and Urban Landscapes. Oxford: Blackwell, 1991.

Lemos, T. M. *Marriage Gifts and Social Change in Ancient Palestine: 1200 BCE to 200 CE*. Cambridge: Cambridge University Press, 2010.

Levin, Adina. "A New Context for Jacob in Genesis and Hosea 12." In *From Babel to Babylon: Essays on Biblical History and Literature in Honour of Brian Peckham*, edited by Joyce Rilett Wood, John E. Harvey, and Mark Leuchter, 226–36. Library of Hebrew Bible/Old Testament Studies 455. New York: T. & T. Clark, 2006.

Lewis, R. L. "The Persuasive Style and Appeals of the Minor Prophets Amos, Hosea, and Micah " PhD diss., University of Michigan, 1958.

Lied, Liv Ingeborg. *The Other Lands of Israel: Imaginations of the Land in 2 Baruch*. Supplements to the Journal for the Study of Judaism 129. Leiden: Brill, 2008.

Low, Setha M. and Denise Lawrence-Zúñiga. "Locating Culture." In *The Anthropology of Space and Place: Locating Culture*, edited by Setha M. Low and Denise Lawrence-Zúñiga, 1–47. Blackwell Readers in Anthropology 4. Malden, MA: Blackwell, 2003.

Lundbom, Jack. "Poetic Structure and Rhetoric in Hosea." *Vetus Testamentum* 29 (1979) 300–308.

———. *Biblical Rhetoric and Rhetorical Criticism*. Hebrew Bible Monographs 45. Sheffield: Sheffield Phoenix, 2013.

Lunn, Nick. "Paronomastic Constructions in Biblical Hebrew." *Notes on Translation* 10.4 (1996) 31–52.

Lyons, Tim. "Situations of a Certain Type and Phone-Tapping 101: A General Semantics Critique of Lloyd Bitzer's 'The Rhetorical Situation.'" *ETC: A Review of General Semantics* 79 (2022) 154–63.

MacIntosh, A. A. *A Critical and Exegetical Commentary on Hosea*. International Critical Commentary. Edinburgh: T. & T. Clark, 1997.

Maisels, Charles Kieth. *The Emergence of Civilization: From Hunting and Gathering to Agriculture, Cities, and the State in the Near East*. London: Routledge, 1990.

Martin, George H. "The Origin and Function of Restoration Passages in the Book of Hosea." PhD diss., New Orleans Baptist Theological Seminary, 1985.

Matthews, Victor H. "Back to Bethel: Geographical Reiteration in Biblical Narrative." *Journal of Biblical Literature* 128 (2009) 149–65.

———. *A Brief History of Ancient Israel*. Louisville: Westminster John Knox, 2002.

BIBLIOGRAPHY

———. "The Determination of Social Identity in the Story of Ruth." *Biblical Theology Bulletin* 36 (2006) 49–54.

———. *The Hebrew Prophets and Their Social World: A Introduction.* 2nd ed. Grand Rapids: Baker, 2012.

———. "Honor and Shame in Gender-Related Legal Situations in the Hebrew Bible." In *Gender and Law in the Hebrew Bible and the Ancient Near East*, edited by Victor H. Matthews, Bernard M. Levinson, and Tivka Frymer-Kensky, 97–112. Journal for the Study of the Old Testament Supplementals 262. Sheffield: Sheffield Academic, 1998.

———. *Manners and Customs in the Bible: An Illustrated Guide to Daily Life in Bible Times.* 3rd ed. Peabody, MA: Hendrickson, 2006.

———. "Marriage and Family in the Ancient Near East." In *Marriage and Family in the Biblical World*, edited by Ken M. Campbell. 1–32. Downers Grove, IL: InterVarsity 2003.

———. *More Than Meets the Ear: Discovering the Hidden Contexts of Old Testament Conversations.* Grand Rapids: Eerdmans, 2008.

———. "Remembered Space in Biblical Narrative." In *Constructions of Space IV: Further Developments in Examining Ancient Israel's Social Space*, edited by Mark K. George, 61–75. Library of Hebrew Bible/Old Testament Studies 569. New York: T. & T. Clark, 2013.

———. "Spatial and Sensory Aspects of Battle in Biblical and Ancient Near Eastern Texts." *Biblical Theology Bulletin* 49 (2019) 82–87.

———. *Studying the Ancient Israelites: A Guide to Sources and Methods.* Grand Rapids: Baker Academic, 2007.

Matthews, Victor H., and Don C. Benjamin. *Social World of Ancient Israel 1250–587 BCE.* Peabody, MA: Hendrickson, 1993.

Mays, James L. *Hosea.* Old Testament Library. Philadelphia: Westminster, 1969.

Mazar, Amihai. *Archaeology of the Land of the Bible: 10,000–586 B.C.E.* Anchor Bible Reference Library. New York: Doubleday, 1992.

Mazor, Yair. "Hosea 5.1-3: Between Compositional Rhetoric and Rhetorical Composition." *Journal for the Study of the Old Testament* 45 (1989) 115–26.

McComiskey, Thomas. "Hosea." In *The Minor Prophets: An Exegetical and Expositional Commentary*, edited by T. McComiskey, 1–237. Grand Rapids: Baker, 2009.

———. "Prophetic Irony in Hosea 1.4: A Study of the Collocation of לי גקם and פקם and Its Implications for the Fall of Jehu's Dynasty." *Journal for the Study of the Old Testament* 58 (1993) 93–101.

McNutt, Paula M. *Reconstructing the Society of Ancient Israel.* Library of Ancient Israel. Louisville: Westminster John Knox, 1999.

Meredith, Christopher. "Taking Issue with Thirdspace: Reading Soja, Lefebvre and the Bible." In *Constructions of Space III: Biblical Spatiality and the Sacred*, edited by Jorunn Økland et al., 75–103. Library of Hebrew Bible/Old Testament Studies 540. New York: T. & T. Clark, 2016.

Merrill, Eugene. *Kingdom of Priests: A History of Old Testament Israel.* 2nd ed. Grand Rapids: Baker, 1996.

Meyers, Carol. *Discovering Eve: Ancient Israelite Women in Context.* Oxford: Oxford University Press, 1988.

———. "Everyday Life in Biblical Israel: Women's Social Networks." In *Life and Culture in the Ancient Near East*, edited by Richard E. Averbeck et al., 185–204. Bethesda, MD: CDL 2003.

BIBLIOGRAPHY

———. "The Family in Early Israel." In *Families in Ancient Israel*, 1–47. The Family, Religion, and Culture. Louisville: Westminster John Knox, 1997.

———. "Material Remains and Social Relations: Women's Culture in Agrarian Households of the Iron Age." In *Symbiosis, Symbolism, and the Power of the Past: Canaan, Ancient Israel, and Their Neighbors from the Late Bronze Age through Roman Palaestina: Proceedings of the Centennial Symposium W. F. Albright Institute of Archaeological Research and American Schools of Oriental Research Jerusalem, May 29–31, 2000*, edited by William G. Dever and Seymour Gitin, 425–44. Winona Lake, IN: Eisenbrauns, 2003.

———. *Rediscovering Eve: Ancient Israelite Women in Context*. Oxford: Oxford University Press, 2013.

———. "Women's Lives." In *Wiley Blackwell Companion to Ancient Israel*, edited by Susan Niditch, 415–32. Wiley Blackwell Companions to Religion. Malden, MA: Wiley Blackwell, 2016.

Millard, A. R. "Israelite and Aramean History in the Light of Inscriptions." In *Israel's Past in Present Research: Essays on Ancient Israelite Historiography*, edited by V. Philips Long, 129–40. Sources for Biblical and Theological Study. Winona Lake, IN: Eisenbrauns, 1999.

Miller, Patrick D., Jr. "The Prophetic Critique of Kings." *Ex Auditu* 2 (1986) 82–96.

———. *Sin and Judgment in the Prophets: A Stylistic and Theological Analysis*. Society of Biblical Literature Monograph Series 27. Chico, CA: Scholars, 1982.

Miller, Robert D. II. "Modeling the Farm Community in Iron I Israel." In *Life and Culture in the Ancient Near East*, edited by Richard E. Averbeck et al., 289–310. Bethesda, MD: CDL, 2003.

Mills, Mary E. *Urban Imagination in Biblical Prophecy*. Library of Hebrew Bible/Old Testament Studies 560. New York: T. & T. Clark, 2012.

Möller, Karl. *A Prophet in Debate: The Rhetoric of Persuasion in the Book of Amos*. Journal for the Study of Old Testament: Supplement Series 372. Sheffield: Sheffield Academic, 2003.

Moon, Joshua N. *Hosea*. Appolos Old Testament Commentary 21. London: InterVarsity, 2018.

Morgenstern, Julian. *Amos Studies*. Vol. 1. Cincinnati: Hebrew Union College, 1941.

Morris, Gerald. *Prophecy, Poetry, and Hosea*. Journal for the Study of the Old Testament Supplement Series 219. Sheffield: Sheffield Academic, 1996.

Muilenburg, James. "The Book of Isaiah: Chapters 40–66." In *The Interpreter's Bible*, edited by George Arthur Buttrick et al., 5:381–773. New York: Abingdon, 1956.

———. "Form Criticism and Beyond." *Journal of Biblical Literature* 88 (1969) 1–18.

Munn, Nancy D. "Excluded Spaces: The Figure in the Australian Aboriginal Landscape." In *The Anthropology of Space and Place: Locating Culture*, edited by Setha M. Low and Denise Lawrence-Zúñiga, 92–109. Blackwell Readers in Anthropology 4. Malden, MA: Blackwell 2003.

Na'aman, Nadav. "Ahab's Chariot Force at the Battle of Qarqar." In *Ancient Israel and Its Neighbors: Interaction and Counteraction*, edited by Nadav Na'aman, 1–12. Winona Lake, IN: Eisenbrauns, 2005.

———. *Ancient Israel's History and Historiography*. Vol. 3: *Collected Essays: The First Temple Period*. Winona Lake, IN: Eisenbrauns, 2005.

———. "Historical and Literary Notes on the Excavations of Tel Jezreel." *Tel Aviv* 24 (1997) 122–28.

BIBLIOGRAPHY

———. "Naboth's Vineyard and the Foundation of Jezreel." *Journal for the Study of the Old Testament* 33 (2008) 197–218.

———. "When and How Did Jerusalem Become a Great City? The Rise of Jerusalem as Judah's Premier City in the Eighth-Seventh Centuries B.C.E." *Bulletin of the American Schools of Oriental Research* 347 (2007) 21–56.

Nakhai, Beth Alpert. "Varieties of Religious Expression in the Domestic Setting." In *Household Archaeology in Ancient Israel and Beyond*, edited by Assaf Yasur-Landau, Jennie R. Ebeling, and Laura B. Mazow, 347–60. Culture and History of the Ancient Near East 50. Leiden: Brill, 2011.

Neef, Heinz-Dieter. "The Early Traditions of Israel in the Prophecy of Hosea—a Review." In *Israel's Past in Present Research: Essays on Ancient Israelite Historiography*, edited by V. Philips Long, 552–56. Sources for Biblical and Theological Study 7. Winona Lake, IN: Eisenbrauns, 1999.

Negenman, J. H. "Geography in Palestine." In *The World of the Bible*, edited by A. S. van der Woude, 21–43. Grand Rapids: Eerdmans, 1986.

Newsom, Carol A. "Selective Recall and Ghost Memories: Two Aspects of Cultural Memory in the Hebrew Bible." In *Memory and Identity in Ancient Judaism and Early Christianity: A Conversation with Barry Schwartz*, edited by Tom Thatcher, 41–56. Semeia Studies 78. Atlanta: Society of Biblical Literature, 2014.

Neyrey, Jerome H. "Gathered around Jesus: An Alternative Spatial Practice in the Gospel of Mark." PhD diss., Notre Dame, 2005.

Niditch, Susan. "A Messy Business: Ritual Violence after the War." In *Warfare, Ritual, and Symbol in Biblical and Modern Contexts*, edited by Brad E. Kelle, Frank Ritchel Ames, and Jacob L. Wright, 187–204. Ancient Israel and Its Literature 18. Atlanta: Society of Biblical Literature, 2014.

Nissinen, Martti. *Prophetie, Redaktion und Fortschreibung im Hoseabuch: Studien zum Werdegang Eines Prophetenbuches im Lichte von Hos 4 und 11*. Alter Orient und Altes Testament 231. Kevelaer: Butzon & Bercker, 1991.

Nissinen, Martti, Choon-Leong Seow, and Robert K. Ritner. *Prophets and Prophecy in the Ancient Near East*. Writings from the Ancient World 12. Atlanta: Society of Biblical Literature, 2003.

Nora, Pierre. *The Realms of Memory: Rethinking the French Past*. Vol. 1: *Conflicts and Divisions*. Translated by Arthur Goldhammer. New York: Columbia University Press, 1996.

Pierre Nora and David P. Jordan, eds. *Rethinking France: Les Lieux de mémoire*. Vol. 1: *The State*. Translated by Mary Seidman Trouville. Chicago: University of Chicago Press, 1999.

Noth, Martin. "Das Deutsche Evangelische Institut für Altertumswissenschaft des Heiligen Landes, Lehrkursus 1954." *Zeitschrift des deutschen Palästina-Vereins* 71 (1955) 42–55.

Olbricht, Thomas H. "The Flowering of Rhetorical Criticism in America." In *The Rhetorical Analysis of Scripture: Essays from the 1995 London Conference*, edited by Stanley E. Porter and Thomas H. Olbricht, 79–102. Journal for the Study of the New Testament Supplement Series 146. Sheffield: Sheffield Academic, 1997.

Parunak, H. Van Dyke. "Oral Typesetting: Some Uses of Biblical Structure." *Biblica* 62 (1981) 153–68.

Patrick, Dale. *The Rhetoric of Revelation in the Hebrew Bible*. Overtures to Biblical Theology. Minneapolis: Fortress, 1999.

Patrick, Dale, and Allen Scult. *Rhetoric and Biblical Interpretation*. Sheffield: Sheffield Academic, 1990.

Patte, Daniel. "Speech Act Theory and Biblical Exegesis." *Semeia* 41 (1988) 85–102.

Peels, H. G. L. "אנק." in *New International Dictionary of Old Testament Theology and Exegesis*, edited by Willem A. VanGemeren, 3:937–40. 5 vols. Grand Rapids: Zondervan, 1997.

Pellow, Deborah. "The Architecture of Female Seclusion in West Africa." In *The Anthropology of Space and Place: Locating Culture*, edited by Setha M. Low and Denise Lawrence-Zúñiga, 160–83. Blackwell Readers in Anthropology 4. Malden, MA: Blackwell, 2003.

Perdue, Leo G. "The Household, Old Testament Theology, and Contemporary Hermeneutics." In *Families in Ancient Israel*, 223–57. The Family, Religion, and Culture. Louisville: Westminster John Knox, 1997.

———. "The Israelite and Early Jewish Family: Summary and Conclusions." In *Families in Ancient Israel*, 163–222. The Family, Religion, and Culture. Louisville: Westminster John Knox, 1997.

Pollock, Susan. *Ancient Mesopotamia: The Eden That Never Was*. Case Studies in Early Societies. Cambridge: Cambridge University Press, 1999.

Poythress, Vern Sheridan. "Canon and Speech Act: Limitations in Speech-Act Theory, with Implications for a Putative Theory of Canonical Speech Acts." *Westminster Theological Journal* 70 (2008) 337–54.

Pratt, Richard L., Jr. "Historical Contingencies and Biblical Predictions." In *The Way of Wisdom: Essays in Honor of Bruce K. Waltke*, edited by J. I. Packer and Sven K. Soderlund, 180–203. Grand Rapids: Zondervan, 2000.

Premnath, D. N. *Eighth Century Prophets: A Social Analysis*. St. Louis: Chalice, 2003.

Pressler, Carolyn. "Achor." In *Anchor Bible Dictionary*, edited by David Noel Freedman, 1:56. New York: Doubleday, 1992.

Prinsloo, Gert T. M. "Place, Space and Identity in the Ancient Mediterranean World: Theory and Practice with Reference to the Book of Jonah." In *Constructions of Space V: Place, Space and Identity in the Ancient Mediterranean World*, edited by Gert T. M. Prinsloo and Christl M. Maier, 3–25. Library of Hebrew Bible/Old Testament Studies 576. New York: Bloomsbury, 2013.

Prinsloo, Gert T. M., and Christl M. Maier, eds. *Constructions of Space V: Place, Space and Identity in the Ancient Mediterranean World*. Library of Hebrew Bible/Old Testament Series 576. New York: T. & T. Clark, 2013.

Pritchard, James B. *Ancient Near Eastern Texts Relating to the Old Testament*. 3rd ed. Princeton: Princeton University Press, 1969.

Rabinow, Paul. "Ordonnance, Discipline, Regulations: Some Reflections on Urbanism." In *The Anthropology of Space and Place: Locating Culture*, edited by Setha M. Low and Denise Lawrence-Zúñiga, 353–62. Blackwell Readers in Anthropology 4. Malden, MA: Blackwell, 2003.

Rainey, Anson F. "Aspects of Life in Ancient Israel." In *Life and Culture in the Ancient Near East*, edited by Richard E. Averbeck et al., 253–68. Bethesda, MD: CDL, 2003.

———. *El Amarna Tablets 359–379: Supplement to J. A. Knudtzon Die El-Amarna-Tafeln*. 2nd ed. Alter Orient und Altes Testament 8. Kevelaer: Butzon & Bercker, 1978.

———. "Institutions: Family, Civil, and Military." In *Ras Shamra Parallels*, edited by Loren R. Fisher, vol. 2, 69–107. Analecta Orientalia 50. Rome: Pontifical Biblical Institute, 1975.

BIBLIOGRAPHY

———. "Looking for Bethel: An Exercise in Historical Geography." In *Confronting the Past: Archaeological and Historical Essays on Ancient Israel in Honor of William G. Dever*, edited by Seymour Gitin et al., 269–73. Winona Lake, IN: Eisenbrauns, 2006.

———. *Teaching History and Historical Geography of Bible Lands: A Syllabus*. Jerusalem: Carta, 2010.

Rainey, Anson F., and R. Steven Notley. *The Sacred Bridge: Carta's Atlas of the Biblical World*. Jerusalem: Carta, 2006.

Resseguie, James L. *Narrative Criticism of the New Testament: An Introduction*. Grand Rapids: Baker Academic, 2005.

Richardson, Tim, and Ole B. Jensen. "Linking Discourse and Space: Towards a Cultural Sociology of Space in Analysing Spatial Policy Discourses." *Urban Studies* 40 (2003) 7–22.

Richter, Sandra. "Eighth-Century Issues: The World of Jeroboam II, the Fall of Samaria, and the Reign of Hezekiah." In *Ancient Israel's History: An Introduction to Issues and Sources*, edited by Bill T. Arnold and Richard S. Hess, 319–49. Grand Rapids: Baker, 2014.

Ricoeur, Paul. *The Rule of Metaphor: The Creation of Meaning in Language*. 3rd ed. London: Routledge Classics, 2003.

Ro, Johannes Un-Sok, and Diana Vikander, eds. *Collective Memory and Collective Identity: Deuteronomy and the Deuteronomistic History in Their Context*. Beihefte zur Zeitschrift für die alttestamentliche Wissenschaft 534. Berlin: de Gruyter, 2021.

Roberts, J. J. M. "The Divided Monarchy." In *The Wiley Blackwell Companion to Ancient Israel*, edited by Susan Niditch, 197–212. Wiley Blackwell Companions to Religion. Malden, MA: Wiley Blackwell, 2016.

Robinson, C. Wheeler. *Corporate Personality in Ancient Israel*. Rev. ed. Philadelphia: Fortress, 1980.

Robker, Jonathan Miles. *The Jehu Revolution: A Royal Tradition of the Northern Kingdom and Its Ramifications*. Beihefte zur Zeitschrift für die alttestamentliche Wissenschaft 435. Berlin: de Gruyter, 2012.

Rocca, Samuel. *The Fortifications of Ancient Israel and Judah 1200–586 BC*. Fortress 91. Oxford: Osprey, 2010.

Rodman, Margaret C. "Empowering Place: Multilocality and Multivocality." In *The Anthropology of Space and Place: Locating Culture*, edited by Setha M. Low and Denise Lawrence-Zúñiga, 204–23. Blackwell Readers in Anthropology 4. Malden, MA: Blackwell, 2003.

Rogerson, John W. *A Theology of the Old Testament: Cultural Memory, Communication, and Being Human*. Minneapolis: Fortress, 2010.

Roubos, K. "Biblical Institutions." In *The World of the Bible: Bible Handbook*, edited by A. S. Van der Woude, 1:350–92. Grand Rapids: Eerdmans, 1986.

Routledge, Robin. "Hosea's Marriage Reconsidered." *Tyndale Bulletin* 69 (2018) 25–42.

Roux, Georges. *Ancient Iraq*. 3rd ed. New York: Penguin, 1992.

Russell, Stephen C. *Images of Egypt in Early Biblical Literature: Cisjordan-Israelite, Transjordan-Israelite, and Judahite Portrayals*. Beihefte zur Zeitschrift für die alttestamentliche Wissenschaft 403. Berlin: de Gruyter, 2009.

Sandy, D. Brent. *Plowshares and Pruning Hooks: Rethinking the Language of Biblical Prophecy and Apocalyptic*. Downers Grove, IL: InterVarsity, 2002.

Satlow, Michael. "The Metaphor of Marriage in Early Judaism." In *Families and Family Relations: As Represented in Early Judaisms and Eraly Christianities: Texts and

BIBLIOGRAPHY

Fictions, edited by Jan Willem van Henten and Athalya Brenner, 13–42. Studies in Theology and Religion 2. Leiden: Deo, 2000.

Schecter, Solomon. *Documents of Jewish Sectaries*, with a Prolegomenon by Joseph A. Fitzmyer. 1910. Reprint, New York: Ktav, 1970.

Schlegel, William. *Satellite Bible Atlas: Historical Geography of the Bible*. Santa Clarita, CA: Masters College, 2013.

Schloen, J. David. *The House of the Father as Fact and Symbol: Patrimonialism in Ugarit and the Ancient Near East*. Studies in the Archaeology and History of the Levant 2. Winona Lake, IN: Eisenbrauns, 2001.

Schmitt, Rüdiger. "War Rituals in the Old Testament: Prophets, Kings, and the Ritual Preparation for War." In *Warfare, Ritual, and Symbol in Biblical and Modern Contexts*, edited by Brad E. Kelle, Frank Ritchel Ames, and Jacob L. Wright, 149–61. Ancient Israel and Its Literature. Atlanta: Society of Biblical Literature, 2014.

Schoors, Antoon. *The Kingdoms of Israel and Judah in the Eighth and Seventh Centuries B.C.E.* Translated by Michael Lesley. Biblical Encyclopedia 5. Atlanta: Society of Biblical Literature, 2013.

Schwartz, Barry. "Where There's Smoke, There's Fire: Memory and History." In *Memory and Identity in Ancient Judaism and Early Christianity: A Conversation with Barry Schwartz*, edited by Tom Thatcher, 7–37. Semeia Studies 78. Atlanta: Society of Biblical Literature, 2014.

Searle, John R. *Speech Acts: An Essay in the Philosophy of Language*. Cambridge: Cambridge University Press, 1969.

Searle, John R., and Daniel Venderveken. *Foundations of Illocutionary Logic*. Cambridge: Cambridge University Press, 1985.

Shanks, Hershel. *The City of David: A Guide to Biblical Jerusalem*. Washington, DC: Biblical Archaeology Society, 1973.

Sheldrake, Philip. *Spaces for the Sacred: Place, Memory, and Identity*. Baltimore: Johns Hopkins University Press, 2001.

Shiloh, Yigal. *Excavations at the City of David 1978–1982: Interim Report of the First Five Seasons*. Vol. 1. Qedem 19. Jerusalem: Institute of Archaeology, 1984.

———. *The Proto-Aeolic Capital and Israelite Ashlar Masonry*. Qedem 11. Jerusalem: Institute of Archaeology and Hebrew University of Jerusalem, 1979.

Simons, J. *The Geographical and Topographical Texts of the Old Testament: A Concise Commentary in XXXII Chapters*. Leiden: Brill, 1959.

Sleeman, Matthew. "Critical Spatial Theory 2.0." In *Constructions of Space V: Place, Space, and Identity in the Ancient Mediterranean World*, edited by Gert T. M. Prinsloo and Christl Maier, 49–66. Library of Hebrew Bible/Old Testament Studies 576. New York: Bloomsbury, 2013.

Smith, Cooper. "The 'Wilderness' in Hosea and Deuteronomy: A Case of Thematic Reappropriation." *Bulletin for Biblical Research* 28 (2018) 240–60.

Smith, D. A. "The Sin of Jehu." *Journal for Semitics* 10 (1998–2001) 112–30.

Smith, Jonathan Z. *To Take Place: Toward Theory in Ritual*. Chicago Studies in the History of Judaism. Chicago: University of Chicago Press, 1987.

Smith, Mark S. "Counting Calves at Bethel." In *"Up to the Gates of Ekron": Essays on the Archaeology and History of the Eastern Mediterranean in Honor of Seymour Gitin*, edited by S. White Crawford et al., 382–94. Jerusalem: The W. F. Albright Institute of Archaeological Research, The Israel Exploration Society, 2007.

―――. *The Early History of God: Yahweh and the Other Deities in Ancient Israel*. 2nd ed. Grand Rapids: Eerdmans, 2002.

Soggin, J. Alberto. *An Introduction to the History of Israel and Judah: Second, Completely Revised and Updated Edition*. Translated by John Bowden. 2nd ed. Valley Forge, PA: Trinity, 1993.

Soja, Edward W. "The City and Spatial Justice." *Justice Spatiale Spatial Justice* (2009) 1–5. http://www.jssj.org.

―――. *Postmetropolis: Critical Studies of Cities and Regions*. Oxford: Blackwell, 2000.

―――. *Thirdspace: Journeys to Los Angeles and Other Real-and-Imagined Places*. Oxford: Blackwell, 1996.

Sperber, Dan, and Deidre Wilson. *Relevance: Communication and Cognition*. 2nd ed. Malden, MA: Blackwell, 1995.

―――. *Relevance: Communication and Cognition*. Cambridge: Harvard University Press, 1986.

Stager, Lawrence E. "The Archaeology of the Family in Ancient Israel." *Bulletin of the American Schools of Oriental Research* 260 (1985) 1–35.

Sternberg, Meir. "The Bible's Art of Persuasion: Ideology, Rhetoric, and Poetics in Saul's Fall." In *Beyond Form Criticism: Essays in Old Testament Literary Criticism*, edited by Paul R. House, 234–71. Sources for Biblical and Theological Study 2. Winona Lake, IN: Eisenbrauns, 1992.

―――. *The Poetics of Biblical Narrative: Ideological Literature and the Drama of Reading*. First Midland Book ed., Indiana Studies in Biblical Literature, edited by Herbert Marks and Robert Polzin, vol. 453. Bloomington: Indiana University Press, 1985.

Stuart, Douglas. *Hosea–Jonah*. Word Biblical Commentary, edited by Bruce M. Metzger, vol. 31. Nashville: Thomas Nelson, 1987.

Sweeney, Marvin A. *The Twelve Prophets*. Berit Olam. Collegeville, MN: Liturgical, 2000.

Tadmor, Hayim. "The Historical Background of Hosea's Prophecies." In *Yehezkel Kaufmann Jubilee Volume: Studies in Bible and Jewish Religion Dedicated to Yehezkel Kaufmann on the Occasion of His Seventieth Birthday*, edited by Menaḥem Haran, 84–88. Jerusalem: Magnes, 1960.

Tappy, Ron E. "The Final Years of Israelite Samaria: Toward a Dialogue between Texts and Archaeology." In *Up to the Gates of Ekron: Essays on the Archaeology and History of the Eastern Mediterranean in Honor of Seymour Gitin*, edited by S. White Crawford, A. Ben-Tor, J. P. Dessel, W. G. Dever, A. Mazar, and J. Aviram, 258–79. Jerusalem: The W.F. Albright Institute of Archaeological Research, the Israel Exploration Society, 2007.

Thiele, Edwin R. *The Mysterious Numbers of the Hebrew Kings*. Edited by John Danilson and Mark Hunt. Grand Rapids: Zondervan, 1983.

Thiselton, Anthony. *New Horizons in Hermeneutics*. Grand Rapids: Zondervan, 1992.

Thomas, Harry Frank. *Atlas of the Bible Lands*. Union, NJ: Hammond World Atlas, 2002.

Thureau-Dangin, F. "L'inscription Des Lions De Til-Barsib." *Revue d'Assyriologie et d'archéologie Orientale* 27 (1930) 11–21.

Tigay, Jeffrey H. *You Shall Have No Other Gods: Israelite Religion in Light of Hebrew Inscriptions*. Harvard Semitic Studies 31. Atlanta: Scholars, 1986.

Tov, Emanuel. *Textual Criticism of the Hebrew Bible*. 2nd rev. ed. Minneapolis: Fortress, 2001.

Trible, Phyllis. *Rhetorical Criticism: Context, Method, and the Book of Jonah*. Guides to Biblical Scholarship: Old Testament Series. Minneapolis: Fortress, 1994.

BIBLIOGRAPHY

Trotter, James Marion. "Reading Hosea in Achaemenid Yehud." PhD diss., Emory University, 1998.

———. *Reading Hosea in Achaemenid Yehud*. Journal for the Study of the Old Testament: Supplement Series 328. London: Sheffield, 2001.

Tuan, Yi-Fu. *Space and Place: The Perspective of Experience*. Minnneapolis: University of Minnesota Press, 1977.

Tull, Patricia K. "Rhetorical Criticism and Intertextuality." In *To Each Its Own Meaning: An Introduction to Biblical Criticisms and Their Application*, edited by Steven L. McKenzie and Stephen R. Haynes, 156–80. Louisville: Westminster John Knox, 1999.

Unger, Merrill F. *Israel and the Arameans of Damascus*. Grand Rapids: Baker, 1980.

Ussishkin, David. "The Credibility of the Tel Jezreel Excavations: A Rejoinder to Amnon Ben-Tor." *Tel Aviv* 27 (2000) 248–56.

———. "The 'Solomonic,' Six-Chambered Gate 2156 at Megiddo Once Again." *Tel Aviv* 47 (2020) 246–55.

———. "Jezreel, Samaria and Megiddo: Royal Centres of Omri and Ahab." In *Congress Volume: Cambridge 1995*, edited by J. A. Emerton, 351–64. Supplements to Vetus Testamentum 66. Leiden: Brill, 1997.

———. "Megiddo and Samaria: A Rejoinder to Norma Franklin." *Bulletin of the American Schools of Oriental Research* 348 (2007) 49–70.

Ussishkin, David, and John Woodhead. "Excavations at Tel Jezreel 1990–1991: Preliminary Report." *Tel Aviv* 19 (1992) 3–56.

———. "Excavations at Tel Jezreel 1992–1993: Second Preliminary Report." *Levant* 26 (1994) 1–48.

———. "Excavations at Tel Jezreel 1994–1996: Third Preliminary Report." *Tel Aviv* 24 (1997) 6–72.

Uziel, Joe. "Middle Bronze Age Ramparts: Functional and Symbolic Structures." *Palestine Exploration Quarterly* 142 (2010) 24–30.

Van De Mieroop, Marc. *A History of the Ancient Near East: Ca. 3000–323 BC*. 2nd ed. Malden, MA: Blackwell, 2007.

Vanhoozer, Kevin J. *Is There a Meaning in This Text? The Bible, the Reader, and the Morality of Literary Knowledge*. Grand Rapids: Zondervan, 1998.

———. "The Semantics of Biblical Literature: Truth and Scripture's Diverse Literary Forms." In *Hermeneutics, Authority, and Canon*, edited by D. A. Carson and John D. Woodbridge, 49–104. 1986. Reprint, Eugene, OR: Wipf & Stock, 2005.

Vatz, Richard. "The Myth of the Rhetorical Situation." *Philosophy and Rhetoric* 6 (1973) 154–61.

Veenhof, K. R. "History of the Ancient Near East to the Time of Alexander the Great." In *The World of the Bible: Bible Handbook*, edited by A. S. Van der Woude, vol. 1, 202–327. Grand Rapids: Eerdmans, 1986.

Vonder Bruegge, John Maxwell. "Mapping Galilee: Josephus, Luke, and John in Light of Critical Geography." PhD diss., Yale, 2011.

Vorster, Johannes N. "Reflecting on the Rhetoric of Biblical Rhetorical Critics." *Neotestamentica* 33 (1999) 293–320.

———. "Why Opt for a Rhetorical Approach?" *Neotestamentica* 29 (1995) 393–418.

Waldman, Nahum M. "The Breaking of the Bow." *Jewish Quarterly Review* 69 (1978) 82–88.

Walsh, Carey. "Why Remember Jezebel?" In *Remembering Biblical Figures in the Late Persian and Early Hellenistic Periods: Social Memory and Imagination*, edited by

Diana V. Edelman and Ehud Ben Zvi, 311–31. Oxford: Oxford University Press, 2013.
Waltke, Bruce K., and M. O'Connor. *An Introduction to Biblical Hebrew Syntax*. Winona Lake, IN: Eisenbrauns, 1990.
Watson, Duane F., and Alan J. Hauser. *Rhetorical Criticism of the Bible: A Comprehensive Bibliography with Notes on History and Method*. Biblical Interpretation Series 4. Leiden: Brill, 1994.
Wazana, Nili. *All the Boundaries of the Land: The Promised Land in Biblical Thought in Light of the Ancient Near East*. Translated by Liat Qeren. Winona Lake, IN: Eisenbrauns, 2013.
Weinstein, James M. "Egyptian Relations with Palestine in the Middle Kingdom." *Bulletin of the American Schools of Oriental Research* 217 (1975) 1–16.
Wenell, Karen J. *Jesus and Land: Sacred and Social Space in Second Temple Judaism*. Library of New Testament Studies 334. New York: T. & T. Clark, 2007.
Wessels, Willie. "At the Potter's Workshop: Jeremiah 18:1-12: A Narrative that Reveals More than Meets the Eye." *HTS Theological Studies* 76 (2020) 1–8.
West, Gerald O. "The Effect and Power of Discourse: A Case Study of a Metaphor in Hosea." *Scriptura* 57 (1996) 201–12.
Whitelam, Keith W. "The Symbols of Power: Aspects of Royal Propaganda in the United Monarchy." *Biblical Archaeologist* 49 (1986) 166–73.
Whiting, Charlotte, and Gloria London. *An Examination of the Stratigraphy and Neolithic-Iron Age Pottery from Tel Jezreel, Area A*. The Annual of ASOR, edited by Kevin M. McGeough, vol. 73. Alexandria, VA: American Society of Overseas Research, 2021.
Williamson, H. G. M. "Jezreel in the Biblical Texts." *Tel Aviv* 18 (1991) 72–92.
———. "Tel Jezreel and the Dynasty of Omri." *Palestine Exploration Quarterly* 128 (1996) 41–51.
Willis, John T. "Symbolic Names and Theological Themes in the Book of Isaiah." *Horizons in Biblical Theology* 23 (2001) 72–92.
Winter, Jay. *Sites of Memory, Sites of Mourning: The Great War in European Cultural History*. Cambridge: Cambridge University Press, 1995.
Wolff, Hans W. *Hosea: A Commentary on the Book of the Prophet Hosea*. Translated by Gary Stansell. Hermeneia. Philadelphia: Fortress, 1974.
———. "The Understanding of History in the Old Testament Prophets." In *Essays on Old Testament Interpretation*, edited by Claus Westermann, 336–55. London: SCM, 1963.
Wray Beal, Lissa M. "Evaluating Jehu: Narrative Control of Approval and Disapproval in 2 Kings 9–10." In *From Babel to Babylon: Essays on Biblical History and Literature in Honour of Brian Peckham*, edited by Joyce Rilett Wood, John E. Harvey, and Mark Leuchter, 214–25. Library of Hebrew Bible/Old Testament Studies 455. New York: T. & T. Clark, 2006.
Wright, Christopher J. H. *God's People in God's Land: Family, Land, and Property in the Old Testament*. Grand Rapids: Eerdmans, 1990.
Wuellner, Wilhelm. "Hermeneutics and Rhetorics: From 'Truth and Method' to 'Truth and Power.'" *Scriptura* S3 (1989).
———. "Where Is Rhetorical Criticism Taking Us?" *Catholic Biblical Quarterly* 49 (1987) 448–63.
Yadin, Yigael. *The Art of Warfare in Biblical Lands: In the Light of Archaeological Discovery*. Translated by M. Pearlman. London: Weidenfeld & Nicholson, 1963.

BIBLIOGRAPHY

Yamada, Shigeo. *The Construction of the Assyrian Empire: A Historical Study of the Inscriptions of Shalmaneser III (859–824 BC) Relating to His Campaigns to the West*. Culture and History of the Ancient Near East 3. Leiden: Brill, 2000.

Yee, Gale A. "'She Is Not My Wife and I Am Not Her Husband': A Materialist Analysis of Hosea 1–2." *Biblical Interpretation* 9 (2001) 345–83.

Yerushlami, Yosef Hayim. *Zakhor: Jewish History and Jewish Memory*. The Samuel and Althea Stroum Lectures in Jewish Studies. Seattle: University of Washington Press, 1982.

Zadok, Ran. "On the Toponomy of the Jezreel Valley and Adjacent Plains." In *The Fire Signals of Lachish: Studies in Archaeology and History of Israel in the Late Bronze Age, Iron Age, and Persian Period in Honor of David Ussishkin*, edited by Israel Finkelstein and Nadav Na'aman, 345–72. Winona Lake, IN: Eisenbrauns, 2011.

Zertal, Adam. "The Heart of the Monarchy: Pattern of Settlement and Historical Considerations of the Israelite Kingdom of Samaria." In *Studies in the Archaeology of the Iron Age in Israel and Jordan*, edited by Amihai Mazar, 38–64. Journal for the Study of the Old Testament Supplements 331. Sheffield: Sheffield Academic, 2001.

Zimhoni, Orna. "Clues from the Enclosure Fills: Pre-Omride Settlement at Tel Jezreel." *Tel Aviv* 24 (1997) 83–109.

———. "The Iron Age Pottery from Tel Jezreel: An Interim Report." *Tel Aviv* 19 (1992) 57–70.

Zulick, Margaret D. "Rhetorical Polyphony in the Book of the Prophet Hosea." PhD diss., Northwestern University, 1994.

Scripture Index

Hebrew Bible/ Old Testament

Genesis

9:22	96
12:8	41
15:5–6	104
21:1	78
28:11–22	41
31:13	41
34	95
35:7	41
50:24–25	78

Exodus

2:6	109
3:6–8	104
9:3–6	104
20:26	96
22:15	107
22:16	107
28:42	96

Leviticus

18:6–19	96
20:10	96
20:11	96
20:17–21	96
26	105
26:9	104

Numbers

25	109
25:1–5	108
32:13	108

Deuteronomy

4:5	106
4:8	106
4:14	106
4:23–24	104
4:36–38	104
4:37	109
4:45	106
5:1	106
5:6–10	105
5:6–7	104
5:8–9	104
5:9	105
5:10	105
5:31	106
6–7	13, 105
6:1–15	104
6:1	106
6:4–5	104
6:10–15	104
6:10–11	104
6:15	104
7:7–8	109
7:11–13	106, 119
7:11	106, 109
8:8–20	109

SCRIPTURE INDEX

Deuteronomy (continued)

8:13	90
11:14	90, 106, 119
17:17	101
22:22	96
23:14	96
24	95
24:1	95
26:17	106
28–30	13, 105
28	90
28:49–51	106
28:68	16
29:5	110
32:39	106

Joshua

5:1–9	123
7	113, 117
7:24–26	113
7:24	115
8:33	117
10:9	88
10:12	115
15:1–12	111
15:5–7	115
15:6–7	113
15:6	114
15:7	114
15:8	115
15:15	88
15:61–62	112
17:2	115
17:3	115
17:16	115
17:52	115
18:16	115
18:21–22	114
19:27	115
24:13	104

Judges

14:15	107
16:5	107

17:7–13	70
19	109

1 Samuel

2:4	85
7:16	41
10:3	41
13:15	88
17	115
17:2	115
17:3	115
17:19	115
17:52	115
29:3	96
29:6	96
29:8	96
31:4	85

2 Samuel

1:1–16	77
1:17–27	85
1:19	85
1:25	85
1:27	85

1 Kings

1:52	96
2:5	79
2:31	79
9:15	67
9:16–17	75
10:18	37
10:29	75
10:31	75
12:22–24	99
12:28–32	40
15:19	88
16:31–33	40
17	76
18:4	12
18:19	40
18:45	58
19:10	75
19:17–18	57

21	74	14:7	36
21:1	54, 58	14:8–14	36
21:17–29	102	14:14	101
21:23	58	14:23–29	81
22:5–28	99	14:25	36
22:10–40	102	14:26–27	101
22:24–27	99	14:28	61, 101
		15:8–12	81
		15:8–10	38, 85
		15:10	78

2 Kings

1:4–5	76	15:14–17	39
6:25	65	15:19–20	39
8:12	34, 59	15:27	39
8:29	58, 74	15:29	39, 85
9:1–10	74	15:30	40
9:7–10	75	15:37—16:9	40
9–10	59, 73–74, 76	17:3–4	40
9:11–16	74	17:4	96
9:15	74	17:13	11, 44
9:16–29	80	20:13	101
9:16	74	23:29–30	77
9:24	74		
9:27	74		
9:30—10:3	54	## 1 Chronicles	
9:33	74	5:16–25	61
9:35–37	74	25:11	64
10	76		
10:1–8	74	## 2 Chronicles	
10:11–17	74		
10:12–14	77	22:7	77
10:16	75	22:8	79
10:18–28	40	22:9	74
10:28	122	28:1–21	40
10:29	40	28:3	79
10:30	39, 75, 85	35:22	77
10:32–33	34, 57, 59	36:15–16	12
12:17–18	34, 59		
13:1–9	81	## Ezra	
13:3	34, 59	9:9	97
13:4–5	35		
13:7	34, 59	## Job	
13:10–13	81		
13:14–19	99	19:8	97
13:17	36		
13:18–19	36		
13: 24–25	36		
13:25	60, 61		

SCRIPTURE INDEX

Psalms

46:10	85
60:8	114
108:8	114
137:7	87

Proverbs

7	98
7:25	98

Isaiah

1:19–20	16
5:5	97
7	40, 44
7:1—9:6	12
9:1	39, 85
9:3	87
9:4	87
10:1–2	37
40–66	20
40–48	20
50:1	96
51:3	96
60–62	12
65:10	114, 116, 117

Jeremiah

2:2	109
3:1	96
3:8	96
7:12	3
7:14	3
7:20	92
7:25–26	109
15:3	78
18:1–12	16
26:1–19	12
26:18–19	17
27–28	75
37:14	12
49:35	85
51:27	79
51:56	85

Lamentations

3:9	97

Hosea

1–3	2, 6, 11, 18, 48, 120, 121
1:1–2a	71
1:1	33, 47, 48, 122
1–2	71, 91
1:2–9	48
1:2–6	48
1:2b–3	71
1:2	72, 79
1:3–9	79
1:4–5	71–72, 76, 90, 91, 97, 123
1:4	33, 71, 72, 77–78, 84–85
1:5	38, 65, 71, 80, 85, 87, 91, 99
1:6–7	71
1:6	72
1:7	38, 47, 80, 86, 99
1:8–9	71
1:8f	48
1:10—2:1	88
1:10–11	87
1:11	71, 102
2	119
2:1–3	88
2:1	47
2:2–13	116
2:2	47, 71, 87–89, 95, 102
2:3	108
2:4–17	48, 97
2:4–15	48, 116
2:4	47, 95
2:5	106, 108
2:6	96–97
2:7	106
2:8	96–97, 106
2:9	89, 91, 106, 117, 119
2:10	36, 84, 106

SCRIPTURE INDEX

Reference	Pages	Reference	Pages
2:11	89, 106, 117, 119	7:11	107
2:12	91, 106, 117	7:14	42
2:13	106	7:16	85
2:14	106, 108, 116–17	8:1	106
2:15–19	84	8:1a	80
2:15	8, 42, 106, 111, 113, 116–17	8:1b–6	80
2:16	108, 116	8:4–6	42
2:17	111, 113, 116–17	8:4	33, 82
2:18–25	48	8:7–8	80
2:19	42	8:7	51
2:20	85	8:9	80, 98
2:21	91	8:10	80
2:22	71, 119	8:11–14	80
2:24–25	51, 91	8:13b	80
2:24	71, 89–91, 119	8:14	47
3:1–5	48	8:14b	80
3:5	89, 100, 102	9:7	12, 118, 126
4:1–3	47	9:8	110
4:1–2	81	9:9	109
4:1	47	9:10	109
4:4–10	47, 122	9:13	76
4:4	47	9:15	96
4:5	126	9:16	76
4:6	107	10	119
4:7	107	10:1	109
4:8	107	10:5–8	42
4:9	107	10:5	42, 123
4:11–19	47	10:6	46
4:11–14	122	10:8	123
4:10–14	42	10:9	109
4:13–14	42	10:11	47, 109
4:13	122	10:12	51
4–14	49, 122	10:13–14	37
4:15	42, 47, 123	10:14	46
4:16	98	11:1	109
5:1	47	11:2	84
5:5	47	11:12	47
5:8	42, 123	12:2	47, 81
5:10	47	12:3	47
5:12	47	12:8–9	37
5:13	46–47	12:11	110
5:14	47, 76	12:14	110
6:4	47	13:1–2	42
6:11	47	13:1	84
7:3–7	33	13:5–8	98
7:7	85	13:5	110
		13:6	110

Hosea *(continued)*

13:9–11	33
13:16	76
14:1	76, 85
14:3	37

Joel

2:12–18	16

Amos

1:1	36
1:3–2:5	47
1:3	34
1:4–5	101
1:9	81
2:2	81
2:6	37, 81
2:7	81
2:8	37, 81, 100
2:9	100
2:10	100
2:12	100
2:14–16	65
3:2–3	81
3:2	109
3:7	110
3:10	81
3:14	42
3:15	37, 81
4:1	42, 100
4:4–5	42
4:4	3, 42
4:12–13	107
5	63
5:3	65
5:5	42
5:7	81, 82
5:10–13	37
5:10–12	100
5:10	81
5:11	81, 101
5:12	81
6:3–4	37
6:3	81
6:4–7	37
6:8	65
6:12	37, 81
6:13	36, 61
7	126
7:1–9	107
7:1–6	16
7:9	82, 100
7:10–17	12, 82
7:10–11	100
7:10	82
7:13	42
7:14–16	110
7:14–15	44
9:13	119

Micah

2:1–2	37
2:8–9	37
3:12	16
7:11	97

New Testament

Matthew

5:12	12
23	24
23:37	12

Acts

7:57	12

Hebrews

11:37	12

Dead Sea Scrolls and Related Texts

3Q15	117

www.ingramcontent.com/pod-product-compliance
Lightning Source LLC
Chambersburg PA
CBHW050818160426
43192CB00010B/1811